John A. Zervopoulos, Ph.D., J.D.

Confronting Mental Health Evidence

A Practical Guide to Reliability and Experts in Family Law

D1615907

ABA

Defending Liberty
Pursuing Justice

SECTION OF
FAMILY LAW

Cover design by ABA Publishing.

Printed in the United States of America

12 11 10 09 08   5 4 3 2 1

Library of Congress Cataloging-in-Publication Data

Zervopoulos, John A.
    Confronting mental health evidence: a practical guide to reliability and experts in family law / By John A. Zervopoulos.—1st ed.
      p. cm.
    ISBN 978-1-59031-704-4
    1. Forensic psychology. 2. Evidence, Expert—United States. 3. Discovery (Law)—United States. 4. Mental health laws—United States. I. Title.

    KF8965.Z47   2008
    347.73'67—dc22

                                            2008022249

Contents

Acknowledgments

Interests start somewhere. Although I had testified as an expert many times and had attended law school, my specific interest in expert evidence issues gelled in 1997 when I was asked to join an ad hoc committee of the Family Law Section of the State Bar of Texas. In 1995, the Texas Supreme Court, adopting the rationale of the landmark 1993 federal *Daubert* case, held in *du Pont v. Robinson* that trial judges have a "heightened responsibility to ensure that expert testimony show some indicia of reliability." The committee's task was to evaluate the effects of the *Robinson* holding on mental health evidence in Texas family law cases. Richard R. Orsinger of San Antonio and Dallas, Texas, ably chaired this committee of Texas lawyers, judges, and mental health professionals. In 1999, the committee published the *Expert Witness Manual* to which I contributed four papers. This two-year committee involvement was the most intellectually stimulating experience I had since law school and spurred my subsequent writing and speaking on issues related to mental health experts, psychology, and the law.

I appreciate the many people who contributed to this book's development and writing. This project began when the Honorable Debra H. Lehrmann of Fort Worth, Texas, asked if I would consider writing a book that would address mental health procedures and evidence issues in family law cases. I am very grateful that she gave me this opportunity, and that she determined to see this project through to its completion. Once I accepted Judge Lehrmann's offer, Erin Quinn, executive editor at the ABA during much of this project, answered my questions graciously and promptly. Later, new editor Louise Benzer worked with me to the book's conclusion. Likewise, Annie Beck of Lachina Publishing Services was very helpful in the manuscript's final editing and production stages.

As I wrote, colleagues and friends willingly gave me their time and expertise to review drafts at various stages. These professionals gave what I expected from them: critical readings that clarified the substance and style of my writing. Kathryn Lanigan Wieser of Dallas, Texas, and Henry H. Robinson of Fort Worth, Texas, provided helpful comments on the legal issues. I greatly appreciated the feedback from Roger L. Greene, Ph.D., who reviewed Part 1 of the book, and Mary A. Connell, Ed.D., ABPP offered useful remarks for the book's opening chapters.

I especially wish to thank three persons. Richard A. Warshak, Ph.D. and Mark R. Otis, Ph.D. encouraged me from the project's beginning and gave valuable feedback in all the book's sections. Their understanding of family dynamics, their keen sensitivity to family difficulties, and their knowledge of applicable research provided me helpful perspectives on several issues I addressed in the book. My writing and practice have benefited from the creative, critical thinking mind-sets Rick and Mark bring to their scholarship and clinical work.

In addition, Professor Daniel W. Shuman of the Dedman School of Law at Southern Methodist University gave me much support and realistic perspective throughout this project. More importantly, Dan's writings and teaching have significantly influenced my thinking and conduct as a forensic psychologist. I have been privileged to be both his student and colleague.

Finally, I wish to dedicate this book to a special woman. As a pediatrician of almost forty years, she was a model professional, committed to her work and especially sensitive to the well-being of her young patients and their families. As a parent, grounded in her faith, she sacrificed for her family and carried out her responsibilities with grace and a natural, kind spirit. Thank you, Mom.

About the Author

John A. Zervopoulos, Ph.D., J.D., ABPP, a psychologist and lawyer, directs PSYCHOL-OGYLAW PARTNERS, a forensic consulting service that helps lawyers understand, organize, and apply social science information in their cases from both the psychological and legal perspectives. In addition, his psychology practice focuses on forensic psychological evaluations, psychotherapy, and mediation. Dr. Zervopoulos has written extensively and has presented to lawyers and mental health professionals on family law and *Frye* and *Daubert* topics. He served on the Expert Witness Committee of the State Bar of Texas Family Law Section and contributed several papers to the committee's published manual. He is a fellow of the American Academy of Forensic Psychology and clinical assistant professor in the Department of Psychiatry at the University of Texas Southwestern Medical Center at Dallas.

Dr. Zervopoulos received his B.A. from Wheaton College (Illinois) in 1974, his Ph.D. in psychology from the University of North Texas in 1981, and his J.D. from Southern Methodist University School of Law in 1993. In 2002, he earned board certification in Forensic Psychology from the American Board of Professional Psychology.

Dr. Zervopoulos is online at www.psychologylawpartners.com and can be contacted by email at jzerv@psychologylawpartners.com.

CHAPTER 1

Introduction and Overview

THE CHALLENGE

How do you know what you say you know? This is the key question the family lawyer should ask when evaluating the reports and testimony of mental health professionals (MHPs), their methods, and the materials that support their conclusions and expert opinions. This question is the foundation of the practical, evidentiary-based model of legal analysis presented in this book. The model empowers family lawyers to effectively handle the difficult psychology-related issues attending their cases and to hold MHPs accountable in court for their conclusions and expert opinions.[1]

Although the question seems straightforward, probing its layers with MHPs unveils a host of ill-defined, yet often used, theories and terms, particularly in divorces that involve children. These include notions of the importance of a primary caretaker, child access schedules, parenting plans, so-called abuse syndromes, parent alienation, and parent relocation.

In addition, divorce is a legal event within the context of a broader emotional process, the seeds of which germinate during the marriage and the by-products of which weigh—sometimes heavily—in the spouses' lives for several years. Divorce evokes deep, psychological feelings and reactions, and because the legal divorce is "no fault," child custody and support disputes can often become proxy battles for parents dealing with the emotional issues that attend the breakup of their marriages. As a result, lawyers may become drawn into the spousal recriminations, thereby finding themselves limited in their ability to effectively manage the psychological aspects of their cases.

Consider the bread and butter of family law: husband and wife, after seven years and two children, decide to divorce. For family lawyers, most of these cases are quite manageable. Most of the time, parents divide their property amicably, agree on how they will deal with their children after the divorce, and settle on the conditions and access schedule under which the noncustodial parent will spend time with the children. Often these parents, with their lawyers, "bargain in the shadow of the law" as they consider how the court might rule on their divorce issues, and they then factor that understanding into their agreements.[2]

After the divorce, many of these parents and their children adapt well to their new post-divorce living arrangements. Some parents use their agreed-upon child access schedules flexibly, depending on their work or other demands or on the children's wishes to spend more time with the noncustodial parent. Other parents value more predictability and arrange their lives around strictly kept schedules that dictate their involvement in their children's lives. Still other parents continue to bear resentment from the marriage and divorce but nevertheless separate their relationship problems from their children's needs and dutifully carry out their parenting responsibilities, albeit in parallel fashion.[3]

Some divorce or post-divorce modification lawsuits, however, are more complicated in that they carry psychological concerns that significantly escalate tensions and ill will. For example, what if one spouse is depressed or angry, even impulsive, when interacting with the other? What if both parents use their child as a go-between for divorce issues they have difficulty resolving between themselves? What if the child resists spending time with one parent and openly favors one over the other? What if the child has been experiencing emotional or behavior problems since the separation and divorce?

In such cases the question becomes how to distinguish common reactions to divorce from other emotional problems that may compromise the children's well-being, both during the divorce and after. Adding the possible layers of substance abuse, domestic violence and child abuse allegations, new marriages, additional siblings, and past counseling confounds the matter.

As complex divorce problems intensify, lawyers may experience difficulty understanding, organizing, and addressing the attendant psychological concerns. Lawyers typically begin to seek relevant information through discovery by obtaining financial records, previous psychotherapy and medical records of family members, previously conducted evaluation reports, children's school reports, and other parent-supplied documents. But obtaining this information is only the first step in managing the psychological issues of a complicated family law case. Knowing what to make of the information, how to organize it, and how to use it is essential to crafting a competent and convincing legal case. To do this, lawyers often retain MHPs to help them manage the materials and provide expert court testimony.

Although MHPs may help lawyers understand, organize, and address psychological issues in these complicated cases, some writers have proposed that MHPs have little, if any, reliable basis upon which to testify when the issues focus on the "best interest of the child"—the primary standard all state courts use to decide child custody cases. For example, because psychological research generally compares groups rather than individuals along different dimensions, questions arise about whether such findings apply to a specific family in court and to that family's legally relevant questions.[4] Other writers contend that the empirical knowledge base is too limited to predict consequences of MHPs' child custody recommendations in a particular case. They criticize MHPs for basing expert opinions on personal biases rather than on accepted research, for utilizing poor evaluation methods, and for misunderstanding the importance of distinguishing the role of a court-involved, or forensic, MHP from that of a therapeutic clinician involved with the litigant.[5]

Differences between law and social science styles and methods of reasoning also raise questions about how MHPs fit in the child custody process in court.[6] For example, a court order is prescriptive; it directs people how to behave. In contrast, the social sciences are more descriptive, seeking to describe behaviors as they actually occur.[7] In addition, a court focuses on the facts of the single case before it to reach its decision, whereas the social sciences focus more on principles and relationships derived from experimental studies of groups of people.[8] Finally, the legal decision-making process values certainty that leads to final decisions in which one party prevails. In contrast, social science conclusions are framed in terms of probability. MHPs are trained to qualify findings and statements and are more likely to view a person's behaviors as multi-determined.[9]

Yet despite criticisms of MHPs in child custody cases and differences in the ways MHPs and the legal system view data and issues, MHPs continue to play a significant role in the family law process. Legislatures and case law have in fact enabled the legal system's reliance on MHPs in child custody cases. For example, note that while the best interest of the child standard is "the primary consideration of the court in determining the issues of conservatorship and possession of and access to the child,"[10] this standard is generally ill-defined, and the trial court has wide discretion when applying it.[11] Consequently, legislatures and courts have tried to guide best interest of the child considerations by freighting their language with psychologically related terms or constructs. For example, Michigan's Child Custody Act of 1970 identifies ten factors for a court to consider when making a child custody determination,[12] yet no definitions are provided for the terms "love," "affection," "other emotional ties," and "moral fitness," among other concepts. The Uniform Marriage and Divorce Act (UMDA)[13] identifies five factors for a judge to consider when making child custody determinations: (1) the wishes of the child's parent or parents as to his or her custody; (2) the wishes of the child as to his or her custodian; (3) the interaction and interrelationships of the child with the parent or parents, siblings, and any other person who may significantly affect the child's best interest; (4) the child's adjustment to home, school, and community; and (5) the mental and physical health of all individuals involved. The UMDA also allows courts to consider any other criterion that might be important in discerning the child's best interest.[14] Clearly, prevailing best interest of the child definitions and guidance—as indeterminate as they appear—beg the involvement of MHPs in child custody cases as consultants to lawyers, as retained experts, and as court-appointed evaluators and experts.

To that end, many MHPs in the past several years have focused on child custody work as a specialty. Several professional organizations have developed standards and guidelines for MHPs involved in these cases;[15] consequently, MHPs have become more sensitized to ensure that their professional relationships with families, lawyers, and courts do not compromise the validity of their methods and opinions. Research, writing, and workshops have mushroomed to address evaluation methodology and psychological aspects of difficult cases. A new journal devoted to child custody work was established in 2005[16] to supplement others that regularly publish papers in the area.[17] In sum, rather than shying from the criticisms, many MHPs have addressed the complaints by seeking to define their expertise in the contexts of the scientific and professional mental health literature.

MEETING THE CHALLENGE: UNDERSTANDING THREE CRITICAL PERSPECTIVES

To best flesh out the central question for MHP experts—"How do you know what you say you know?"—and meet the challenge of evaluating reports and testimony of MHPs, family lawyers should understand, separately and jointly, three key perspectives. First, lawyers must recognize important emotional dynamics that underlie their clients' behaviors and thinking during the divorce process. Lawyers must also view and understand mental health testimony from two other perspectives: the legal and the psychological.

The first critical perspective, the emotional perspective, addresses the emotional dynamics of divorce that underlie spouses' behaviors and thinking. These dynamics provide useful insights about spouses' actions and motivations in a given case and sensitivities to what issues might address the children's best interests. Key events leading to the marital separation may also foretell issues that facilitate or frustrate the divorce's resolution. Understanding the nature of impasses that stall progress in settling certain tough issues may help lawyers propose constructive and creative steps to move forward.

The second critical perspective, the legal perspective, addresses the legal principles by which lawyers must evaluate the reports and testimony of MHPs. Lawyers must consider whether the opinions of MHPs are reliably based and, therefore, admissible by the court, and how the admissibility of opposing experts' opinions may be challenged. Examining mental health testimony from a legal perspective presents challenges. In most state court jurisdictions, *Frye*[18] or *Daubert*[19] principles govern the admissibility of expert testimony, but for several reasons family courts have not been awash with *Frye* or *Daubert* challenges. Neither *Frye* nor *Daubert* requires trial judges to raise questions of admissibility of expert testimony on their own motion. Trial lawyers must identify and object to such issues,[20] but some may be uncertain about how to apply the *Frye* or *Daubert* principles to mental health testimony or may fear that raising *Frye* or *Daubert* concerns with the opposing counsel's mental health experts might undermine their own expert's testimony.[21] In addition, *Daubert* requires the judge to be the evidence gatekeeper. The appellate standard of review for assessing a trial court's decision to admit an expert's testimony is whether the court abused its discretion by acting without reference to guiding rules and principles.[22] Therefore, the lawyer practicing before a judge who does not dismiss the testimony of a qualified expert may believe that it would be futile to appeal that judge's ruling admitting the testimony.[23]

The third critical perspective, the psychological perspective, addresses MHPs' conclusions and the means and methods by which MHPs reached those conclusions and resulting expert opinions. The analysis can be confusing in the layers that must be addressed:

- MHPs come to court with different kinds of professional qualifications; not all are equivalent. What do these qualifications mean, and what level of competence is defined by a particular qualification?
- How may lawyers evaluate the methods by which MHPs arrive at their conclusions and opinions?
- How do MHPs use psychological testing results to support their opinions?
- How have MHPs guarded against the influence of biases when gathering or evaluating the data that inform their opinions?
- How do MHPs handle special issues—allegations of domestic violence, child abuse, child resistance to visitation, and interference with custodial access, as well as concerns about access schedules for young children and relocation—that complicate child custody cases?

- How do MHPs justify their child access schedule recommendations? And how might a prospective relocation of one parent with the children impact the schedule and the children's relationships with each parent?

In sum, by considering the conclusions of MHPs from three key perspectives—the emotional perspective, the legal perspective, and the psychological perspective—lawyers will enhance their abilities to:

- evaluate the quality of mental health materials and testimony;
- present their courtroom arguments in a manner that sharpens their own expert's presentation;
- critique their opponent's expert effectively; and
- provide the court with a logical, understandable guide for their *Frye* or *Daubert* arguments.

In the end, the lawyer will be able to address most effectively the central question for MHPs: "How do you know what you say you know?"

THE ROADMAP

This book is divided into three sections. Part 1 includes Chapters 2, 3, and 4 and addresses the three critical perspectives lawyers must understand to manage mental health materials and expert testimony. Chapter 2 addresses key emotional dynamics of the divorce process that will help family lawyers better understand the underlying concerns of their clients and their clients' spouses that may facilitate or impede the progress of their cases.

Chapter 3 examines mental health testimony from the legal perspective. First, we discuss and deconstruct the *Frye* and *Daubert* lines of cases and note key evidentiary principles in each. Then, from these principles, we consider a practical four-step *Frye-Daubert* Analysis Model with which to evaluate MHPs' opinions and testimony. We look carefully at how to apply each step of the model—problems at any step may be grounds for challenging the admissibility of an MHP's expert testimony. The model will help lawyers understand and organize the methods, testimony, and expert opinions of MHPs.

Chapter 4 uses the *Frye-Daubert* Analysis Model as a framework to address the psychological perspective in family law cases. From an admissibility standpoint, "[T]he district court should ensure that the opinion . . . will have a reliable basis in the knowledge and experience of the discipline."[24] Understanding the standards, methods, and ethics MHPs bring to family law cases is essential for lawyers to evaluate and manage mental health materials and expert testimony. We explore how MHPs' views of each step in our model can help lawyers construct more compelling evidentiary arguments to the court and more informed cross-examination questions by discussing several key issues:

- experts' professional qualifications
- the critical issue of the roles MHP experts adopt in their forensic tasks
- the methods MHPs use to gather their data, including the use and misuse of psychological testing
- biases that may compromise the quality of MHP experts' conclusions and opinions
- MHPs' use of research in expert testimony
- the debate about whether MHP experts should offer opinions on the ultimate issue in family law cases

At the chapter's end, we present a model for organizing child custody evaluations to illustrate how lawyers may focus MHPs on the objectives of such evaluations rather than on concerns less relevant to the parents' capacities to care for their children.

Part 2 assists lawyers in meeting the challenge of the most difficult of the *Frye-Daubert* tasks: exposing analytical gaps in empirical and logical reasoning that tie experts' methods and data to their opinions. Courts may view opinions with analytical gaps that are too wide as unreliable and, therefore, inadmissible.[25] With a view toward closing these gaps, we first discuss the scientific–critical thinking mindset that provides the prism through which *Frye-Daubert* questions should be considered. Then, we will use that mindset to describe six means, illustrated with several issues that could arise in family law cases, by which MHP experts may hide analytical gaps in their empirical and logical reasoning. As a result, lawyers will learn to expose analytical gaps hidden by:

- overly abstract psychological concepts
- "common sense" notions unsupported by empirical or logical reasoning
- *ipse dixit* assertions whereby experts offer opinions devoid of support
- reliance on general acceptance factors absent in other support
- misapplication or misrepresentation of research
- confirmation bias

Finally, Part 3 discusses issues that arise when lawyers seek to obtain mental health records. Lawyers sometimes encounter roadblocks when they negotiate the interplay of patient confidentiality, privacy laws represented by the Health Insurance Portability and Accountability Act (HIPAA)[26] and the psychotherapist-patient privilege. Questions about whether and how psychologists should release test data to lawyers add to the mix. We look at how these concerns overlap, suggest ways to manage them, and point to useful resources to access for further guidance.

Dealing with mental health issues and information in family law cases may at times seem confusing—even daunting. But appreciating the emotional dynamics of divorce and organizing the legal case and arguments around the practical, four-step *Frye-Daubert* Analysis Model presented in this book will help lawyers address the key question to MHPs—"How do you know what you say you know?"—thereby meeting the challenge of evaluating MHPs' reports and testimony.

NOTES

1. Throughout this book, unless noted differently, MHPs include psychologists, psychiatrists, social workers, licensed counselors, and marriage and family therapists.

2. *See* Robert H. Mnookin & Lewis Kornhauser, *Bargaining in the Shadow of the Law: The Case of Divorce*, 88 YALE L.J. 950 (1979).

3. *See* PHILLIP M. STAHL, PARENTING AFTER DIVORCE (2000).

4. GARY B. MELTON ET AL., PSYCHOLOGICAL EVALUATIONS FOR THE COURTS 12–13 (2d ed., 1997).

5. *See* William T. O'Donohue & A.R. Bradley, *Conceptual and Empirical Issues in Child Custody Evaluations*, 6 CLINICAL PSYCHOL.: SCI. & PRAC. 310 (1999); *see also* Robert E. Emery, Randy K. Otto & William T. O'Donohue, *A Critical Assessment of Child Custody Evaluations*, 6 PSYCHOL. SCI. PUB. INT. 1 (2005).

6. C. Haney, *Psychology and Legal Change: On the Limits of Factual Jurisprudence,* 4 LAW & HUM. BEHAV. 147, 158 (1980).

7. *Id.* at 163.

8. *Id.* at 164.

9. *Id.* at 164, 168.

10. TEX. FAM. CODE § 153.002 (parallels language of the best interest standard in most jurisdictions).

11. *See* Gillespie v. Gillespie, 644 S.W.2d 449, 451 (Tex. 1982).

12. Mich. Comp. Laws § 722.23.

13. Uniform Marriage and Divorce Act (1973), 402 9A U.L.A. 561 (1988) [hereinafter UMDA].

14. *Id.*

15. American Academy of Child and Adolescent Psychiatry, *Practice Parameters for Child Custody Evaluation,* 36 J. AM. ACAD. CHILD & ADOLESCENT PSYCHIATRY (1997) [hereinafter *Psychiatry Parameters*]; American Psychological Association, *Guidelines for Child Custody Evaluations in Divorce Proceedings,* 47 AM. PSYCHOL. 677 (1994) [hereinafter *APA Child Custody Guidelines*]; Association of Family and Conciliation Courts, *Model Standards of Practice for Child Custody Evaluation,* 45 FAM. CT. REV. 70 (2007) [hereinafter *AFCC Child Custody Standards*].

16. *Journal of Child Custody.*

17. *See, e.g., Family Court Review* and the *Journal of Divorce and Remarriage.*

18. Frye v. United States, 293 F. 1013 (D.C. Cir. 1923).

19. Daubert v. Merrell Dow Pharmaceuticals, 509 U.S. 579 (1993).

20. Daniel W. Shuman & Bruce D. Sales, *Daubert's Wager,* 1 J. FORENSIC PSYCHOL. PRAC. 69, 71 (2001).

21. John A. Zervopoulos, *Robinson/Daubert and Mental Health Testimony: The Sky Is Not Falling,* 64 TEX. B.J. 350, 352 (2001).

22. *See* Broders v. Heise, 924 S.W.2d 148, 151 (Tex. 1996); *see also* General Electric Co. v. Joiner, 522 U.S. 136, 138–39 (1997).

23. Zervopoulos, *supra* note 21, at 352.

24. Watkins v. Telsmith, Inc., 121 F.3d 984, 991 (5th Cir. 1997).

25. *See Joiner,* 522 U.S. at 146.

26. Pub. L. No. 104–191, 42 U.S.C. § 1320d-1, *et seq.*

PART 1

Three Critical Perspectives

CHAPTER 2

The Emotional Perspective

Why must family lawyers appreciate emotional concerns of their clients when handling a divorce case? Although the question seems elementary, lawyers dismiss these concerns at their peril. At such times, relatively straightforward cases with an extra twist or two may become more difficult, and issue-laden cases, particularly those involving children, may spin out of control. Older research measuring the effects of life changes over a twelve-month period has noted divorce and marital separation as the second and third most stressful experiences to which people might be exposed.[1] More contemporary findings confirm conventional wisdom that spouses' decisions to divorce are rarely easy and that the divorce process exacts a heavy emotional toll.[2] High divorce rates increase the likelihood that people are aware of these emotional concerns from their own experiences (as adult spouses or as children of divorce) or from the experiences of family members and friends.

Any lawsuit is imbued with emotional elements—inherent in all human interactions. But as matters become more personal and intimate, the parties' emotional lives may, unexpectedly and dramatically, impact the lawsuit. Family law concerns entangle spouses' current difficulties—marital problems, child-related issues, financial concerns, and decision-making patterns—and may invoke ghosts of childhood experiences. Issues from previous marriages and relationships may further stir the potion. While most people who divorce will eventually find their emotional bearings, attorneys encounter their clients at the beginning stages of the process.

In sum, divorce is more than just a legal concern. Pauline Tesler, in her work on collaborative law, notes that a divorcing couple must address their "relational estate" as well as their property and other legal interests.[3] The relational estate includes the spouses' emotional dynamics and the respect spouses give each other in their interactions and co-parenting tasks. This notion is particularly important because a divorce that includes children, while a significant life event in itself, is really a transition within the family's overall timeline. Children generally benefit when they can understand divorce as a transition from one kind of family relationship to another, rather than as a time when their relationship with either parent was severed. If family lawyers learn to appreciate the relational estates of their clients' divorces, even apart from other pressing legal issues, they will manage their clients' cases more effectively. As a result, whether considering mediation or settlement options or when preparing for trial, lawyers will be less likely to entangle themselves in their clients' emotional struggles. An added benefit may be the appreciation of a satisfied client whose divorce was handled competently and sensitively in the midst of a trying time.

THE EMOTIONAL EFFECTS OF DIVORCE AND RESILIENCY

Much research and writing in the past twenty years—including countless books and articles in the popular press—have explored the emotions in family relationships affected by divorce, including spouses' relationships with each other, parents' relationships with their children, and how these relationships are affected by the family's new realities. Much of this literature focused on the negative effects of divorce on children.[4] But later research using quantified measures of adjustment and comparisons with non-divorce families paints a more nuanced picture of divorce's long-term effects on family members.

While the experiences of separation and divorce may upend family members' emotional lives in the short term, the experiences for most spouses do not leave lasting negative emotional effects.[5] In fact, many divorced spouses, over time, use the stressful and confusing divorce experiences to grow personally and seek new opportunities.[6]

Psychologists who have studied divorce point to the notion of resiliency to explain how many adults adjust their lives after divorce. They note that protective factors and risk factors interact to impact post-divorce emotional and life adjustments. These factors determine a person's resiliency, or capacity to adapt, when encountering difficulties and recovering from perceived or actual setbacks.[7] Protective factors include: social maturity, emotional autonomy, self-confidence, social support, work satisfaction, and a new intimate relationship. In contrast, risk factors include: behaviors associated with antisocial personality, impulsivity, anxiety and ongoing depression, promiscuity, and continued obsessive attachments to the former spouse.[8] People with more protective factors do better; those with more risk factors do worse. But even this balance is contextual—a protective factor appropriate at one time may not be so at another time.[9]

More recent research on the emotional effects of divorce also paints nuanced pictures of the long-term effects of divorce on children. Short term, children often are confused about why their parents are separating and divorcing, and even children with strong emotional attachments to caring parents may become quite distressed.[10] Many children express surprise and sadness at their parents' decision to divorce, even though they may have witnessed loud and aggressive arguments or physical altercations between their parents. Commonly, children pine for their parents' reconciliation. In addition, these children may become depressed and anxious, act out behaviorally, or blame the parent whom they perceived "broke up" the family. But the research shows that though divorce increases children's risk of psychological, academic, and social problems, the great majority of children whose parents divorce function, over time, with the same competence as children whose parents are married.[11]

As with adults, the notion of resiliency—encompassing protective and risk factors—helps to explain how children may adapt to the life changes of divorce. Good parenting that balances emotional warmth, reasonable limits, and consistency may be the most important protective factor for children whose parents are divorcing.[12] Such authoritative parenting, in contrast to overly indulgent or authoritarian styles, creates predictability in the child's home life, fosters mutual trust between the parent and child, and engenders respect of the parent by the child.[13] In addition, children with easier, adaptable temperaments tend to adjust more readily to divorce's changes. Children with more difficult temperaments—demanding, anxious, impulsive—are more challenging to parents under the best of circumstances and even more so during a divorce.[14] Also, children with good social skills tend to attract others who will support them, while children who experience difficulties relating with others may find themselves with less support to help navigate the troubling effects of their family breakups.[15] Notably, persistent conflict between parents following separation and divorce is a prime stressor and risk factor for children.[16]

Some writings have emphasized long-term negative emotional consequences of divorce on children.[17] Emery noted that these writings were based primarily on clinical interviews during which the children expressed their pained feelings about the past divorce, leading the researchers to focus primarily on the children's distress. In addition, those researchers did not compare the adjustments of children of divorce with those of children from non-divorce homes. In contrast, Emery concluded—from his and others' research based on quantified measures of mental health problems among young adults from both divorce and non-divorce homes—that most young adults whose parents divorced when they were children did well but still had painful memories about the divorce. Emery found that the resilience of these young adults grew around the pain, not in its absence.[18] Hetherington noted from her research that most young adults from divorced families looked similar to their contemporaries from non-divorce homes and observed, "[A]lthough they looked back on their parents' breakup as a painful experience, most were successfully going about the chief tasks of young adulthood: establishing careers, creating intimate relationships, building meaningful lives for themselves."[19]

In sum, divorce is an emotionally difficult period. Adults and children express their unsettledness during that period through emotional symptoms and uncharacteristic acting-out behaviors. But most adults regain their emotional bearings. And, over time, the life adjustment of most children whose parents divorced is not different from the adjustment of children whose parents did not divorce. It appears that emotional resiliency in adults and children contributes to the likelihood of good post-divorce adjustment: as noted earlier, people with more protective factors do better, while those with more risk factors do worse.

THREE KEYS TO UNDERSTANDING PROBLEM DIVORCES

In addition to understanding normal, long-term emotional responses to divorce, family lawyers should attune themselves to three key issues when trying to understand problem divorces:

1. The spouses' different perceptions of their marriages and the effects of those perceptions on the decision to separate and divorce
2. The emotional impact of events around the marital separation
3. The sources of impasses, or impediments, to resolving the divorce

Family lawyers should attune themselves to three key issues when trying to understand problem divorces:

1. The spouses' different perceptions of their marriages and the effects of those perceptions on the decision to separate and divorce
2. The emotional impact of events around the marital separation
3. The sources of impasses, or impediments, to resolving the divorce

Of course, underlying these key issues is the reality that many people during divorce experience difficulties managing their emotions in situations they might have handled more appropriately during the marriage or in their lives in general. Anger, sadness, guilt, anticipation, shame, embarrassment, humiliation, and relief are but some of the emotions mixed in the divorce cauldron. And, added to the increased tension and verbal sparring, couples may even engage in isolated, uncharacteristic post-separation physical altercations—at times, witnessed by the children—that become fodder for later domestic violence allegations.[20] Divorcing spouses vary in their capacities to understand and manage these difficult divorce-engendered feelings. How the spouses manage their emotions in the context of these three key issues will give lawyers insights about their clients and their clients' spouses during the legal divorce process.

The First Key—Recognizing "His" and "Her" Marriage

Spouses often view their marriages differently, a phenomenon that has been referred to as "his" and "her" marriage.[21] Differences in life experiences, resources, perceptions, and coping styles contribute to these different views of the marriage. These differences create dissimilar styles by which spouses relate to each other and seek to meet their marital needs and expectations.[22] As the couple experiences more problems, their different views and expectations of the marriage may diverge further, and "his" and "her" marriages may take on lives of their own, retrospectively redefining the marriage's meaning and goals in each spouse's mind. At such times, spouses may feel both justified and shamed by their behaviors with each other. If the problems persist and the spouses harden their own marital view as "the way it was," the conflict may become entrenched. These spouses will experience more difficulty when they seek to resolve their divorce issues.

The notion of "his" and "her" marriage also helps to explain emotional dynamics of the marital separation and post-separation period. At the separation, few spouses mutually agree that a divorce is best for the marriage. In most troubled marriages, the separation occurs when one spouse leaves and the other is left. The leaver and the spouse left behind are usually at different places in their feelings and thinking about the marriage or the specter of divorce.[23] Typically, the leaver has thought about divorce for some time: emotionally grieving the marriage loss; thinking about how life will be after the separation and divorce; and, often, considering living arrangements and accommodations for the children.

The spouse left behind is in a different emotional place. Typically, this spouse is surprised, even stunned, by the leaver's separation announcement and departure. While the leaver contemplated divorce for a while, perhaps even for years, the spouse left behind, although recognizing the marriage was troubled, may not have anticipated the marriage's sudden end. These spouses become depressed and uncertain about why the marriage is ending, and they often offer to do whatever may be necessary to reconcile the marriage.[24]

The interactions between these separated spouses take on characteristic styles.[25] Plaintive pleas for reconsideration and promises of change by the left behind spouse often pervade interactions between the spouses early in the separation period. The leaving spouse may then feel guilty and respond to the left spouse's appeals. But as the left spouse's hopes for reconciliation are then raised, the leaving spouse rebounds away from the relationship, sometimes in anger. And the cycle continues. Clearly, such spouses, at the separation, will not be at the same stable, emotional place; they will not be for a while. But it is during this time that the spouses retain their lawyers to start the task of obtaining a legal divorce. While most spouses will, over time, adapt to the reality of their divorce, many spouses during the separation period still struggle with their cycling emotions: the leavers, wishing to move ahead quickly with the divorce process (perhaps too ready to accommodate unreasonable financial and child custody demands), and the left behind spouses, aching to pull the reins on a perceived unrestrained process.[26]

In sum, understanding that spouses perceive their marriages differently is the first key that can help family lawyers gain further insight into what is happening with their clients and clients' spouses during the divorce process. These divergent marital perceptions predictably generate distinct emotional reactions by the time the spouses contact their family lawyers. Those reactions then may rigidify and define positions that frustrate subsequent problem solving during the divorce process.

The Second Key—Understanding the Marital Separation Events

What happened during the marital separation day is a second key factor family lawyers should understand when weighing the emotional dynamics of the divorces they handle. Most couples view the separation day as the day their marriage ended. Couples often cannot recall the date their divorce was final, but they clearly recall when they separated. The separation often is a time of major emotional, and often physical, disruption, even disorganization. The family's future at the time is unknown.[27] What happens at the separation strongly influences the post-separation perceptions spouses will have of each other. Understanding what happened on the separation day often provides insight into the later motivations, thinking, and behaviors of both spouses.

The private and the public aspects of the marital separation combine to generate spouses' emotional reactions. Johnston and Campbell described two types of separations that decrease the likelihood that the spouses will appropriately manage their post-separation emotions to resolve the divorce: the unexpected, traumatic separation; and the ambivalent separation.[28] Unexpected, traumatic separations include those of sudden desertion, humiliating involvement of a lover, or uncharacteristic violence. In response, the aggrieved spouse may experience an enormous betrayal of trust and may react in uncharacteristic ways. Subsequently, the spouses will begin to redefine each other's character in polarized, negative ways and "rewrite" the marriage's history. Over a short period, countless ambiguous interactions during the marriage that were resolved with good will, the expectations of good intentions, or forgiveness begin to coalesce around the new negative, pejorative theme. As a result, these spouses may claim that they finally discovered who the other spouse really was; "his" and "her" marriages—discussed in the first key to understanding problem divorces—then show themselves in graphic relief. If these "redefinitions" stand uncorrected, they will provide rationales for distrusting the other spouse's motivations, for resisting agreements that could resolve key divorce issues—whether related to money, property, or children[29]—and for seeking "vindication" in court.

A second kind of marital separation that may characterize divorcing couples is the ambivalent separation. In these separations, couples have difficulty making decisions about the divorce because they cannot let go of the marriage and, as a result, resist settlement decisions or finalizing their divorces. Their post-separation periods are characterized by repeated separations and reunions. Essentially, these couples cannot live together or apart.[30]

While the different separation styles may begin as private marital struggles, the separation and decision to divorce eventually become public. Then, both the leaving spouse and the left behind spouse must deal with reactions of family, friends, workmates, and, at times, religious or other communities in which they have been involved.[31] Often, the spouses kept their marital troubles under wraps, sharing their problems with only a select few friends or counselors. But after the separation, other friends and acquaintances, in response to questions about why the couple are divorcing, may be unsatisfied with generic answers of incompatibility. In the face of this ambiguity, the leaving spouse may bear the primary "blame"—after all, the leaver chose to leave. In contrast, the left behind spouse often is viewed as the one trying mightily to reconcile the marriage. When perceived that way, the left behind spouse may hold fast to the victim role in order to maintain the moral edge in the marital conflict and, possibly, to extract guilt-induced concessions in later settlement negotiations or in mediation. Each spouse has his or her constructed story that in bitter divorces may form rationales for trial strategy or settlement accommodations, or develop into entrenched, negative myths about the other.[32]

In sum, understanding what happened at marital separation is a second key that can help the family lawyer gain further insight into what is happening with the client and the client's spouse during the divorce process and after. What happened at the separation may lead spouses to "redefine" their partners in new, often more negative, ways and frustrate the development of even a modicum of trust that is important to negotiate divorce agreements.

The Third Key—Recognizing Sources of Impasses to Resolving the Divorce

Recognizing the sources of impasses between the spouses that heighten tension and, thus, impede the divorce's resolution is the third key to helping family lawyers gain insight into the dynamics of a difficult divorce. Couples are at an impasse when they are stuck, and problem solving seems dead in the water. The divorce negotiations cannot move forward without working through that obstacle. At such times, spouses' positions have hardened—at least as they see it—and neither is willing to concede. Each spouse reinforces the other's hardened positions in cycles of mutual behaviors that only "prove" the other's views.[33] Johnston and Campbell provide a useful model to help untangle these dynamics and target the impasses' sources. They posit that elements of impasses may occur, separately or jointly, on three levels: the external, the interactional, and the intrapsychic.[34]

At the external level, significant others may stoke the conflict by supporting the spouses' claims, particularly as those claims reflect one-sided, negative accounts from "his" or "her" side of the marriage.[35] For example, extended family members, including parents, grandparents, and siblings of a spouse, may weigh into the divorce problems, sympathetically resonating with the loved one's pain. New spouses, in child custody modification actions, may seek to rescue their aggrieved spouses from the "bad" former spouse. In addition, MHP therapists who misunderstand their roles and professional obligations in their clients' child custody cases may give cover to spouses who feel they must hold fast to their hardened positions. Such MHPs may assert that a child is fearful of the noncustodial parent or has been abused by that parent while not having interviewed that supposedly feared parent or seen the child with that parent. Or, such MHPs may opine that a child has been abused by a parent with whom those professionals have had no contact. In addition, such MHPs may urge the client parent—without knowing the family's history or marital dynamics—to withhold the child from the other parent's contact in violation of court orders or otherwise encourage the client parent to continue the child custody fight when realistic negotiated options are possible. Even lawyers may become so emotionally overinvolved in these cases that they lose professional perspective and exacerbate the conflicts. Spouses who overrely on these significant others on the external level deflect responsibility for decisions or negotiation options by invoking the advice of these strong advocates with hopes that these advocates will help them prevail in court.

At the interactional level, the second impasse level, continuation of the spouses' conflictual marriage relationship may cause impasses when these spouses try to resolve an important divorce issue. If the couple fought often in their marriage, saving face by not yielding to the other spouse's hardened position, particularly during this emotional period, may just reprise previous problem-solving situations. In addition, marital separation dynamics—the traumatic separation or ambivalent separation types discussed earlier—and their resultant feelings of humiliation, loss, betrayal, and fear of the future may contribute to impasses at the interactional level. Finally, a child's emotional and behavioral problems may contribute to an impasse at this level.[36] For example, two parents may fight to a standstill over their child's misbehavior, one accusing the other of poor discipline, and the other parent upset that the accuser will not see the necessity of having the child examined for attention deficit hyperactivity disorder.

At the intrapsychic level, the third impasse level, the spouses' individual emotional reactions to the separation or divorce may create barriers leading to impasses in resolving certain divorce-related issues. Because spouses experience a number of different emotional reactions during this period, they are unlikely to be at the same emotional place in the divorce's emotional cycle. In addition, not everyone deals with stress, divorce-related or otherwise, similarly. Some people are better able than others to manage conflicted feelings and difficult circumstances. Others may be so ready to escape the marriage that they dismiss—too readily, too harshly, and with little, if any, insight—the other spouse's emotional reactions to the changed circumstances.

And the feelings of some spouses may, in the extreme, energize characteristic, enduring patterns of thinking and behaving that are inflexible and self-defeating.[37] Such spouses may seek to protect themselves emotionally from the perceived hurts of the separation or divorce by refusing to settle or by seeking personal and public vindications by taking the custody case to trial. They may cast their battle as good versus bad. Often spurious abuse allegations are traced to emotional or personality disorders of bitter spouses or those seeking vindication in court;[38] these allegations must be distinguished from credible allegations through careful and reliable evaluations. Finally, some couples experience such ambivalence about the divorce that they impede efforts to resolve important issues that would bring the divorce process to an end.

In sum, identifying whether sources of impasses are external, interactional, and/or intrapsychic will provide family lawyers with insights into the actions and motivations of their clients or their clients' spouses. But just having the insights may not suggest easy impasse resolutions. For example, if an impasse is due solely to the influence of a spouse's parents (external), that concern might be easily addressed. But if the impasse also stems from a traumatic separation (interactional) and other individual emotional problems (intrapsychic), all three levels would be implicated, making the impasse more ingrained. Keep in mind that impasses arise from coping strategies—albeit often self-defeating—spouses use to protect themselves from the emotional effects and uncertainties of the impending divorce. In such cases, family lawyers might seek the advice of an MHP knowledgeable about marital and divorce dynamics to help fashion strategies that either break down or sidestep the impasse.

Family law matters involve personal and intimate concerns of spouses that may significantly impact the legal divorce or modification actions. Family lawyers will be able to understand better the context of conclusions and opinions by MHP experts when they recognize and monitor the emotional effects of divorce during the course of a contentious family law case.

NOTES

1.   *See* Holmes & Rahe, *Holmes-Rahe Life Changes Scale,* 11 J. PSYCHOSOMATIC RES. 213 (1967).

2.   *See* E. MAVIS HETHERINGTON & JOHN KELLY, FOR BETTER OR FOR WORSE: DIVORCE RECONSIDERED 2 (2002).

3.   *See* PAULINE TESLER, COLLABORATIVE LAW: ACHIEVING EFFECTIVE RESOLUTION IN DIVORCE WITHOUT LITIGATION (2001).

4.   *See, e.g.,* JUDITH S. WALLERSTEIN & S. BLAKESLEE, SECOND CHANCES: MEN, WOMEN, AND CHILDREN A DECADE AFTER DIVORCE (1989).

5.   *See* HETHERINGTON & KELLY, *supra* note 2, at 5–7 (2002).

6.   *Id.* at 65.

7.   *Id.* at 71.

8.   *Id.* at 67–93.

9.   *Id.* at 89.

10.   *See* JUDITH S. WALLERSTEIN & JOAN B. KELLY, SURVIVING THE BREAKUP (1980).

11.   ROBERT E. EMERY, THE TRUTH ABOUT CHILDREN AND DIVORCE 66 (2004).

12.   HETHERINGTON & KELLY, *supra* note 2, at 127–28.

13.   *Id.* at 128.

14. *Id.* at 147–48.

15. *Id.* at 148–49.

16. *See* Robert E. Emery, *Interparental Conflict and the Children of Discord and Divorce,* 92 Psychol. Bull. 310 (1982); *see also* Joan B. Kelly & Robert E. Emery, *Children's Adjustment Following Divorce: Risk and Resilience Perspectives,* 52 Fam. Rel. 352 (2003).

17. *See, e.g.,* Elizabeth Marquardt, Between Two Worlds: The Inner Lives of Children of Divorce (2005); *see also* Wallerstein & Blakeslee, *supra* note 4.

18. Emery, *supra* note 11, at 81.

19. Hetherington & Kelly, *supra* note 2, at 7.

20. Janet R. Johnston & Linda E.G. Campbell, *A Clinical Typology of Interparental Violence in Disputed-Custody Divorces,* 63 Amer. J. Orthopsychiatry 190 (1993).

21. *See* Jesse Bernard, The Future of Marriage (1975). *See also* Walter R. Schumm, Anthony P. Jurich, Stephan R. Bollman & Margaret A. Bugaighis, *His and Her Marriage Revisited,* 6 J. Fam. Issues 221 (1985); and Maureen R. Waller & Sara S. McLanahan, *"His" and "Her" Marriage Expectations: Determinants and Consequences,* 67 J. Marriage & Fam. 53 (2005).

22. Hetherington & Kelly, *supra* note 2, at 23–42.

23. *See* Constance R. Ahrons, The Good Divorce 89–92 (1994); *see also* Robert E. Emery, Renogotiating Family Relationships, 33–40 (1994).

24. *See* Ahrons, *supra* note 23, at 89–92.

25. *Id.*

26. *See* Emery, *supra* note 23, at 36–40.

27. *See* Ahrons, *supra* note 23, at 109–18.

28. Janet R. Johnston & Linda E.G. Campbell, Impasses of Divorce 14–15 (1988).

29. *Id.*

30. *Id.* at 15.

31. Ahrons, *supra* note 23, at 90.

32. *Id.* at 91.

33. Johnston & Campbell, *supra* note 28, at 12.

34. *Id.* at 12.

35. *Id.*

36. *Id.* at 12–13.

37. *See* American Psychiatric Association, Diagnostic and Statistical Manual of Mental Disorders (4th ed., Text Revision 686, 2000) [hereinafter DSM-IV-TR].

38. Johnston & Campbell, *supra* note 28, at 16.

CHAPTER 3

The Legal Perspective

After recognizing key emotional dynamics of divorce, family lawyers must consider the legal perspective—the second of three critical perspectives—when they evaluate the reports and testimony of MHPs. The legal perspective centers on determining the reliability and admissibility of MHPs' conclusions and expert opinions. The practical four-step model presented in this chapter will help family lawyers gauge the clarity and potential usefulness of the mental health materials and testimony they consider in their cases and organize their admissibility arguments.

In most jurisdictions, the rules of evidence allow an expert witness to offer opinions in court if the expert is qualified to offer those opinions and if those opinions "will assist the trier of fact to understand the evidence or to determine a fact in issue."[1] Some jurisdictions still impose the older, more stringent standard that the knowledge imparted by the expert be "beyond the ken" of an ordinary person.[2] One principle recognized consistently is that expert testimony must be reliable to assist the trier of fact. The two seminal cases giving rise to the standards for evaluating expert testimony are *Frye v. United States*[3] and *Daubert v. Merrell Dow Pharmaceuticals*.[4] Legal reliability refers to the "trustworthiness" of the evidence.[5] In his influential 1980 review of *Frye*, Professor Paul Giannelli asserted that "the probative value of scientific evidence is connected inextricably to its reliability: if the technique is not reliable, evidence derived from the technique cannot be relevant."[6]

What standard, then, should the court use to ensure the reliability and, thus, the admissibility of the evidence or testimony? While courts in the nineteenth and early twentieth centuries relied primarily on the expert's qualifications to decide whether to admit that expert's testimony, today's state courts, as mentioned earlier, look to variants of two tests to gauge that testimony's evidentiary reliability and admissibility: the *Frye* test and the *Daubert* test. In this chapter, we will look at each test and then draw on shared principles to build a practical four-step model for addressing the legal quality of mental health reports and testimony. While developing the model's steps, we will also examine how MHPs' practice guidelines, ethics codes, and prevailing practices provide rich sources with which to measure the quality and reliability of MHPs' expert testimony.

THE *FRYE* TEST

Introduction and Concerns

The *Frye* test arose in a 1923 federal D.C. Circuit case to address the admissibility of evidence derived from a crude precursor to the polygraph machine. The question was this: How should the court determine whether novel scientific techniques are reliable enough to be admitted into evidence? In a frequently quoted phrase, the *Frye* court wrote: "[W]hile courts will go a long way in admitting expert testimony deduced from a well-recognized scientific principle of discovery, the thing from which the deduction is made must be sufficiently established to have gained general acceptance in the particular field in which it belongs."[7] *Frye*, in contrast to the prior approach that required only qualified experts to support expert testimony, held that expert opinions must be generally accepted by the relevant scientific community—a standard beyond initial experimentation.[8] The *Frye* test assumed that an accepted scientific technique would have undergone extensive testing in the relevant scientific community.[9] In sum, *Frye* established a method to ensure the reliability of scientific evidence by directing "that those most qualified to assess the general validity of a scientific method will have the determinative voice."[10] In other words, the scientific community would act as a kind of technical jury.[11]

But while *Frye* brought definition—beyond just the expert's qualifications—to the task of gauging the admissibility of expert testimony based on novel scientific techniques, the standard itself raised other questions. These questions continue to provide bases for examining scientific expert testimony in *Frye* jurisdictions or in *Daubert* courts when experts seek to invoke the *Daubert* factor of "whether the theory or technique has been generally accepted as valid by the relevant scientific community."[12] Namely:

- In what relevant scientific community is the novel technique accepted? That is, a more general group of experts or a more select group within the general group?
- What percentage of those in the relevant scientific community must accept the technique for the technique to be generally accepted?[13]
- May a single witness alone sufficiently represent, or attest to, the views of an entire scientific community regarding the reliability of the new technique or principle?[14]
- How much empirical research—if any—supporting the technique is sufficient to be deemed accepted by the relevant scientific community?[15]
- Courts have often cited legal and scientific publications to satisfy the general acceptance standard—"a type of judicial notice."[16] But courts using these publications are not judicially noticing the validity of a technique; rather, they are taking judicial notice of articles, texts, and other publications, both legal and scientific, in attempting to determine whether general acceptance has been achieved.[17] How valid, or "trustworthy," are these publications? And have all the relevant articles been presented to the court, including those that question the validity of the novel technique?[18]
- Because the *Frye* test is intended to gauge the admissibility of novel scientific evidence, how much extrapolation to untested situations should be permitted and still allow the technique to be admitted into evidence?
- What must be accepted: the underlying scientific principle, the technique applying it, or both?[19]

- Finally, Professor Giannelli noted that "perhaps the most important flaw in the *Frye* test is that by focusing attention on the general acceptance issue, the test obscures critical problems in the use of a particular technique."[20] While a particular technique might be generally accepted, how that technique is used by the expert or whether alternative methods may be more valid might highlight the weaknesses in the generally accepted technique used by the expert.

The Different Faces of *Frye*

Despite these concerns, a number of states continue to use *Frye*'s general acceptance test to gauge the admissibility of scientific evidence, although they may employ *Frye* differently. While the principle inquiry is the same, different *Frye* applications emphasize various *Frye* concerns when gauging the reliability of the expert's testimony. A sampling of those concerns shows how different jurisdictions use *Frye* and highlights points with which to examine or cross-examine experts in both *Frye* and *Daubert* jurisdictions—there is some overlap in the analyses because the general acceptance test is one factor the judge may consider in a *Daubert* jurisdiction to gauge the reliability of the expert's methods and testimony.[21]

To apply the general acceptance test, lawyers first must ask how "general acceptance in the field" is defined. The Arizona Supreme Court observed that the reliability inquiry is not scientific "nose-counting." Rather, the degree of acceptance in the scientific community, the novelty of the scientific principle, and the existence of specialized literature on the subject should be considered.[22]

The California Supreme Court concluded that general acceptance means a consensus—not an absolute unanimity of views—drawn from a typical cross-section of the relevant, qualified scientific community. But mere "numerical majority" of expert opinion regarding the technique is insufficient;[23] rather, a clear majority of the relevant scientific community must accept the expert's proffered methodology before expert testimony can be admitted.[24] Further, a "scientific consensus by major voices in the scientific community" is consistent with *Kelly/Frye*.[25] Further, the court noted that when evaluating whether a scientific technique meets the general acceptance standard, courts should consider the quality, as well as the quantity, of the scientific literature and opinion supporting or opposing the technique.[26]

The Florida Supreme Court echoed these assertions when it stated that while general acceptance of a technique in the scientific community can be established if a clear majority of that community's members support the technique, trial courts also must consider the quality of the evidence supporting or opposing a new scientific technique.[27] Further, "mere numerical majority support or opposition by persons minimally qualified to state an authoritative opinion is of little value."[28]

A second *Frye* issue over which states have struggled is whether the general acceptance test applies to generally accepted methods only, to the expert's methods and reasoning from the data derived from those methods, or to an expert's ultimate opinion.[29] For example, in *People v. Wesley*, the New York Court of Appeals found that the *Frye* test gauges "whether there is general acceptance in the relevant scientific community that a technique or procedure is capable of being performed reliably."[30] In Florida, while the *Frye* test is applied in a four-step process when expert opinion testimony concerns a new or novel scientific principle,[31] "the burden is on the proponent of the evidence to prove the general acceptance of both the underlying scientific principle and the testing procedures used to apply that principle to the facts of the case at hand."[32] In *Lofgren v. Motorola, Inc.*, an Arizona trial court held that a court must scrutinize an expert's reasoning as well as the methodology employed.[33]

A third *Frye* issue over which states have differed is whether *Frye* should apply only to novel scientific evidence or to all scientific testimony. Recall that the *Frye* decision itself focused on a crude form of polygraphy, a novel scientific technique at the time. In California state courts, the *Kelly/Frye* doctrine—California's complement to the *Frye* test—applies only to new scientific techniques.[34] The same holds in Arizona.[35] The Pennsylvania Supreme Court, while it has applied the *Frye* test to novel scientific evidence, has not established whether *Frye* may also apply to all expert evidence.[36] But in *Thomas v. West Bend Co.*,[37] the Pennsylvania Superior Court—the appellate court below the Pennsylvania Supreme Court—held that general acceptance "applies not only to new inventions, but whenever science enters the courtroom."

An important *Frye* issue for mental health testimony is whether the test should apply to social science evidence. It appears that *Frye* generally has not applied to social science evidence except in some cases for so-called social science explanative theories, such as post-traumatic stress disorder, battered wife syndrome, and child sexual abuse syndrome.[38] For example, in a case involving repressed memories, the Arizona Supreme Court noted that "*Frye* is inapplicable when a qualified witness offers relevant testimony or conclusions based on experience and observation about human behavior for the purpose of explaining that behavior."[39] That court noted similar exceptions for mental health testimony in rape cases and on child abuse accommodation syndrome.[40] California's Supreme Court recognized in *People v. Stoll*[41] that the MMPI and the MCMI, which are standard psychological tests, were not new to psychology or the law and that diagnostic use of written personality inventories has been established for decades.[42] Consequently, the court concluded that this testing was not subject to a *Frye* analysis. The *Stoll* court also acknowledged, "We have never applied the *Kelly/Frye* rule to expert medical testimony, even when the witness is a psychiatrist and the subject matter is as esoteric as the reconstitution of a past state of mind or the prediction of future dangerousness, or even the diagnosis of an unusual form of mental illness not listed in the diagnostic manual of the American Psychiatric Association."[43]

In sum, the *Frye* test, while not the admissibility standard in federal courts, still is the primary test to determine admissibility of scientific evidence in many state courts. But states differ in the ways they apply *Frye* and the elements they emphasize in their *Frye* versions. Despite *Frye*'s longtime use, many questions about its assumptions and application remain. Defining the relevant scientific community in which a particular technique is accepted is but one key concern. In addition, it appears that *Frye* is applied infrequently when the admissibility of social science evidence is at issue; in such cases, courts may look more to experts' qualifications and allow the jury to decide the weight to give those experts' opinions. Nevertheless, understanding *Frye*'s strengths and weaknesses and its various uses will provide family lawyers useful fodder for both direct- and cross-examination of experts in court.

THE *DAUBERT* TEST

Introduction

The *Daubert* test is the other test that many state courts have adapted to gauge evidentiary reliability and admissibility of expert scientific evidence. *Daubert* principles were introduced in a 1993 U.S. Supreme Court case, *Daubert v. Merrell Dow Pharmaceuticals.*[44] Two subsequent cases, *General Electric v. Joiner*[45] and *Kumho Tire Co., Ltd. v. Carmichael,*[46] fleshed out and clarified those principles. This case trilogy established that the Federal Rules of Evidence, not the *Frye* test, provide the proper standard for the admission of expert testimony in federal courts.[47] The *Daubert* Court reasoned that nothing in Federal Rule of Evidence 702 (governing expert testimony in federal courts) established "general acceptance" as the absolute prerequisite to admissibility of expert testimony.[48] Rather, "the trial judge must ensure that any and all scientific testimony or evidence admitted is not only relevant, but reliable."[49]

The relevance requirement incorporates traditional relevancy analysis under Rules 401 and 402 of the Federal Rules of Evidence. Rule 401 defines relevant evidence as that which has "any tendency to make the existence of any fact that is of consequence to the determination of the action more probable or less probable than it would be without the evidence." Rule 402 provides that all relevant evidence is admissible unless rendered inadmissible by the Constitution, an Act of Congress, the Rules of Evidence, or other rules prescribed by the Supreme Court. Rule 402 further provides that "evidence which is not relevant is not admissible."

In addition, the *Daubert* Court held that all scientific testimony or admitted evidence must be based on reliable, or trustworthy, methodology[50] and is not applied only to novel scientific techniques or evidence.[51] The trial judge, as the evidence gatekeeper, must assess "whether the reasoning or methodology underlying the testimony is scientifically valid and whether that reasoning or methodology properly can be applied to the facts in issue."[52] The Court proposed a nonexclusive list of "general observations" to help the trial judge determine the validity of the methodology underlying the expert's opinion(s):[53]

- the extent to which the theory or technique has been or can be tested
- whether the theory or technique has been subjected to peer review and publication
- the known or potential rate of error of the particular scientific technique
- whether the theory or technique has been generally accepted as valid by the relevant scientific community

The *Daubert* Court emphasized that this inquiry, envisioned by Rule 702, was flexible,[54] and even noted that other authorities have presented their own different set of factors.[55] Nevertheless, the Court noted that the inquiry's "overarching subject is the scientific validity—and thus the evidentiary relevance and reliability—of the principles that underlie the proposed submission."[56]

Joiner, the second case in the *Daubert* trilogy, focused on what standard an appellate court should apply in reviewing a trial court's decision to admit or exclude expert testimony under *Daubert*. The Supreme Court in *Joiner* held that abuse of discretion was the appropriate standard.[57] The *Joiner* Court also stretched the *Daubert* reliability analysis from just an examination of the expert's methodology to include the expert's conclusions and opinions.[58]

Kumho Tire, the third case in the *Daubert* trilogy, addressed the question of whether the *Daubert* inquiry applied only to "scientific knowledge." The Supreme Court held that *Daubert's* general principles applied in federal courts to all expert testimony covered by Rule 702, not just "scientific knowledge."[59] However, the Court stated, "a trial court should consider the specific factors identified in *Daubert where they are reasonable measures of the reliability of expert testimony*" (emphasis added).[60] Nevertheless, the Court emphasized that the objective of the *Daubert* requirement was "to ensure the reliability and relevancy of expert testimony," even though the expert presented acceptable qualifications.[61]

While the Supreme Court in *Daubert* intended to present trial judges with a flexible way to assess the reliability of scientific testimony, doubters questioned whether trial judges could accomplish this task effectively. Chief Justice Rehnquist, in his *Daubert* dissent, noted that while he agreed that judges had gatekeeping responsibilities in deciding whether to admit expert testimony, he did not believe that those responsibilities imposed on them "either the obligation or the authority to become amateur scientists in order to perform that role."[62] For example, Chief Justice Rehnquist noted that while he had confidence in federal judges, he himself was "at a loss to know what is meant when it is said that the scientific status of a theory depends on its 'falsifiability.'"[63] Subsequent research has shown that judges understand the less technical, traditional *Daubert* factors (general acceptance, peer review, and publication) but not the more technical ones (falsifiability and error rate), and that judges prefer looking to general acceptance and expert qualifications when weighing the admissibility of psychological evidence.[64]

Further, some expert testimony, such as mental health testimony or economic valuations, may not easily fit the *Daubert* factors. How, then, may the reliability of such expert testimony be assessed? Two principles emerge from state and federal cases that hearken to *Daubert*: the Applicable Professional Standards Test and the Analytical Gap Test. *Watkins v. Telsmith*, relying on *Daubert*, highlighted the first principle, noting that "the [district] court should ensure that the opinion comports with *applicable professional standards* outside the courtroom, and that it will have a reliable basis in the knowledge and experience of the discipline."[65]

The second principle, the Analytical Gap Test, arose in the *Joiner* decision—the second case in the *Daubert* trilogy. The Supreme Court recognized that "conclusions and methodology are not entirely distinct from one another. . . . [N]othing in either *Daubert* or the Federal Rules of Evidence requires a district court to admit opinion evidence which is connected to existing data only by the *ipse dixit* of the expert. A court may conclude that there is simply too great an *analytical gap* between the data and the opinion proffered."[66] The Texas Supreme Court complement case to *Kumho Tire* added to the *Joiner* quotation: "[I]t is not so simply because an expert says it is so."[67] In stating the importance that the expert's opinion be supported by data, the *Joiner* Court broadened *Daubert's* objective by emphasizing that the analysis would be applied not only to methods but also to the expert's reasoning, conclusions, and proffered opinion.[68]

Keeping pace with *Daubert* case law, the second part of Rule 702 (see in italics) was added in 2000 to reflect *Daubert* basics:

> If scientific, technical, or other specialized knowledge will assist the trier of fact to
> understand the evidence or to determine a fact in issue, a witness qualified as an expert
> by knowledge, skill, experience, training, or education, may testify thereto in the form

of an opinion or otherwise, *if (1) the testimony is based upon sufficient facts or data, (2) the testimony is the product of reliable principles and methods, and (3) the witness has applied the principles and methods reliably to the facts of the case.*

As with the *Frye* test, several states have adopted variations of the *Daubert* approach to guide the trial judge when evaluating expert testimony or evidence.[69] Some states use *Daubert* in some cases but not others, and other states interpret *Daubert* differently. A few states apply some combination of *Frye* and *Daubert*.[70] And some *Daubert* states that have adopted the Federal Rules of Evidence have not incorporated the added *Daubert*-influenced language of amended Rule 702.

Applying *Daubert* in Bench Trials

States differ about what family law issues may be litigated before juries. For example, only Texas allows juries to decide whether parents should be appointed as sole or joint managing custodians of the children. The judge, however, subsequently decides how the parenting rights and duties—for example, education and medical decisions, and access schedules—are to be allocated between the parents and which parent in a joint managing custody arrangement will establish the child's primary residence.[71] Despite the jury options for Texas family law clients and their lawyers, less than 1 percent of all family law dispositions in 2003 were resolved through a jury trial.[72]

The extensive use of bench trials in family law matters begs the question of whether *Daubert* admissibility principles apply in such trials. If there is no jury needing protection from scientifically shoddy expert testimony, does the *Daubert* analysis apply? The government in *Seaboard Lumber Co. v. United States*[73] argued that because *Daubert* emphasized the trial judge's gatekeeping role to prevent jurors from having to consider expert opinions lacking sound scientific basis, a *Daubert* analysis of expert opinions in a bench trial was inapplicable. But the *Seaboard Lumber* court held that while judicial evidentiary gatekeeping concerns were "of less import in a bench trial . . . the *Daubert* standards of relevance and reliability for scientific evidence must nevertheless be met." Judge Richard Posner, in a subsequent case, wrote that judges in bench trials should, while following *Daubert*, have discretion "to admit evidence of borderline admissibility and give it the (slight) weight to which it is entitled."[74] In addition, while *Daubert*'s primary purpose was to protect jurors from considering unreliable expert testimony, *Daubert*'s principles serve other ends: to protect opponents from having to expend resources to counter untrustworthy testimony; to keep the courts from wasting time and resources; and to guard the integrity of the system from seeming reliance on bad science.[75]

In sum, the *Daubert* trilogy of cases, like *Frye*, provides a rich framework by which to judge expert evidence.[76] The trial judge may use the nonexclusive *Daubert* factors to gauge the reliability, or trustworthiness, of certain aspects of mental health testimony—for example, to examine certain psychological tests, proffered diagnoses, or new or unconventional theories. But for testimony or evidence to which the *Daubert* factors do not apply—such as some elements of a child custody study or other evaluation protocols—the judge is free to use other reliability indices, as long as the judge's ruling is not an abuse of discretion. Practically, trial and appellate courts might differ in what expert evidence or testimony is deemed admissible in any particular case. Finally, besides *Daubert*'s listed factors, the

Daubert line of cases points to two other tests to assess whether the expert's evidence is reliable: the Applicable Professional Standards Test and the Analytical Gap Test.

COMPARING *FRYE* AND *DAUBERT*

The *Frye* and *Daubert* tests propose different approaches to address the reliability of expert testimony. The tests differ in that *Frye* looks to the general acceptance of an expert's assertion among a community thought to understand the issue, while *Daubert* charges the trial judge to evaluate directly the opinion's scientific basis.[77] The tests also may differ in what evidence the court might admit: under *Daubert*, testimony that is well based but not generally accepted may be admitted into evidence, while under *Frye*, that testimony may not be admitted.[78] The opposite also may show a difference: under *Frye*, testimony that may not be as scientifically sound but that has gained general acceptance may be admitted into evidence, while under *Daubert*, that testimony might be excluded.[79]

But *Frye* and *Daubert* also share important features. Bernstein argues that case law under *Frye* is slowly converging with *Daubert* views.[80] Shuman notes that these tests share a common concern with relevance and reliability, and they both recognize the importance of separating an assessment of the expert's qualifications from an assessment of the reliability of the expert's methods and procedures.[81] The decisions in both cases recognized that while the testifying experts were qualified, the qualifications alone did not ensure the reliability of the experts' methods or procedures. One key lesson is that expert opinions are not admissible just because someone with a diploma says they are so.[82] Thus, once the expert's qualifications satisfy the court, the central question to the expert is clear-cut: "How do you know what you say you know?" *Frye* and *Daubert*'s shared laser beams of relevance and reliability focus on that question.

A *FRYE-DAUBERT* ANALYSIS MODEL: APPLYING SHARED PRINCIPLES

The two tests arising out of the *Daubert* cases, the Applicable Professional Standards Test and the Analytical Gap Test, form the legal and logical tools by which to analyze the reliability of mental health expert testimony in both *Frye* and *Daubert* jurisdictions. These tests are linchpins of a *Frye-Daubert* Analysis Model (see box below) that will help family lawyers gauge the quality of experts' materials and testimony.

The *Frye-Daubert* Analysis Model requires four steps:

1. Determine whether the witness is qualified as an expert by knowledge, skill, experience, training, or education.
2. Determine whether the expert's methods follow applicable professional standards of the relevant professional specialty.
3. Evaluate the empirical and logical connections between the data arising from the expert's methods and the expert's conclusions.
4. Gauge the connection between the expert's conclusions and the proffered expert opinion.

While this four-step analysis seems straightforward, its application may be tricky. Problems often arise in family law cases where both legal and psychological concepts may be quite abstract, and experts are asked questions that are nested within other questions.[83] For example, addressing the best interest of the child may involve examining children's needs, parents' competencies, family relationships, and factors outside the family. And each of these concerns begs other questions, all producing responses that will require indicia of reliability to be admitted.

In sum, the family lawyer should gauge the evidentiary reliability of the expert's testimony for each question that supports the overall issue the testimony addresses.[84]

> Lawyers who use this *Frye-Daubert* Analysis Model to evaluate experts in their cases will give themselves opportunities to organize and manage mental health issues in their cases effectively and, at the same time, help the court follow the expert examination themes and admissibility arguments.

Step One—Determine Whether the Witness Is Qualified as an Expert.

Gauging the qualifications of a witness offering an expert opinion to the court predates *Frye* and is an element of expert witness testimony defined by Rule 702 of the Federal Rules of Evidence. But what specifically in the proposed expert's background will convince the court that the testimony is trustworthy? May any witness with knowledge, skill, experience, training, or education in the subject at issue be qualified to testify as an expert?

The *Kumho Tire* Court noted that "there are many different kinds of experts, and many different kinds of expertise."[85] Ordinarily, courts will look to the expert's claimed expertise and the demands of the proposed testimony.[86] Courts, while flexible about expert witness qualifications, employ practical, albeit sometimes rough, guidelines. For instance, expert testimony involving medical issues often requires an M.D. or a doctorate in a related scientific field. But consider two other examples from *Gammill v. Jack Williams Chevrolet*, a 1998 Texas Supreme Court case[87] where the relevance and reliability of an expert witness's testimony related to the witness's skills and experiences. In the first example, the court considered a situation in which a lawyer might want to explain to the jury how a bumblebee is able to fly. Certainly, the court explained, an aeronautical engineer might be a helpful witness, applying general flight principles to the case of the bumblebee, even if the engineer had never seen one. Or, if the lawyer wanted to prove that bumblebees always take off into the wind, a beekeeper with no scientific training would be an acceptable witness if the proper foundation related to the beekeeper's first-hand observations—unrelated to any formal training—was laid. The court concluded: "In other words, the beekeeper does not know any more about flight principles than the jurors, but he has seen a lot more bumblebees than they have."[88]

In the second example, the Texas Supreme Court noted that an experienced car mechanic would not be required to resort to engineering principles to provide relevant and reliable expert testimony about problems with a car's performance[89]—think of Marisa Tomei's turn in the movie *My Cousin Vinny* as a car mechanic expert witness whose qualifications were based on knowledge derived from her experiences in a car mechanic's shop. Finally, the Advisory Committee Notes for Rule 702 of the Federal

Rules of Evidence assert: "If the witness is relying solely or primarily on experience, then the witness must explain how that experience leads to the conclusion reached, why that experience is a sufficient basis for the opinion, and how that experience is reliably applied to the facts."[90]

How closely, then, must the expert's qualifications match the requirements of the case? Case law looks at how the expert's qualifications "fit" the issues the expert will address. For example, *Gammill*, the aforementioned Texas Supreme Court case, noted that "[j]ust as not every physician is qualified to testify as an expert in every medical malpractice case, not every mechanical engineer is qualified to testify as an expert in every products liability case."[91] The court further noted that "trial courts must ensure that those who purport to be experts truly have expertise concerning the actual subject about which they are offering an opinion."[92] Several federal cases state this same principle,[93] while other cases provide that although generalists may testify as experts on specialty areas, their lack of expertise in those areas is a matter of weight for the trier of fact.[94]

In sum, the issues about which the expert will testify must be considered when examining a witness's qualifications to testify as an expert. Courts differ on how to weigh the "fit." But a court's decision about whether the proposed expert's qualifications pass muster will be overturned on appeal only for abuse of discretion.

Step Two—Determine Whether the Expert's Methods Follow Applicable Professional Standards of the Relevant Professional Specialty.

The keys to considering whether MHP experts' methods follow Applicable Professional Standards of the relevant professional specialty lie in two areas: (1) learning to use MHPs' ethical codes and practice guidelines that relate to experts' involvement in legal cases, and (2) ensuring that the procedures MHPs use to gather information upon which their opinions are based are accepted in the relevant professional field and can provide a basis for reliable testimony. Recall the two-pronged basis for the Applicable Professional Standards Test: "[T]he [district] court should ensure that the opinion comports with *applicable professional standards* outside the courtroom, and that it will have a reliable basis in the knowledge and experience of the discipline."[95]

Ethical codes and professional guidelines provide a rich source of material to test whether MHPs' expert testimony comports with applicable professional standards. Shuman and Greenberg proposed that ethical rules and professional guidelines—which arise from professional standards and peer review—may assist courts by serving as "red flags" to raise potential problems with the reliability of expert testimony. They stated: "[W]hile compliance with a profession's ethical code or guidelines provides no assurance that the reasoning and methodology underlying the testimony is scientifically valid, failure to comply with [the code or guidelines] is powerful evidence that the reasoning and methodology may be invalid."[96]

Before exploring how ethical codes and professional guidelines may be used to test the reliability of the MHP's expert testimony, it is necessary to distinguish between ethical code standards and practice guidelines. Consider the following documents: the *Ethical Principles of Psychologists and Code of Conduct* (hereinafter *APA Ethics Code*); the *Specialty Guidelines for Forensic Psychologists* (hereinafter *Forensic Specialty Guidelines*); and the American Psychological Association's *Guidelines for Child Cus-*

tody Evaluations in Divorce Proceedings (hereinafter *APA Child Custody Guidelines*). The *APA Ethics Code* notes the contrast between "ethical standards [that] set forth enforceable rules for conduct as psychologists" and "aspirational goals to guide psychologists toward the highest ideals of psychology."[97] In addition, other guidelines published by APA hearken to the distinction between "ethical standards" and "aspirational goals." For example, the *Forensic Specialty Guidelines* "provide an aspirational model of desirable professional practice by psychologists . . . when they are engaged regularly as experts and represent themselves as such in an activity primarily intended to provide professional psychological expertise to the judicial system."[98] The *APA Child Custody Guidelines* contain similar language, noting that the guidelines are aspirational in intent, that they are not intended to be either mandatory or exhaustive, and that their goal is to promote proficiency in using psychological expertise when conducting child custody evaluations.[99]

In sum, ethics codes differ from guidelines; lawyers evaluating MHPs' expert testimony by referencing guidelines should understand the difference. Ethics codes are mandates of minimal levels—the floor—for acceptable professional practice. If MHPs fall short, they may be subject to disciplinary review and, at worst, may be required to give up their licenses to practice. In contrast, practice guidelines (e.g., the *APA Child Custody Guidelines* or the *AFCC Child Custody Standards*)[100] educate MHPs or lay consumers about best practices and generally describe methods and practices to which MHPs might "aspire" in their work. Guidelines are not intended to be mandatory or exhaustive and may not be applicable to every professional and clinical situation.[101]

Should lawyers then treat MHPs' mandatory ethical standards and applicable aspirational guidelines differently? I believe that lawyers should view these as distinctions with few differences. That is, while ethical standards are enforceable rules of conduct for MHPs to which MHPs must comply, forensic MHPs should bear the burden of explaining why they might deviate from applicable guidelines in a particular case.

How, then, may lawyers support the position that MHP experts should conform their evaluations to "aspirational guidelines," a position to which psychologists, for example, might assertively object? The *APA Ethics Code*, while noting that the Preamble and General Principles are aspirational, emphasizes that those principles "should be considered by psychologists in arriving at an ethical course of action and may be considered by ethics bodies in interpreting the Ethical Standards."[102] Also, the *Forensic Specialty Guidelines*[103] and *APA Child Custody Guidelines*[104] purport to "amplify" or "build upon" the *APA Ethics Code*. Further, the *APA Child Custody Guidelines* "are intended to help practitioners interact with the legal system, families, and children in a way that preserves ethical standards and clarifies professional roles."[105] Deviating from applicable guidelines should not be rationalized easily by MHP experts.

In addition to following their respective ethics codes and applicable guidelines, MHPs will usually follow protocols or accepted procedures to gather information that forms the bases of their expert opinions. Because no child custody evaluation protocol as a whole has been validated empirically to address specific custody-related questions, how may MHPs support the reliability of an evaluation's procedures that purport to support their expert opinions? Or, what are the applicable professional standards that "have a reliable basis in the knowledge and experience of the MHP's professional field?"[106]

Lawyers must ensure that MHP experts do not try to shoehorn reliability into an unreliable, or "untrustworthy," method, even by a method purportedly held as "generally accepted" in the field in which the expert is offering testimony. For example, questionable techniques practiced by some sexual abuse investigators that "validate" sexual abuse allegations may invoke this concern. Also, *Kumho Tire* notes that *Daubert*'s general acceptance factor—akin to the *Frye* test—does not help to show that an expert's testimony is reliable "where the discipline itself lacks reliability."[107] Likewise, *Black v. Food Lion*, a 1999 Fifth Circuit Court of Appeals case, noted that an expert's use of general methodology—in this case, an accepted protocol in rendering an opinion that the plaintiff's slip-and-fall injury caused fibromyalgia—"cannot vindicate a conclusion for which there is no underlying medical support."[108]

How might these issues apply to child custody evaluations? Survey research of MHPs who conduct child custody evaluations has established a common set of procedures for these evaluations. Recent surveys confirmed earlier findings about the most prevalent data collection procedures employed by MHPs in child custody evaluations.[109] In addition, this research is supported by the recommended procedures of other published MHPs who specialize in conducting child custody evaluations.[110] Finally, the child custody guidelines of major professional mental health organizations, which are developed by committees of experts within those organizations, recommend that the custody evaluator follow a comprehensive set of procedures similar to that highlighted in the literature before proffering custody recommendations.[111] Hence, the survey research, the recommended procedures of other published psychologists, and the various professional guidelines define a common set of procedures that could support an expert custody opinion in court. MHPs conducting child custody evaluations should explain any deviations from these procedures. These procedures include:

- individual interviews of the parents
- individual interviews of the child
- interviews with significant others, including stepparents, teachers, health care providers, and counselors, among others
- observations of the child jointly with each parent
- some psychological testing
- review of the child's school records

Given that a set of procedures exists that is generally accepted in the professional mental health literature for conducting child custody evaluations, should lawyers assume that all methods MHPs use within those accepted procedures to conduct child custody evaluations will produce reliable data upon which to base an expert opinion? Or, may experts base their opinions on data they collect simply because they claim that the methods that generated the data are generally accepted in the professional community they represent? Clearly, the answer to both questions is no; such testimony puts the cart before the horse.[112] The underlying data should be independently evaluated to determine if the opinion itself is reliable.[113] If the data supporting opinion testimony are unreliable—even from ostensibly generally accepted methodology—any opinion drawn from that data likewise is unreliable.[114]

Step Three—Evaluate the Empirical and Logical Connections Between the Data Arising from the Expert's Methods and the Expert's Conclusions.

The third step—after gauging whether the expert witness is qualified to offer an opinion on an issue before the court, and after considering whether the mental health expert's methods follow applicable professional standards of the relevant professional specialty—is to examine the empirical and logical connections between the data arising from the expert's methods and the expert's conclusions. Note the difference between an expert's conclusions and opinion. The expert's conclusions from the gathered data still fall squarely in the social science realm. For example, do the evaluation data support the expert's conclusion that the father is depressed and that the father's depression compromises his ability to relate to his child? Or, do the data suggest that the mother has a personality disorder that affects her parenting style? In contrast, the expert's opinion applies the conclusions to the legal question before the court. Two examples of legal questions that might elicit an expert's opinion are these: When considering the best interest of the child, which parent should establish the child's primary residence? What access schedule should a parent with a history of physical abuse have with the child?

Experts reach their conclusions by organizing the data gathered from their evaluation methods. Data from unreliable methods cannot lead to reliable conclusions.[115] Recall *Joiner*: "[C]onclusions and methodology are not entirely distinct from one another"[116]—a broadening of *Daubert*, which focused primarily on the experts' methodologies. The tie between data and conclusions makes sense—and is legally required.

Even so, the connections that experts make between their evaluation data and conclusions may not be as tight as experts try to present. The lawyer's key to handling this issue is to understand that experts essentially link data to conclusions by interpretation and synthesis, which are products of their knowledge, experiences, and training. Lawyers should keep in mind the adage that "there is much that may slip between the cup and the lip." Even when experts use empirical research to support the connection, they must decide that the research applies properly and adequately to this specific individual before drawing conclusions. For example, psychological research has shown that depressed parents as a group have less to give emotionally and physically to their young children, which may negatively impact their children's development.[117] Assume that a parent in a child custody evaluation presents as depressed during the evaluation interviews and produces a significant clinical depression scale elevation on a generally accepted psychological test. How will the MHP expert apply the group research underlying the test interpretation—most social science research is group-developed—to this individual parent? It is at this point that the MHP interprets evaluation and research data and synthesizes them to form conclusions about the parent being evaluated. Recall that *Joiner*'s "analytical gap" need not be fully bridged to satisfy the court's reliability requirement. Rather, the gap just cannot be "too great."

If, then, interpretation and synthesis are key elements of how experts develop their conclusions, how broad may the "analytical gap" become before it is "simply too great"? Recall that the trial court's task "is to make certain that an expert, whether basing testimony upon professional studies or personal experience, employs in the courtroom the same level of intellectual rigor that characterizes the practice of an expert in the relevant field."[118] The less "rigorous" the analysis, and the greater the gaps between the expert's methods, data, and conclusions, the less reliable, or trustworthy, those conclusions will be.

Step Four—Gauge the Connection Between the Expert's Conclusions and the Proffered Expert Opinion.

This is the final step when assessing the reliability of mental health expert testimony. But while the previous steps—qualifications, methodology, and the data-to-conclusions links—were strictly social science–based, gauging the connections between experts' conclusions and their proffered opinions has a different character. In this step, MHPs seek to apply their social science–based conclusions to legal standards. Common legal standards in family law include the "best interest of the child," termination of parental rights criteria, and sexual or physical abuse definitions in family or criminal law. These legal standards are codified in state statutes or outlined by case law. While none of these standards was derived from social science studies or defined by a generally accepted group in the field, the standards are heavily freighted with social science concepts and terms that are usually general and abstract. Are these just lay concepts, or should MHPs provide the court with expertise to define or flesh out these notions? Given that these legal standards represent public policy statements about how society wants the legal system to handle certain family problems, do MHPs even have the expertise to provide expert opinions about the legal issue at hand?

The issue of offering expert opinions or recommendations on the ultimate issue in the case is vigorously debated among forensic psychologists.[119] Some who believe that experts should not offer opinions on a particular case's legal standard emphasize the reality that such opinions are inference-based.[120] These critics insist that there is little, if any, scientific basis for experts to proffer opinions on the legal standard at issue. In contrast, others believe that MHPs may provide opinions useful to the court if those opinions are based on reliable data.[121]

If the expert offers an opinion—and most will—the lawyer's task is to examine the inferences that link the expert's conclusions to the expert's opinions. Several issues that we will address more fully later in this book should be examined. For example, does the expert appropriately unpackage the legal standard to address elements of that standard? Or, does the expert take the abstract standard as a whole and blindly assume that everyone will agree to its definition? Are the expert's inferences supported by data derived from reliable methodology? What from the expert's methods or manners of considering data from those methods might bias the inferences that inform the expert's opinion on the legal standard? While these may seem like complicated questions, this step in the analysis boils down to our primary question of experts: "How do you know what you say you know?" The *APA Child Custody Guidelines* highlight this issue well, noting that "recommendations (expert opinions on the legal standard in a child custody case) are based on articulated assumptions, data, interpretations, and inferences based upon established professional and scientific standards."[122] Viewing the analytical gap analysis as an opportunity to explore the connections experts make between their social science–based conclusions and the legal standards under consideration in court provides much cross-examination fodder as well as a guide to tightening your own expert's testimony.

SUMMARY

The legal perspective is the second of three critical areas for family lawyers to consider when they organize and manage mental health materials and critique mental health testimony, whether from their own or an opposing party's experts. This perspective addresses whether MHPs' opinions are reliably based and, therefore, admissible by the court, and how the admissibility of opposing experts' opinions may be challenged.

The practical four-step legal analysis model presented in this chapter incorporates shared principles from the *Frye* and *Daubert* cases to assess the legal reliability and strength of MHPs' expert testimony and the quality of work MHPs use to support their testimony. But lawyers must employ the model step-by-step to use it effectively. To ask whether the expert's testimony, as a whole, reliably supports the opinion is not a useful way to gauge the quality of the expert's testimony or supporting work—such a molar approach will be perceived as too abstract, unfocused, and confusing. Instead, lawyers should look at each step of the model in sequence, addressing the issues that each step demands. Problems at any step of the analysis may be grounds for the court to find the expert's testimony—in part or in whole—inadmissible.[123] Using this model, lawyers will sharpen their own experts' presentations, effectively critique their opponents' experts, and provide the court a roadmap for their *Frye-Daubert* analyses.

NOTES

1. FED. R. EVID. 702.
2. DAVID L. FAIGMAN ET AL., MODERN SCIENTIFIC EVIDENCE 23 (2d ed. 2005).
3. Frye v. United States, 293 F. 1013 (D.C. Cir. 1923).
4. Daubert v. Merrell Dow Pharmaceuticals, 509 U.S. 579 (1993).
5. *Daubert,* 509 U.S. at 590, n.9.
6. Paul C. Giannelli, *The Admissibility of Novel Scientific Evidence:* Frye v. United States, *a Half Century Later,* 80 COLUM. L. REV. 1197, 1235 (1980).
7. *Frye,* 293 F. at 1014.
8. Giannelli, *supra* note 6, at 1205.
9. *Id.*
10. *Id.* at 1207. *See also* United States v. Addison, 498 F.2d 741, 743 (D.C. Cir. 1974).
11. People v. Barbara, 255 N.W.2d 171, 194 (Mich. 1977).
12. *Daubert,* 509 U.S. at 594.
13. Giannelli, *supra* note 6, at 1211.
14. *Id.* at 1215 (citing People v. Kelly, 549 P.2d 1240, 1248 (Cal. 1976)).
15. *Id.* at 1213.
16. *Id.* at 1217.
17. *Id.*
18. *Id.* at 1218.
19. *See* Mark R. Kapusta, *Daubert Versus Flanagan: Comparing Standards for the Admissibility of Scientific Evidence in Florida State and Federal Courts,* 68 FLA. B.J. 38, 40 (1994).
20. Giannelli, *supra* note 6, at 1226.
21. *Daubert,* 509 U.S. at 594.
22. Logerquist v. McVey, 1 P.3d 113 (Ariz. 2000).
23. People v. Leahy, 882 P.2d 321, 336–37 (Cal. 1994).
24. *Id.* at 336.
25. *Leahy,* 882 P.2d at 336 (citing People v. Shirley, 723 P.2d 1354 (Cal. 1982)).

26. *Leahy,* 882 P.2d at 336.

27. Brim v. State, 695 So. 2d 268, 272 (Fla. 1997).

28. *Id.*

29. David A. Bernstein, Frye, Frye *Again: The Past, Present, and Future of the General Acceptance Test,* 41 JURIMETRICS J. 385, 393 (2001).

30. People v. Wesley, 633 N.E.2d 451, 461 (N.Y. 1994).

31. Ramirez v. State, 651 So. 2d 1164, 1166–67 (Fla. 1995).

32. *Id.* at 1168.

33. 1998 WL 299925 (Ariz. Super. Ct. 1998).

34. *Leahy,* 882 P.2d at 332 (citing *Stoll,* 783 P.2d at 710); People v. Kelly, 549 P.2d 1240, 1244 (Cal. 1976).

35. *Logerquist,* 1 P.3d at 128.

36. CYNTHIA H. CWIK & JOHN L. NORTH, SCIENTIFIC EVIDENCE REVIEW: ADMISSIBILITY AND USE OF EXPERT EVIDENCE IN THE COURTROOM 136 (2003).

37. 760 A.2d 1174 (Pa. Super. Ct. 2000), *appeal denied by* 781 A.2d 147 (Pa. 2001).

38. Bernstein, *supra* note 29 (citing Michael K. Graham, *The* Daubert *Dilemma: At Last a Viable Solution?,* 179 F.R.D. 1, 7 (1998)).

39. *Logerquist,* 1 P.3d at 123.

40. *Id.* at 121.

41. People v. Stoll, 783 P.2d 698 (1989).

42. *Id.* at 712.

43. *Id.* at 711 (citation omitted).

44. 509 U.S. 579 (1993).

45. 522 U.S. 136 (1997).

46. 526 U.S. 137 (1999).

47. *Daubert,* 509 U.S. at 589.

48. *Id.* at 588.

49. *Id.* at 589.

50. *See id.* at 590, n.9, n.11.

51. *Id.* at 592.

52. *Id.* at 593.

53. *Id.* at 593–94.

54. *Id.* at 594.

55. *Id.* at 594, n.12.

56. *Id.* at 594–95.

57. *Joiner,* 522 U.S. at 146.

58. *Id.*

59. *Kumho Tire,* 526 U.S. at 147.

60. *Id.* at 152.

61. *Id.*

62. *Daubert,* 509 U.S. at 600–601 (Rehnquist, J., dissenting).

63. *Id.* at 600.

64. Veronica B. Dahir, James T. Richardson, Gerald P. Ginsberg, Sophia I. Gatowski, Shirley A. Dobbin & Mara L. Merlino, *Judicial Application of* Daubert *to Psychological Syndrome and Profile Evidence,* 11 PSYCHOL. PUB. POL'Y & L. 62, 75 (2005).

65. Watkins v. Telsmith, Inc., 121 F.3d 984, 991 (5th Cir. 1997) (emphasis added).

66. *Joiner,* 522 U.S. at 146 (emphasis added).

67. Gammill v. Jack Williams Chevrolet, 972 S.W.2d 713, 726 (Tex. 1998).

68. *See Joiner,* 522 U.S. at 146.

69. *See* FAIGMAN ET AL., *supra* note 2, at 13 n.8 for discussion of states having accepted *Daubert* principles for admitting expert evidence.

70. *Id.*

71. TEX. FAM. CODE § 153.071.

72. STATE OF TEXAS OFFICE OF COURT ADMINISTRATION, STATEWIDE ACTIVITY SUMMARY—CIVIL, JUVENILE, AND OTHER PROCEEDINGS (2004).

73. Seaboard Lumber Co. v. United States, 308 F.3d 1283, 1301–02 (Fed. Cir. 2002).

74. SmithKline Beecham Corp. v. Apotex Corp., 247 F. Supp. 2d 1011 (N.D. Ill. 2003), *aff'd* 2004 WL 868425 (Fed. Cir. 2004).

75. FAIGMAN ET AL., *supra* note 2, at 20.

76. *Id.* at 21.

77. *See* Michael J. Saks & David L. Faigman, *Expert Evidence after* Daubert, 1 ANN. REV. L. & SOC. SCI. 105, 119 (2005).

78. *Id.*

79. *Id.*

80. Bernstein, *supra* note 29, at 388.

81. Daniel W. Shuman, *The Role of Mental Health Experts in Custody Decisions,* 36 FAM. L.Q. 135, 139 (2002).

82. *Id.,* citing *Joiner,* 522 U.S. at 146.

83. Daniel W. Shuman & Bruce D. Sales, *The Impact of* Daubert *and Its Progeny on the Admissibility of Behavioral and Social Science Evidence,* 5 PSYCHOL. PUB. POL'Y & L. 3, 12 (1999).

84. *Id.*

85. *Kumho Tire,* 562 U.S. at 150.

86. FAIGMAN ET AL., *supra* note 2, at 24.

87. Gammill v. Jack Williams Chevrolet, 972 S.W.2d 713 (Tex. 1998).

88. *Id.* at 724–25.

89. *Id.* at 722.

90. FED. R. EVID. 702 advisory committee's note.

91. *Gammill,* 972 S.W.2d at 719.

92. *Gammill,* 972 S.W.2d at 719 (quoting Broders v. Heise, 924 S.W.2d 148, 152 (Tex. 1996). *Broders* also notes, "(O)ur holding does not mean that only a neurosurgeon can testify about the cause in fact of death from an injury to the brain, or even that an emergency room physician could never so testify. What is required is that the expert has 'knowledge, skill, experience, training, or education' regarding the specific issue before the court which would qualify the expert to give an opinion on that particular subject." *Broders,* 924 S.W.2d at 153; *see also* Christopherson v. Allied-Signal Corp., 939 F.2d 1106, 1112–13 (5th Cir. 1991), *cert. denied,* 503 U.S. 912 (1992) (one possessing a medical degree is not qualified to give an opinion on every medical question).

93. *See* FAIGMAN ET AL., *supra* note 2, at 26 n.3.

94. *See id.* at 26, n.4.

95. Watkins v. Telsmith, Inc., 121 F.3d 984, 991 (5th Cir. 1997) (emphasis added).

96. Daniel W. Shuman & Stuart A. Greenberg, *The Role of Ethical Norms in the Admissibility of Expert Testimony,* 37 A.B.A. JUDGES J. 4 (1998).

97. American Psychological Association, *Ethical Principles of Psychologists and Code of Conduct,* 57 AM. PSYCHOL. 1597 (2002) [hereinafter *APA Ethics Code*].

98. Committee on Ethical Guidelines for Forensic Psychologists, *Specialty Guidelines for Forensic Psychologists,* 15 LAW & HUM. BEHAV. 655 (1991) [hereinafter *Forensic Specialty Guidelines*].

99. American Psychological Association, *Guidelines for Child Custody Evaluations in Divorce Proceedings,* 47 AM. PSYCHOL. 677 (1994) [hereinafter *APA Child Custody Guidelines*].

100.   Association of Family and Conciliation Courts, *Model Standards of Practice for Child Custody Evaluation,* 45 FAM. CT. REV. 70 (2007) [hereinafter *AFCC Child Custody Standards*].

101.   American Psychological Association, *Determination and Documentation of the Need for Practice Guidelines,* 60 AM. PSYCHOL. 976 (2005) [hereinafter *APA Practice Guidelines*].

102.   *APA Ethics Code, supra* note 97.

103.   *Forensic Specialty Guidelines, supra* note 98.

104.   *APA Child Custody Guidelines, supra* note 99, at 677.

105.   *APA Practice Guidelines, supra* note 101, at 977.

106.   *Watkins,* 121 F.3d at 991.

107.   *Kuhmo Tire,* 526 U.S. at 151.; *see also* FED. R. EVID. 702 advisory committee's note.

108.   Black v. Food Lion, 171 F.3d 308 (5th Cir. 1999).

109.   James N. Bow, *Review of Empirical Research on Child Custody Practice,* 3(1) J. CHILD CUSTODY 23, 44 (2006); K.A. Lafortune & B.N. Carpenter, *Custody Evaluations: A Survey of Mental Health Professionals,* 16 BEHAV. SCI. & L. 207 (1998); M.J. Ackerman & M.C. Ackerman, *Custody Evaluation Practices: A Survey of Experienced Professionals (Revisited),* 28 PROF. PSYCHOL.: RES. & PRAC. 137 (1997); W.G. Keilin & L.J. Bloom, *Child Custody Practices: A Survey of Experienced Professionals,* 17 PROF. PSYCHOL.: RES. & PRAC. 338 (1986).

110.   JONATHAN W. GOULD, CONDUCTING SCIENTIFICALLY CRAFTED CHILD CUSTODY EVALUATIONS (2d ed. 2006); Beth Clark, *Acting in the Best Interest of the Child: Essential Components of a Child Custody Evaluation,* 29 FAM. L.Q. 19 (1995); PHILIP M. STAHL, CONDUCTING CHILD CUSTODY EVALUATIONS (1994).

111.   *APA Child Custody Guidelines, supra* note 99; American Academy of Child and Adolescent Psychiatry, *Practice Parameters for Child Custody Evaluation,* 36 J. AM. ACAD. CHILD & ADOLESCENT PSYCHIATRY (1997); *AFCC Child Custody Standards, supra* note 100.

112.   Havner v. Merrell Dow Pharmaceuticals, 953 S.W.2d 706, 712 (Tex. 1997).

113.   *Id.* at 713.

114.   *Id.* at 714.

115.   *Id.*

116.   *Joiner,* 522 U.S. at 146.

117.   *E.g.,* Geraldine Downy & James C. Coyne, *Children of Depressed Parents: An Integrative Review,* 108 PSYCHOL. BULL. 50 (1990).

118.   *Kumho Tire,* 562 U.S. at 152.

119.   *APA Child Custody Guidelines, supra* note 99, at 679.

120.   *See, e.g.,* Timothy M. Tippins & Jeffrey P. Wittmann, *Empirical and Ethical Problems with Custody Recommendations: A Call for Clinical Humility and Judicial Vigilance,* 43 FAM. CT. REV. 193 (2005).

121.   *See, e.g.,* RICHARD ROGERS & DANIEL W. SHUMAN, CONDUCTING INSANITY EVALUATIONS 46 (2d ed. 2000).

122.   *APA Child Custody Guidelines, supra* note 99, at 679.

123.   *See In re* Paoli Railroad Yard PCB Litigation Mabel Brown, 35 F.3d 717 (3rd Cir. 1994), which notes that conclusions must be supported by good grounds for each step in the analysis. Any step that renders the analysis unreliable under the *Daubert* factors renders the expert's testimony inadmissible.

CHAPTER 4

The Psychological Perspective

INTRODUCTION

The psychological perspective is the third of three critical perspectives for family lawyers to consider when they organize, manage, and critique mental health materials and critique mental health testimony. The psychological perspective addresses how forensic MHPs should conduct their work to produce legally reliable conclusions and opinions. Again, the challenge to MHPs: "How do you know what you say you know?"

While the elements of the four-step *Frye-Daubert* Analysis Model presented in the preceding chapter build a framework with which to organize legal thinking about mental health testimony, lawyers must also recognize who MHP experts are and the means by which they reach their conclusions and resulting expert opinions. In addition, lawyers should appreciate key issues with which MHPs grapple when MHPs define the scope of their involvements in the legal system.

A helpful way to organize psychological perspective issues is to track the framework of our *Frye-Daubert* Analysis Model. We will begin with *Step One*, which addressed expert witness qualifications in the model, by examining who are the MHPs involved in the legal system and how their relationships with attorneys and courts should be defined. To those ends, we will discuss the varied professional identities and qualifications MHPs bring to court and how those differences might reflect what these experts offer a particular case. Then we will address how to choose an MHP expert and how the manners in which MHPs manage their roles in the case—vis-à-vis the lawyers and the parties, respectively—reflect MHPs' competence and professional credibility.

After exploring these beginning issues, we will move to *Step Two* of our analysis model to probe the methods MHPs use to gather the data upon which they base their expert opinions. For example, we will look at how MHPs draw on interviews and records to collect their data. Then we will examine how MHPs use—and misuse—psychological tests to generate data for their conclusions and opinions.

Once we discuss MHPs' methods, we will address *Step Three* by focusing on the conclusions MHPs reach from their derived data. First, we will look at thinking biases that may infect and color the inferences MHPs draw from their data and what MHPs should do to guard against those biases. Then we will discuss how MHPs use research to support their conclusions and how lawyers can challenge loose, inappropriate, or inapplicable citations of social science literature. Next, we will discuss MHPs' uses of DSM-IV-TR and syndromes to support inferences and conclusions.

Then we will address *Step Four* of our *Frye-Daubert* Analysis Model: the opinions MHPs offer in court. Forensic psychologists have debated whether they should offer expert opinions on the ultimate legal issue in a particular case unless required by law. As we explore that debate, you will become attuned to the arguments and, thereby, gain important clues about how to address those opinions—in both direct- and cross-examinations.

Finally, we will complete discussion of the psychological perspective by presenting a practical, functionally oriented evaluation model that lawyers may use to gauge how effectively MHPs organized their data and addressed the case concerns.

STEP ONE—MHP QUALIFICATIONS AND USE AND THE PSYCHOLOGICAL PERSPECTIVE

Professional Identities and Qualifications

MHPs come to court with one or more professional identities: psychologist, psychiatrist, social worker, marriage and family therapist, and professional counselor, among others. Each identity reflects the expert's education, training experiences, and expertise, suggesting areas in which the expert may be able to offer reliable expert opinions. Also, the various professions differ in the guidance they provide about how their respective members should conduct themselves in legal cases—some professions offer explicit, prescriptive standards; others offer little, if any, direction. State law governs licensing requirements and practice rules of each profession, while national professional organizations, some more highly regarded than others, offer specialties and board certifications for particular practice areas. Following are brief descriptions of these professional identities and the training required in each, as well as comments on major board certifications MHPs may present to highlight their training and qualifications.

Psychology

Psychology is the scientific study of the behavior of individuals and their mental processes.[1] Psychologists apply research and theoretically derived principles to many aspects of people's lives, addressing relationship and individual concerns across the developmental span, in families, and in organization structures and systems. In addition, psychologists diagnose and treat symptoms of mental disorders, including those of anxieties, mood disorders, thought disturbances, attention problems, or substance abuse. One particular expertise of psychologists is the use and interpretation of psychological tests. These tests may generate useful hypotheses about people's emotional states, cognitive capacities, and interaction styles, whether in the contexts of private psychotherapy and assessment or of forensic evaluations, by offering information about how an individual's performance compares to that of groups or categories of people.

Psychologists' training prior to licensure involves three steps. First, psychologists attend graduate school in a program that results in a Ph.D. (Doctor of Philosophy) degree or a Psy.D. (Doctor of Psychology) degree. While a Ph.D. program places greater emphasis on research, the American Psychological Association (APA) accredits programs with either degree, and states allow candidates with either degree to sit for psychology licensing examinations. Graduate programs accredited by the APA have been vetted for quality in psychology graduate education and training. In addition, APA recognizes eleven psychological specialties;[2] graduate programs emphasize training in one or more specialty areas.

The second training step for most psychologists involves two years of pre-license clinical experience: one year before the doctorate degree is conferred, usually as a full-year structured and supervised internship, and one year after the degree is conferred in a formal externship or in a supervised work arrangement. In both years, the prospective psychologist's work must be supervised by a licensed psychologist.

Finally, prospective psychologists seeking certification and licensure sit for a written examination. Some states also require an oral examination for licensure.

While most psychologists practice with the general psychology license issued by the states in which they practice, some seek further expertise and credentials in one or more specialized areas. The American Board of Professional Psychology (ABPP), the oldest credentialing organization in psychology,[3] is a respected example of a credentialing board in professional psychology—the ABPP has provided certification in designated psychology specialties since 1947[4] and, since its inception, has been unofficially recognized by the APA as the certification body for specialty in psychology.[5] The ABPP defines a specialty as a distinct area in the practice of psychology that connotes special competency acquired through an organized sequence of formal education, training, and experience.[6] Forensic psychology is one designated specialty that the ABPP certifies through the American Board of Forensic Psychology (ABFP). Forensic psychology is "the application of the science and profession of psychology to questions and issues relating to law and the legal system."[7] The ABFP's credentialing process includes the following:

- Strict requirements for education, licensing, supervision, and experience
- Verification of stated credentials
- Ethics review by contacting state psychological associations and licensing boards
- The submission of work products in two areas of expertise in the candidate's forensic psychology practice for review by Board Certified Examiners
- Successful completion of a written examination covering forensic psychology areas and issues—including knowledge of relevant case law—and a three-hour oral examination conducted by a committee of Board Certified Examiners in the two areas of expertise represented by the candidate's submitted work products and in the ethics that apply to practice represented by those work products.[8]

While other organizations offer board certifications or diplomate status in various forensic psychology fields, lawyers should ensure that such certifications are not distributed by "certification mills." In one humorous, yet sobering, account, a psychologist credentialed his cat, Zoe D. Katze, Ph.D., with an organization that described its diplomate status as "limited to a select group of professionals who, by virtue of their extensive training and expertise, have demonstrated their outstanding abilities in regard to their specialty"—the psychologist had only to submit Dr. Katze's "résumé" and pay the application fee.[9] We will discuss more fully the issue of evaluating board certification claims when we discuss choosing an expert for a family law case.

Psychiatry

A psychiatrist is a physician who specializes in the diagnosis and treatment of people suffering from mental disorders as well as in the prevention of such disorders.[10] Psychiatrists explore the biological, psychological, and social components of their patients' functioning as they fashion treatment plans.[11] Among their treatment tools, psychiatrists may prescribe medicines to alleviate or control symptoms arising from diagnosed mental disorders, which may include anxiety, thought disturbance, mood disorders, obsessive thinking and behaviors, attention problems, or substance abuse concerns.

Psychiatrists' training typically includes several steps. First, psychiatrists must complete a general medical education and internship leading to a Doctor of Medicine (M.D.) degree or a Doctor of Osteopathy (D.O). degree; while M.D. and D.O. training differ in emphasis, states authorize holders of either degree to become licensed to practice medicine. After licensure, most physicians seeking to practice psychiatry receive further specialized training in a three- to four-year residency program, although completing such a residency program is not required for physicians to represent themselves as psychiatrists.

While most psychiatrists will begin practice after completing their residency program, some pursue further training and board certification from the American Board of Psychiatry and Neurology (ABPN), a member board of the American Board of Medical Specialties (ABMS). The certifications in psychiatry and neurology are distinct, each with its own prerequisites. The psychiatry board certification candidate must have trained in a psychiatry residency program, unless the program was an approved combined training program.[12] After the candidate's application is approved, the candidate sits for a two-part examination. Part I is an all-day written examination that includes questions from all fields of general psychiatry, including life cycle development, behavioral and social sciences, psychiatric disorders, diagnostic procedures and treatment, and other special topics.[13] Part II is a two-hour oral examination that addresses the candidate's assessment and examination skills.[14]

After board certification in psychiatry, psychiatrists may choose further certification in a "subspecialty." Two subspecialties of interest for family lawyers are Forensic Psychiatry and Child and Adolescent Psychiatry.[15] Forensic Psychiatry is a "subspecialty of psychiatry in which scientific and clinical expertise is applied to legal issues in legal contexts embracing civil, criminal, and correctional or legislative matters. Forensic psychiatry should be practiced in accordance with guidelines and ethical principles enunciated by the profession of psychiatry."[16] To become board certified in forensic psychiatry, candidates must already be certified in general psychiatry, must have completed one year of specialized fellowship training—post-residency—in forensic psychiatry, and must sit for a written examination covering legal and psychiatric issues over the broad range of concerns in which forensic psychiatrists might become involved, including child- and family-related issues.[17]

Candidates for board certification in the subspecialty of Child and Adolescent Psychiatry must be certified in general psychiatry. Then, they must complete two years of residency training in child and adolescent psychiatry and sit for a written examination covering theory and issues related to child and adolescent development, psychopathology, and consultation.[18]

Social Work

As with psychologists and psychiatrists, social workers are licensed and regulated by the states in which they practice. Social workers may appear in family law cases in several ways: as court-appointed child custody evaluators, as private therapists, or as Child Protective Services caseworkers or abuse investigators.

Typically, social workers involved in family law cases will have attained a bachelor's degree in social work (BSW) or a master's degree in social work (MSW), and then, as a condition for licensure, will have fulfilled experience requirements and passed a national written examination administered by the Association of Social Work Boards. Afterwards, MSW-level social workers may attain additional expertise and credentials by several means: by fulfilling education and experience requirements listed in the state's licensing statutes, by earning the Academy of Certified Social Workers (ACSW) accreditation, or by attaining the Diplomate in Clinical Social Work (DCSW)—social work's highest certification. While a master's degree in social work is required for these credentials, examinations are not required. The DCSW requires five years of postgraduate clinical social work experience, three more than required for the ACSW.[19] These certifications operate under the auspices of the National Association of Social Workers (NASW). The NASW is the largest membership organization of professional social workers in the world. The NASW aims to enhance the professional growth and development of its social worker members, to create and maintain professional standards, and to advance sound social policies.[20]

While the NASW offers nine social work specialty practice areas, none is devoted to forensic practice, despite the fact that many social workers, particularly those who work child welfare cases, interact with the legal system. Further, social work standards of practice offer little guidance on how to manage forensic issues, roles, and relationships.[21] Nevertheless, in recognition of social workers' involvements as expert witnesses, the NASW, in 1997, published a booklet titled *Social Workers as Expert Witnesses*. This booklet provides social workers with some information about the role of an expert witness and examples of some cases in which social workers have provided expert testimony.[22]

Professional Counseling

Licensed Professional Counselors (LPCs) apply mental health and human development principles by counseling, assessing, and consulting with individuals, groups, or organizations.[23] LPCs may become involved in family law cases in a number of ways—for example, by counseling with a family member before, during, or after the divorce process or by conducting custody evaluations.

As with the other mental health disciplines, LPCs' licensure and practice are regulated by the state in which they practice. To be licensed, LPCs must have a master's or doctoral degree in counseling or a counseling-related field[24] from an accredited college or university. In addition, applicants for the license must have had, as a part of their graduate training, a supervised practicum experience that was primarily counseling in nature. No internship, residency, or post-degree clinical training is required for licensing.

The leading national credentialing body for professional counselors is the National Board for Certified Counselors (NBCC). The NBCC's certification program recognizes counselors who have met predetermined standards in their training and experience and who have demonstrated adequate performance on the National Counselor Examination for Licensure and Certification.[25] The NBCC's primary credential is the National Certified Counselor (NCC). The NBCC also offers three specialty certifications—School Counseling, Clinical Mental Health Counseling, and Addictions Counseling.[26] The professional counseling organizations offer no specialty designation for forensic-related work or guidance on how to manage court-related issues, roles, or relationships.

Marriage and Family Therapy

Marriage and Family Therapists (MFTs) address relationship problems and mental and emotional disorders within the context of family and larger social systems.[27] MFTs emphasize the impact of the family system on individual behaviors. For example, while many MHPs might emphasize treating children individually for their problems, MFTs may instead explore whether the child's problems reflect problems in family functioning—for example, is a boy's academic struggling during a contentious divorce an effort to force his arguing parents to unite in concern over his school misfortunes? This systems-oriented approach opens analysis of individual problems to other family members and explores the effects of each member's actions on the entire family system. This approach may generate creative options to help family members understand and deal with their problems. While members of other mental health professions may incorporate a systems perspective in their views of the family, many MFTs are specially trained in this approach. Some MFTs also incorporate approaches as varied as cognitive-behavior therapy and psychodynamic concepts into their treatments of marital and family problems.

Almost all states regulate MFTs[28] and detail the education and licensing requirements for the practice of marriage and family therapy. The American Association of Marriage and Family Therapists (AAMFT) has provided the major impetus for development and licensing of the practice of marriage and family therapy.

Marriage and family therapy is a distinct professional discipline with graduate and postgraduate programs. Three education options are available for those interested in becoming a marriage and family therapist: a master's degree (two to three years), a doctoral program (three to five years), or a postgraduate clinical training program (three to four years). Historically, marriage and family therapists have come from a wide variety of educational backgrounds, including psychology, psychiatry, social work, nursing, pastoral counseling, and education.[29]

Sorting Through the Qualifications Maze

In addition to different professional identifications, MHPs may tout board diplomates or other similar certifications to support their claimed expertise. The "alphabet soup-like" listing of letters behind experts' recognizable degree abbreviations may seem both impressive and confusing. But, as noted earlier in the account of the psychologist who credentialed his cat, specialty certifications are not equivalent or fungible, whether within or across professional identities. Criteria of credentialing boards may differ dramatically: some boards are little more than "vanity boards" that readily offer certifications upon receipt of an application fee and unverified experiences, while other boards attempt to verify the applicant's education, training, skills, knowledge, and practice abilities.[30] The two leading and most respected specialty credentialing entities are the American Board of Professional Psychology (ABPP), with its thirteen specialties[31] (the American Board of Forensic Psychology, or ABFP, is an ABPP member board), and the American Board of Medical Specialties (ABMS), with eight subspecialties under the General Psychiatry specialty[32] given by the American Board of Psychiatry and Neurology (ABPN), an ABMS member board (Forensic Psychiatry is an ABPN subspecialty).

How should one evaluate the qualities of other board certifying entities? First, use the requirements discussed earlier for the psychologists' ABFP and the psychiatrists' Forensic Psychiatry subspecialty as standards.[33] Next, explore the nature of the certification examination—does the examination test the knowledge and skills of the prospective specialist, or is it merely a perfunctory exercise? In addition, note whether the certification's title fits the expert's training—for example, don't let an MHP without previous medical training claim diplomate or fellow status in forensic medicine. Besides helping you to understand the nature of the credential, this investigative process may provide much fodder for cross-examination.

Of course, the credentials issue begs the question posed earlier of whether an MHP who has had some coursework and work experiences as a counselor, psychotherapist, or evaluator and who touts seemingly impressive certifications is thereby qualified to testify as an expert. The legal answer is the same as before: case law looks at how the expert's qualifications and testimony "fit" the issues the expert will address. But psychologists are guided by professional standards and guidelines that are more specific. The *APA Guidelines for Child Custody Evaluations in Divorce Proceedings* address the "fit" concern from psychologists' perspective, utilizing a functional, practical approach—irrespective of board certification. These guidelines note that "competence in performing psychological assessments of children, adults, and families is necessary but not sufficient. Education, training, experience, and/or supervision in the areas of child and family development, child and family psychopathology, and the impact of divorce on children help to prepare the psychologist to participate competently in child custody evaluations."[34] In addition, these guidelines state that if issues of child abuse, neglect, family violence, or other problems arise in the course of a child custody evaluation and these issues are not within the scope of a particular evaluator's expertise, "the psychologist [should seek] additional consultation, supervision, and/or specialized knowledge, training, or experience in child abuse, neglect, and family violence to address these complex issues."[35] More generally, the *APA Ethics Code* notes that "psychologists provide services . . . only within the boundaries of their competence, based on their education, training, supervised experience, consultation, study, or professional experience."[36] Lawyers should test these qualification and competence issues as they size up their own experts or cross-examine opposing experts. As a result, lawyers will gain a better sense about whether the quality of MHPs' work products or testimony might pass muster in light of the courts' insistence on reliable, trustworthy expert testimony.

Choosing MHP Experts: Distinguishing Qualities

Family lawyers know that not all prospective experts are created equal: some experts know much about the clinical and research aspects of the issue before the court; many experts, in their behavior and dress, display a competent professional courtroom demeanor; others are able to communicate difficult concepts in simple ways to jurors; and a few experts combine all these elements. Choosing the right expert is not easy. While a literature review on choosing experts is beyond this book's scope, lawyers should consider key issues when they retain MHP experts for various tasks in their cases or when they critique opposing counsel's experts.

Federal and State Rules of Civil Procedure distinguish two kinds of experts: testifying experts and consulting experts.[37] Because testifying and consulting experts play different roles within a case, certain qualities lawyers might value for one expert may be less important for another expert. For example, communication skills and the ability to convey credibility to a jury are more important for the testifying expert than for the consulting expert.

But consider several qualities important for both types of expert:

- *Clinical and evaluation experiences in the areas that the MHP is retained to address.* This quality has both practical and legal significance. Generally, MHPs with clinical and evaluation experiences outside the courtroom and with experiences interacting with legal cases will better grasp the issues before the court. For example, an MHP with little experience treating or evaluating children may only have "book sense" notions about children's reactions to divorce and lack firsthand appreciation of the emotional struggles these children may experience. If this MHP consults with the lawyer, the lawyer may miss key issues with which to cross-examine the opposing expert and omit real-life perspectives that could enrich arguments to the court.

  The MHP's lack of clinical and evaluation experiences on issues before the court may also create problems for the MHP testifying expert. An MHP's expert testimony may be admitted into evidence on grounds other than past experiences or skills—recall Texas's *Gammill* case, cited in an earlier chapter, which noted that "trial courts must ensure that those who purport to be experts truly have expertise concerning the actual subject about which they are offering an opinion."[38] However, one might legitimately question whether an MHP testifying expert has the requisite expertise without the clinical or evaluation experiences on the issue being addressed in court. The exception, of course, is if the MHP expert is testifying to educate the court about how the professional literature addresses the issue before the court. Even so, recall *Kumho Tire*'s directive that the trial court's task "is to make certain that an expert, whether basing testimony upon professional studies or personal experience, employs in the courtroom the same level of intellectual rigor that characterizes the practice of an expert in the relevant field."[39]

- *Knowledge of the professional literature in the areas that the MHP is retained to address.* Lawyers often overlook examining their expert's knowledge of the professional literature. Do not fall into the trap of retaining MHP experts without gauging their knowledge of the professional literature. The lawyer does not have to know all the literature before determining whether the prospective expert can comfortably answer questions about significant issues in the field that will be the subject of court testimony. But some awareness of mental health issues in the case can be gained easily and quickly by an Internet search, a review of a seminar paper, or a short phone call to a colleague. Use that awareness to question the prospective MHP expert about how the professional literature addresses the case issues; if the MHP cannot answer readily, ask him or her to get back to you shortly with a satisfactory response or consider choosing another expert.

  The MHP's knowledge of the professional literature that addresses case issues is important for at least two reasons. First, that knowledge establishes the MHP as conversant with how the profession views relevant issues. For example, in a bitter child custody case with sexual abuse allegations, it is important for the expert to be aware of research related to how the allegation first arose, how the child was questioned by a concerned parent, how the child was interviewed by child welfare authorities, and whether the child was influenced into making the statements alleged to be an "outcry." Merely stating an opinion about the allegations without calling upon the professional literature for support will keep potentially valuable information from the lawyer, will detract from the expert's credibility when testifying, and may draw objections from opposing counsel as to whether the expert's testimony should be admitted—recall the directive from *Joiner's* Analytical Gap Test noted earlier: "(I)t is not so simply because an expert says it is so."[40]

Second, MHPs should know the professional literature because the literature may raise alternative, competing hypotheses to case issues. Good forensic psychology practice demands that psychologists consider and weigh rival hypotheses in the issues they examine as they conduct their forensic activities.[41] If MHP experts do not know the literature, they will be less likely to know what alternative hypotheses should be considered. Further, these MHPs will be unlikely to address the general acceptance of the methods they use to reach their conclusions and opinions. Finally, lawyers who rely on MHP experts who do not know the relevant professional literature will be deprived of vital information that might help them understand their cases better and improve their direct- and cross-examinations in depositions and in trial.

- *Professional associations to which the MHP expert belongs.* Membership in professional organizations is an important, yet often overlooked, quality when choosing an MHP expert. Association affiliations, at minimum, reflect MHPs' professional identifications and areas of interest. An added benefit to knowing this information about opposing counsels' experts is that some professional associations endorse practice guidelines that members may be expected to follow or adopt. But note that an MHP may belong to different professional associations, each with its own practice guidelines for particular forensic tasks. For example, a psychologist may belong to the American Psychological Association (APA) and to the Association of Family and Conciliation Courts (AFCC)— an interdisciplinary association of MHPs, lawyers, judges, and other court personnel interested in family issues in courts. The APA and the AFCC each has its own guidelines for conducting child custody evaluations; most psychologists belonging to both groups probably will elect to hold themselves to the APA's guidelines.

- *The MHP's professional reputation.* The MHP's professional reputation may be an important element in building the perception of credibility in court. A popular adage is that it takes years to build a reputation and a few seconds to lose it. Today, the Internet makes it possible to shrink further the time needed to affect one's reputation. Ask your colleagues about your prospective MHP expert. Find out if the expert's testimony has ever been excluded by any court, or whether the expert has ever been refused qualification as an expert on any subject matter.[42] Also, find out if the expert has ever been disciplined by a professional organization or licensing board.[43] And check the Internet. While not everything you read may be truthful—some of it may even be slanderous—be assured that opposing counsel will do that same Internet search. Know what is out there, and ask your prospective expert about concerns you discover. Don't be surprised later.

- *The MHP's publications and presentations.* Publications and presentations are two indicators of an MHP's professional interests and often reflect the MHP's special areas of expertise. In particular, highlight those that will relate to the prospective expert's testimony. But also examine, with the prospective expert, the nature of the publications and presentations; with the opposing counsel's expert, go over each one, item by item. Do not be surprised later by discovering that your expert has "padded" the vita, or résumé.

- *Ideological or gender bias.* Many family law issues have become politically charged, with mothers' rights, fathers' rights, and children's rights advocacy groups all staking their claims to various family court issues. MHPs, often with good intentions, are drawn into these battles—sometimes touting research support and other times voicing only personal beliefs they feel are inherently best for families. For example, some experts may be biased toward placing young children with mothers, other MHPs may be biased against relocation of children to a residence far away from one parent, some experts may be viewed as "fathers' rights" advocates, and some take an inflexible "always believe the children" approach to abuse allegations. Other experts may support or associate themselves with websites that exclusively help mothers or fathers gain custody of their children. MHP experts with ideological or gender-based agendas are not inclined to view family situations from various perspectives or to examine alternate hypotheses or explanations of the concerns before the court. Lawyers should find out if their testifying experts have demonstrated ideological or gender biases in their work or past testimony—knowing those biases, perceived or real, ahead of time will enable lawyers to defuse the effects of later challenges. Conversely, look for biases in the opposing counsel's experts; you will be richly rewarded during cross-examination if you discover any and are able to frame those experts' testimony with those biases.
- *Communication skills.* Obviously, an MHP expert's communication abilities comprise a vital skill set on the witness stand. Witness preparation experts believe that witnesses who communicate clearly will be perceived as credible and persuasive.[44] A witness who speaks confidently and assertively rather than hesitantly and who avoids "hypercorrect" or overly formal speech is viewed as more effective.[45] And witnesses are more believable when they testify in a conversational manner and are responsive to the questions asked without having to rely on jargon or technical, abstract terms.[46]

Nonverbal communication also affects others' perception of a witness's competence. Research findings in this area suggest that "effective communicators make frequent eye contact with attorneys and jurors—especially while talking—use illustrator gestures, lean forward slightly, have a relaxed posture, face their head and body toward their audience, express genuine emotions, and speak at a moderately fast rate using a loud voice with variations in pitch."[47]

Using MHP Experts: The Matter of Professional Roles

Lawyers will gain important insights into the professional objectivity MHPs bring to their cases when they note how MHPs manage relationships in those cases. The matter of professional roles speaks to this issue.

Lawyers may engage experts for different tasks in a given case—as consulting or testifying experts;[48] rules of civil procedure distinguish these roles. But apart from understanding their legally defined expert roles, forensic MHPs also are ethically required to manage the professional roles they adopt in cases in which they are involved. MHPs are taught from the beginning of their training the importance of defining and clarifying roles in their professional relationships. Roles guide MHPs in two ways: they enable MHPs to define their tasks in given situations, and they prescribe the nature of MHPs' relationships with the persons or entities to which MHPs provide services. For example, in the familiar therapist and patient relationship, an MHP's task may be to help an adult patient deal with the emotional pain of a recent marital separation. But the nature of the psychotherapy relationship ethically prohibits the MHP from becoming involved in a romantic relationship with the patient during the course of psychotherapy and for a period beyond.[49]

Dual-role relationships occur when MHPs assume two or more roles within a single case.[50] Dual-role relationships, although discouraged, are not prohibited by the *APA Ethics Code*. But "a psychologist refrains from entering into a multiple relationship if the multiple relationship could reasonably be expected to impair the psychologist's objectivity, competence, or effectiveness in performing his or her functions as a psychologist, or otherwise risks exploitation or harm to the person with whom the professional relationship exists."[51] In the example above, a professionally unethical dual-role relationship would occur if the MHP were to become involved in a business venture or a romantic relationship with the patient—a combination of a professional role with a personal role.

Two other types of MHP dual-role relationships that may compromise the reliability and integrity of experts' testimony may be less obvious to lawyers: when MHPs inappropriately assume a second, conflicting role within a case, and when MHPs adopt conflicting professional roles.[52] The former generally occurs in the relationship between the MHP and the lawyer, and the latter in the relationship between the MHP and the lawyer's client. Let's examine these two MHP dual-role relationships.

Dual-Role Relationships Between the Lawyer and Expert

While rules of evidence seek to ensure that expert testimony is reliable or trustworthy,[53] MHPs' ethical codes and professional guidelines also call for expert witness reliability, emphasizing that MHP forensic experts approach their roles in neutral, impartial manners, even when retained by one party.[54] If the MHP adopts dual roles in the relationship with an attorney—where the MHP's task is unclear or the nature of the MHP's relationship with the lawyer is blurred—the reliability of the MHP's testimony may become compromised before the court.

MHPs may be engaged in family law cases in at least four ways. First, MHPs may be court-appointed to conduct family evaluations that address custody and possession issues or particular concerns of certain family members—for example, the depression of one of the parents, the special needs of a child, or domestic violence allegations. In such a role, the MHP's tasks are defined by the court order, and the MHP's relationship with the lawyer is as an impartial expert. The MHP expert does not advocate for either party. Nevertheless, this principle does not preclude MHPs from forcefully representing the data and reasoning upon which their conclusions and opinions are based.[55]

Second, lawyers may retain MHPs to testify about the professional literature or practices of an issue before the court.[56] For example, the lawyer may want to retain an MHP expert to educate the judge or jury about the research and literature on children diagnosed with attention deficit/hyperactivity disorder and the importance for such children of structure in home and school. Third, lawyers may retain MHPs to conduct evaluations of their clients to be used in court that may, for example, address parenting capacity or substance abuse problems. Finally, lawyers may hire MHPs to consult about key issues in the case, to help plan the theory or theme of the case, to help pick a jury, to prepare clients for testimony, to manage difficult clients, or to help appraise the quality of the opposing mental health expert's work or prospective testimony.

While these separate tasks or roles seem straightforward, tensions may arise in the lawyer and expert relationship that could pull the MHP into a problem dual-role relationship. Because such a relationship impairs "the psychologist's objectivity, competence, or effectiveness in performing his or her functions as a psychologist,"[57] the expert's testimony could, at the least, be perceived as unduly biased.

One way lawyers and MHPs may understand the dual-relationship issue is to consider the two ways mentioned earlier of how roles guide MHPs in a given case—roles enable MHPs to define their tasks in given situations, and roles prescribe the nature of MHPs' relationships with the persons or entities to which MHPs provide services—and to apply this thinking to the court's demand that experts testify reliably. For example, if an MHP is court-appointed to conduct a child custody evaluation, the nature of the MHP's relationships with the court and the attorneys is clear: the evaluator should take reasonable steps to refrain from ex parte communication with the court and with attorneys of the parties. While this rule may vary slightly in different jurisdictions, it, nevertheless, is clear. It is easy to see that if the court-appointed MHP violates this rule, depending on the nature of the violation, the MHP's conclusions and opinions may be compromised, at least by the perception of bias, and, thus, be less likely to provide a basis for trustworthy expert testimony.

But if the lawyer retains an MHP for the task of conducting a parenting evaluation of a client who has experienced substance abuse problems, may the MHP offer expert opinions concerning that evaluation at trial and also help the attorney develop the case, both before and during trial—say, as a jury consultant or a case adviser? This status could be a dual-relationship problem for the MHP: while the court demands reliable expert witness testimony, the expert, in this case, would also be on the lawyer's "team"—hardly a situation in which the court could presume impartial, trustworthy testimony. A testifying expert, even if retained by a lawyer, is obliged to offer testimony, derived from reliable methods, that is not driven by a desire to reach a particular outcome.[58] Sometimes the line is difficult to draw. MHPs differ in their views of how much testifying experts should assist attorneys who retain them about the varied issues upon which they will offer opinions. For example, should testifying experts assist in deposition preparation of the opposing expert or in preparing cross-examination questions of the opposing expert? Some MHPs contend that assisting the retaining lawyer in such tasks allows MHPs to gain relevant but otherwise unattainable data that could inform their conclusions—at times, the best way to hear from the other party is through that party's testimony. Other MHPs and lawyers suggest that lawyers may remedy this dual-relationship concern by retaining a different MHP for trial preparation and assistance, ensuring that the testifying expert's task remains that of proffering reliable, independent testimony that will assist the trier of fact.[59]

However, what if the family lawyer initially retains an MHP as a consultant but later decides that the MHP should change roles by conducting an evaluation of the client and then offering expert testimony in court based on that evaluation? This scenario differs from the acceptable situation in which the MHP is retained to review materials prior to committing either to conduct an evaluation that would lead to expert testimony or to consult with the lawyer as the case develops from pretrial through trial.[60] If the MHP is engaged with the lawyer as a consultant and then changes roles to an evaluator who will testify, legitimate questions should arise during testimony about the MHP's bias and, thereby, whether the MHP's opinions are trustworthy given the MHP's previous consultant role.[61]

Finally, what if a family lawyer retains an MHP to conduct a similar evaluation but the lawyer decides not to put the MHP on the stand to offer an expert opinion from the evaluation? May the MHP then assist the lawyer with trial preparation? This switch from expert witness to consultant would be acceptable because the court would not have to judge the reliability of the MHP's testimony—there would be no testimony to judge. But in this case the MHP must meet a basic condition to avoid a dual-relationship ethical problem: there must be an agreement that under no circumstances would the MHP return to the role of impartial evaluator and testifying expert.[62]

The professional forensic mental health literature provides a range of positions on the dual-relationship issue, with most writers either advocating no dual-role involvement whatsoever or recommending limited, carefully explained involvement.[63] These issues highlight the imperative that MHPs, when they testify, should provide impartial, reliable information to the courts in their fields of competence.[64]

Reconciling Dual-Relationship Tensions Between Lawyers and Experts

Because MHPs, at times, find these role issues difficult to sort through, they often feel pressured to adopt inappropriate dual-relationships with lawyers or pulled to testify beyond what their data will allow.[65] Lawyers may also wonder why the same MHP expert cannot be both a testifying witness and a consultant in the same case.[66] These tensions drive many MHPs to the uneasy conclusion that they must choose between professional integrity and a win-lose, advocacy approach that they believe may harm children and ongoing co-parenting relationships.

Shuman and Greenberg address this concern from a different, but helpful, perspective. They assert that pitting professional integrity against advocacy is a false choice. Instead, they promote a model that permits MHPs to be ethical, persuasive, impartial, and helpful in their expert witness roles.[67] Shuman and Greenberg emphasize that an expert's credibility is essential to being an effective advocate, and that credibility derives from the expert's impartiality. An expert's absence of impartiality compromises the expert's claims of objectivity and the strength of the lawyer's case.[68]

Shuman and Greenberg offer five principles to integrate the demands of the MHP expert witness and lawyer relationship:[69]

- Competence
- Relevance
- Perspective
- Balance
- Candor

Each principle speaks to mental health experts' responsibilities in the manners in which they testify and offer conclusions and opinions in court. This framework also provides lawyers valuable standards with which to guide their direct examinations and useful "hooks" with which to structure their cross-examinations.

Competence, the first principle, is a central concern in psychology. The *APA Ethics Code* states that psychologists provide services only in areas within the boundaries of their competence based on their education, training, supervised experience, consultation, study, or professional experience.[70] Shuman and Greenberg assert that the competence of psychologists to provide forensic services is issue specific and contextual.[71] They note that when considering whether to become involved in a case, "experts should first identify each legal question on which their opinion is being sought and then determine if and how their competence permits them to offer an expert opinion to assist in the resolution of these legal questions."[72] Clearly, this notion hearkens to the *Daubert* cases that look at how the expert's qualifications "fit" the issues the expert will address. And recall the Texas Supreme Court case discussed earlier noting that "trial courts must ensure that those who purport to be experts truly have expertise concerning the actual subject about which they are offering an opinion."[73] During direct- or cross-examination, lawyers should be "issue specific" when questioning experts about their competence to testify about each legal question to which the experts will offer an opinion. Such questioning will enhance an expert's credibility or, conversely, open up possibilities for *Frye-Daubert* challenges, if not encourage the court to place less weight on the expert's testimony.

Relevance, Shuman and Greenberg's second principle, addresses information the expert witness should disclose. The authors' assert that "the expert's unilateral obligation of disclosure only applies to information relevant to issues on which the expert's opinions have been sought."[74] Further, they maintain that experts have no obligation to disclose information that is not relevant to the issues in question, unless, of course, the court deems the information relevant and not privileged. When adopting this principle, expert witnesses are more likely to appear neutral and credible to the fact finder.[75] The *Forensic Specialty Guidelines* have a comparable provision.[76] Lawyers should be sensitive to nonrelevant information offered by experts to support the experts' conclusions and opinions. For instance, suppose, in a child custody dispute, a mother in her mid-thirties reports that, as an adolescent, she had a difficult relationship with her father. If, solely based on this information, the expert concludes that this mother is unable to have healthy relationships with men and, therefore, lacks the capacity to parent her preschool son adequately, this testimony would be inappropriate. Or, suppose a mother reports that she used cocaine twice ten years ago and has not used any drugs since then. This information alone is not relevant to her current capacity as a parent. In both examples, use of nonrelevant information on which to base an expert opinion would compromise the expert's credibility as well as expose the unreliability of the expert's testimony.

Perspective, Shuman and Greenberg's third principle, encourages MHPs to examine evidence that might support or refute each party's perspective—"an expert witness who is uninformed of the parties' differing perspectives can hardly be expected to be a credible witness."[77] The *Forensic Specialty Guidelines* note that "the forensic psychologist maintains professional integrity by examining the issue at hand from all reasonable perspectives, actively seeking information that will differentially test plausible rival hypotheses."[78] Lawyers may expose confirmation biases or other biases when they ask MHP experts to relate the differing perspectives attending each legal question that they considered in forming their conclusions and opinions.

Balance, Shuman and Greenberg's fourth principle, addresses the notion that "the expert has an obligation to assign a fair weight to each (perspective) . . . and not to allow the inherent pressures of the situation to influence this decision-making."[79] Shuman and Greenberg warn that the absence of balance created by not considering rival hypotheses in an evenhanded manner renders the expert an ineffective advocate for whatever opinions the expert reaches.[80] Considering different plausible perspectives is an important step in the process of forming an opinion. Considering those perspectives fairly speaks to a balanced approach when forming opinions and testifying about those opinions.

Candor, the fifth principle, refers "to the forthrightness with which psychological experts present their analysis."[81] The expert is not to testify as the "hired gun" who provides favorable testimony because the lawyer paid for it or to ensure future work from that lawyer. Experts should not selectively disclose relevant information about an opinion to aid or disadvantage a party.[82] Rather, the expert's opinions should apply and reflect "the knowledge and experience of the discipline."[83] *Trigon Ins. Co. v. United States* emphasizes that "it is specifically not an expert's position to advocate for a party, lest the witness ceases to be an expert whose testimony is valuable because he or she is not an advocate and becomes, instead, just another legal practitioner for the client."[84]

Shuman and Greenberg assert that these five principles integrate for MHP experts "the idealistic *APA Ethics Code* in the rough-and-tumble adversary system."[85] Lawyers will recognize that expert testimony that does not reflect these principles will likely be tinged with bias if not driven by personal or politically based agendas. Consequently, expert testimony not based on these principles is unlikely to be trustworthy and, therefore, unlikely to benefit the courts, MHPs and lawyers, or the litigants.[86]

Dual-Role Relationships Between the MHP Expert and the Lawyer's Client

Besides monitoring potential dual-role relationship problems in the family lawyer and MHP relationship, family lawyers also should recognize problems inherent in dual-role relationship issues between the MHP and the lawyer's client. The most prevalent of such concerns is that of MHPs testifying as experts on behalf of their own patients and then offering opinions on the ultimate legal issues in the case. For example, should an MHP who has been a parent's therapist testify and offer expert opinions about whether the court should designate that parent's home as the child's primary residence? While, on its face, one might see much benefit for such testimony—after all, who knows that parent's parenting abilities and emotional state better?—such testimony could present role conflicts. The primary rationale against the "dual role" of therapist versus expert witness is that a therapist has a different relationship with the patient than does an expert witness evaluator. Therapists are usually highly invested in their patients' welfare and rightfully concerned that publicly offering candid opinions about their patients' deficits could seriously impair their patients' trust in them.[87] On the other hand, the primary client of the expert evaluator-witness is the hiring attorney or the court. In sum, therapist "experts" who engage in conflicting therapeutic and forensic relationships heighten the danger that they will be more concerned with the patient's legal case outcome than with the testimony's accuracy.[88]

Greenberg and Shuman, in an influential article, describe ten differences between therapeutic and forensic relationships.[89] Among the differences, they distinguish the cognitive set and evaluative attitude of the therapist versus the forensic evaluator towards a client: the therapist is supportive, accepting, and empathic, while the forensic evaluator is neutral, objective, and detached.[90] In addition, the goal of the professional in relation to the client differs: the therapist attempts to benefit the patient by working within the therapeutic relationship, while the forensic evaluator advocates for the result and implications of the evaluation for the court's benefit.[91] Another important difference relates to the "scrutiny applied to the information utilized in the process and the role of historical truth": therapists take most of their information from the client with little independent scrutiny of that information, while forensic evaluators supplement the client's reports with reports by collaterals—teachers, past counselors, family members, babysitters or other caretakers—and other records; the client's word is not enough.[92]

Several mental health professional guidelines and ethics codes address this dual-role relationship directly, although all warn against the dangers of conflicts of interest. For example, the *APA Child Custody Guidelines* note that "although the court may require the psychologist to testify as a fact witness regarding factual information he or she became aware of in a professional relationship with a (therapy) client, that psychologist should generally decline the role of an expert witness who gives a professional opinion regarding custody and visitation issues unless so ordered by the court."[93] The *Forensic Specialty Guidelines* recommend that "forensic psychologists avoid providing professional services to parties in a legal proceeding with whom they have personal or professional relationships that are inconsistent with the anticipated relationship."[94]

Psychiatry guidelines express similar cautions. The *Practice Parameters for Child Custody Evaluation* of the American Academy of Child and Adolescent Psychiatry note: "It is extremely important for the clinician to understand the differences in roles and to keep these roles separate. Wearing 'two hats'—therapist and forensic evaluator—with a family is inappropriate, and it complicates both the therapy and the evaluation."[95] And the *Ethics Guidelines for the Practice of Forensic Psychiatry*, in commentary to the section titled *Honesty and Striving for Objectivity*, note that "the forensic evaluation and the credibility of the practitioner may also be undermined by conflicts inherent in the differing clinical and forensic roles. Treating psychiatrists should therefore generally avoid acting as an expert witness for their patients or performing evaluations of their patients for legal purposes."[96] Problems resulting from this dual-role relationship are of a practical and ethical nature.[97]

But consider another scenario: While the professional literature emphasizes the distinction between therapist and forensic evaluator, may a therapist counseling with a child or parent going through a divorce ethically offer the court useful, reliable information apart from recommendations on the ultimate legal issue in the case? Or, is such a therapist prohibited from offering any opinions because of dual-role relationship concerns? Two situations suggest that therapists may provide the court important information about family members who engage them for counseling: (1) courts often order family members into counseling for specific purposes—for example, helping the children through the emotional stress of the divorce—and (2) family members themselves may have already been in counseling with therapists who may be able to give the court helpful information for its decisions about the family. In these situations, the MHP's treating expert role is to intervene therapeutically in the family—a different role from that of a forensic evaluator.[98]

What are the MHP treating expert's role boundaries in these situations? Because treating experts do not have access to the breadth of information (represented by document reviews, psychological test data, contacts with collateral sources, and a fact-finding focus) of forensic evaluators, they should not offer opinions on ultimate legal questions before the court—for example, child custody, visitation issues, validity of abuse allegations.[99] But treating MHPs may offer expert opinions on patients' diagnosis and behavior patterns in counseling.[100] Also, among other issues, treating MHPs may offer opinions on the counseling's progress or lack thereof, or, with adequate basis, if the counseling has not yet begun, what conditions might best contribute to the probability that counseling might benefit the patient or family. Again, the concern focuses on whether the role MHPs adopt in a particular case allows them to provide the court trustworthy information to help decide the case. To meet this concern, MHP treating experts should understand and acknowledge limitations in their role, information base, and treatment methods and thus limit their conclusions and opinions.[101]

STEP TWO—METHODOLOGY AND THE PSYCHOLOGICAL PERSPECTIVE

While *Step One* of our *Frye-Daubert* Analysis Model addressed MHPs' qualifications, *Step Two* addressed whether the MHPs' methods follow *applicable professional standards* of the relevant specialty. Understanding MHPs' approaches to methodology is vital when addressing this step of the analysis. Recall that the *Frye* principle emphasizes that methods be generally accepted by the relevant scientific community—also one of *Daubert*'s factors. In addition, note *Kumho Tire*'s charge that the expert "employs in the courtroom the same level of intellectual rigor that characterizes the practice of an expert in the relevant field,"[102] and *Daubert*'s reminder that "the expert's opinion will have a reliable basis in the knowledge and experience of his discipline."[103] In this section, we will discuss methodology used in evaluations to generate and organize data that form the bases of much MHP testimony in family law cases. The methods include forensic interviewing, use of third-party or collateral information, and psychological testing. Understanding how MHP evaluators use these methods will provide lawyers with valuable information by which to gauge the quality of their own experts' work and useful tools with which to assess and cross-examine the work of opposing experts.

Guidelines and Protocols Informing Methodology

In general, protocols are sets of procedures developed for professionals to guide their application of methods and to direct their decision making in various clinical or assessment tasks. Some organizations distinguish between structured protocols and guidelines, noting the former as more formal, even scripted, and the latter as generalized guides to good practice based upon empirical findings and professional consensus.[104]

In essence, protocols and guidelines define or describe procedures by which MHPs collect the data upon which they form their conclusions and opinions. Some protocols have strong experimental support. For example, the *NICHD Investigative Interview Protocol*—designed to maximize the amount of information in interviews of alleged child sexual abuse victims—used research to note that children give more accurate information about past events when asked open-ended questions, when presented with more focused questions only after exhausting open-ended questions, and when probed with option-posing questions only to elicit essential information at the interview's end.[105] Other protocols were developed from generally accepted procedures that professionals use to gather information by systematically weighing alternate hypotheses in decision-tree formats; clinical medical protocols that physicians use to rule diagnoses in or out are examples of these protocols.[106]

As noted earlier, a set of procedures has been recognized and gained acceptance in the social science literature for child custody evaluations. The procedures include the following:

- individual interviews of the parents
- individual interviews of the children
- interviews with significant others, including stepparents, teachers, health care providers, and counselors, among others
- observations of the child jointly with each parent
- some psychological testing
- review of the children's school records

But even if MHPs use these procedures to gather evaluation data, are all methods used within a generally accepted set of procedures, guidelines, or protocols automatically accorded the mantle of reliability? Of course, the answer is no. As noted earlier, lawyers must ensure that MHP experts do not try to shoehorn reliability into an unreliable or "untrustworthy" method, even if that method is applied within a set of procedures or a protocol that may be "generally accepted" in the field in which the expert is offering testimony. If a method or reasoning within the generally accepted set of procedures or protocol is unreliable, the procedure set or protocol as a whole, and the expert's resulting conclusions, may also be judged unreliable. For example, in *Black v. Food Lion*, a 1999 Fifth Circuit Court of Appeals case, the plaintiff alleged that her slip-and-fall injury in a grocery store caused fibromyalgia. The court ruled that there was insufficient data from the medical literature to indicate whether causal relationships exist between trauma and fibromyalgia.[107] Further, the court asserted that an expert's use of general methodology—in this case, an accepted protocol in rendering an opinion in terms of reasonable medical probability—"cannot vindicate a conclusion for which there is no underlying medical support."[108]

At times, MHPs use unreliable methods—often accepted within a limited group of MHPs—in family law evaluations to generate data from within the structure of generally accepted child custody evaluation procedures. For example, while interviewing a child, the evaluator might conceptualize the child's play or drawings as "projections" of the child's emotional state or wishes. But drawn human figures depicting the "self" may represent, if anything, children's perceptions of themselves, or of what they wish themselves to be, or of actual or perceived impairments, or of compensation for real or perceived shortcomings, or of "a combination of these factors."[109] And interpretations of these projective-type responses may reveal more about the examiner's theoretical orientation or favorite hypotheses than the examinee's personality dynamics.[110] As a result, these kinds of techniques on their own, while accepted within a group of clinically oriented MHPs, cannot generate—even as elements of a generally accepted set of child custody procedures—the kind of reliable or trustworthy data that the court should consider.

Prudent lawyers will unpackage MHPs' evaluation procedures by challenging the methods and the methods' elements for logical and empirical indices of reliability. Toward that goal, let us examine three main elements of a child custody evaluation: forensic interviews, third-party informant contacts, and psychological testing.

Forensic Interviews

Forensic interviews represent a key method by which MHPs gain information upon which to base their conclusions and opinions. For instance, parents tell the stories of their separations and divorces and their concerns for their children during interviews in child custody evaluations. In the process, parents will "put their best foot forward" while attempting to persuade MHPs that their concerns are legitimate. Such interviews are not merely sets of verbal interactions. They also are social interactions during which parents—and at times, children—will actively seek to persuade and impress.

Forensic MHPs and parent interviewees interact with very different agendas. Forensic MHPs must bring a forensic perspective to the interview. As therapists, MHPs are trained to respond to their clinical patients with empathy and guidance in order to help their patients understand or alleviate emotional hurt or to manage relationships more effectively. But MHPs conducting forensic interviews must curb their use of empathy "in a manner unusual for clinical practice but essential for fair, ethical, evaluative interaction."[111] Recall the basic distinctions between the therapist and forensic roles discussed earlier: the therapist is supportive, accepting, and empathic with his or her patients, while the forensic evaluator's approach is neutral, objective, and detached, offering to the court the evaluation's results and implications for the court's benefit.[112] Child custody evaluators, for example, who slip into "therapeutic" roles may compromise their objectivity and confuse parents' understanding of the evaluation's purposes. This problem also arises if evaluators attempt to "mediate" a settlement between the parties under the guise that the evaluator knows the family better than most others and has developed a rapport with each family member. Do not allow this serious dual-relationship problem to develop, despite the apparent good intentions. Family lawyers should insist—for their clients' sakes—that MHPs involved with their clients understand their roles and stick to them.

Parent interviewees also have different agendas than clinical patients.[113] Clinical patients engage MHPs to help alleviate emotional pain or problem relationships. But parent interviewees in forensic evaluations engage MHPs to accomplish their legal goals—for example, custody of their children. The stakes are high, and many such parents do not lack in their efforts or tactics to persuade MHP evaluators.

Besides providing parents and children opportunities to relate their wishes and concerns, good forensic interviewing enables MHPs to gain more reliable information from parents and children by providing opportunities to explore complaints, concerns, and assets from different perspectives. As noted earlier, standard forensic psychology practice demands that psychologists consider and weigh rival hypotheses in the issues they examine as they conduct their forensic activities.[114] Research also supports this practice: empirical data suggest that clinicians become more accurate in their decision making and less prone to biased thinking when they actively consider alternative explanations.[115]

On what, then, should forensic interviews focus? The answer seems simple: interviews should address the referral question. But on closer scrutiny, the focus may be more complex. For example, a referral question to evaluate whether a parent is clinically depressed or is experiencing a bipolar disorder is fairly targeted—of course, this question could be extended to address the extent to which this problem impacts parenting. In contrast, a broader, typical child custody question that asks with which parent the child should live during the school week is more complicated. How might the evaluator or potential expert examine this question? What issues are relevant and important to consider?

Professional guidelines and literature provide some direction. The *APA Child Custody Guidelines* emphasize that the "focus of the evaluation is on parenting capacity, the psychological and developmental needs of the child, and the resulting fit . . . . Psychopathology may be relevant to an evaluation, insofar as it has impact on the child or the ability to parent, but it is not the primary focus."[116] In addition, the *APA Child Custody Guidelines* note that "the values of the parents relevant to parenting, ability to plan for the child's future needs, capacity to provide a stable and loving home, and any potential for inappropriate behavior or misconduct that might negatively influence the child also are considered."[117] The *APA Child Custody Guidelines* view parenting as a functionally oriented capacity, not as an abstract notion that is summarily negated by psychopathology. That is, how does each parent, with each one's abilities, interact with the child to meet the child's needs; what are the reasons for any noted parenting deficits; and how may those deficits be remedied to benefit the parent and the child?[118] This approach forces psychologists to conform their conclusions to the scientific and professional literature on parenting issues. Also, a functionally oriented approach to the evaluation is more likely to survive admissibility challenges in court because that approach will tend to be more centered in the scientific and professional literature, and the conclusions will be logically "connected" to the evaluation data—a key requirement in *Step Three* of our analysis model presented in the preceding chapter. In a child custody or parenting evaluation, looking only to parents' emotional difficulties or only to allegations raised by one parent against the other does not sufficiently address the legal issue from a functional approach. In either case, the lawyer could convincingly argue that the analytical gap between the data and the best interest opinion is too great to address reliably the court's concern.

Interviews with children raise their own challenges. The quality of children's reports is a joint product of their cognitive and social maturities, their experiences outside formal interviews, and the interview context.[119] Children below the age of four are not good candidates for reliable verbal interviews. The less developed the child's language, the greater the risks that the child's statements will be misinterpreted or that the child will misinterpret the interviewer's questions.[120] Also, young children tend to remember less information and provide briefer accounts of their experiences than older children, and they tend to forget information faster as well.[121]

Experiences outside children's formal MHP interviews may also affect the quality of the children's reports. For example, adults may instill negative, even false, stereotypes of others in children, and children's reports about events involving those negatively stereotyped people may be easily influenced by those stereotypes.[122] Also, adults can influence children to produce false reports even when interview questions are not suggestive.[123] In addition, children's reports can be influenced by exposure to misinformation from their parents.[124]

Issues within the interview may also affect the quality of children's reports. For example, a line of research notes that children generally are cooperative and compliant participants in verbal interactions, and, at times, attempt to make their answers consistent with what they see as the questioner's desire[125]—good interviewers will let children know at the outset that they have the option to say they do not know the answer to a question.[126] Also, interviewers with biases about the experiences of children interviewees tend to elicit more false information from children[127] as they mold the interviews to elicit statements that are consistent with those biases and that avoid inconsistent evidence.[128] In addition, children interviewed in an accusatory context—with comments such as "You'll feel better once you've told" and "Are you afraid to tell?"—will tend to yield more false information.[129]

In sum, while children may provide reliable reports in the right interview context, many factors may affect the quality of those reports. And while many of these principles were studied in the context of forensic interviews of suspected sexually abused children, these concerns and the research also speak to children's reports in other family law matters, such as child custody or visitation cases.[130] These issues will be addressed again in Chapter 8 when sexual abuse allegations are discussed in the context of exposing confirmatory bias in MHP experts' reports and testimony.

Third-Party or Collateral Information

The second of three main elements in child custody evaluations involves collecting and reviewing third-party or collateral information. There is near-universal agreement in the professional literature that collateral interview data and record reviews are critical components of a comprehensive forensic child custody evaluation.[131]

Clinical interviews alone of the parties usually cannot provide enough reliable data upon which to support credible evaluation conclusions. As noted earlier, parents and others involved in family law cases tend to present themselves positively and minimize issues that reflect unfavorably on their cases. Often, information from sources outside the clinical interview will offer MHPs opportunities to explore issues with parents that the parents were unprepared or less than willing to relate. Collateral interviews or third-party information provide a broader picture of the family beyond the four walls of the evaluator's office as well as opportunities for MHPs to check the plausibility of parties' accounts of key incidents or claims relevant to the legal case. For example, if a father says that his fifth-grade daughter living with him has done well in school in the previous six weeks, a report card or a telephone interview with the teacher will check the father's assertion. Third-party information may also reveal a party's motivations and capacities and further test developing evaluation hypotheses.[132] In sum, careful review of records, gathering of personal history, and interviews with family members, teachers, counselors, and medical professionals will develop more accurate pictures of the parties and their personal and legal concerns than what could have been developed solely from interviews with the parties themselves.

Of course, usefulness of third-party information increases with the credibility of those reports.[133] Usually, professionals—counselors, teachers, physicians—are viewed as credible informants, with family members and friends presumed less objective. But this rule is not fixed: some counselors, based on an ongoing relationship with one parent who consistently talks negatively about the other parent, may offer very biased opinions about a child's concerns, while some family members may give useful descriptions about a parent or child. Heilbrun noted four problems that might compromise the credibility of third-party informants: bias, expertise, suggestibility, and memory loss.[134] Bias may be more prevalent when sources are family, friends, or new spouses in custody modification cases. At times, bias may even creep into the reports of ostensibly neutral professionals—with a teacher, for example, in whose class a mother may be a parent-assistant. Problems of expertise occur when sources of third-party information lack sufficient training or experience in dealing with certain mental disorders and, thus, are unable to address those concerns adequately. Suggestibility concerns arise when third-party informants are influenced by an MHP's leading questions that may reflect the MHP's bias. And memory loss problems may be evident when a third-party informant cannot adequately recall details of certain incidents of interest to the MHP.[135]

Obtaining information from multiple collateral sources—informants and records—is particularly important when evaluating allegations of parent-child violence. Interestingly, mothers, fathers, and children may give discrepant reports—for different reasons—of the frequency and type of parent-child violence. Consequently, lack of agreement among family members in these cases should not be considered simply a reliability issue.[136]

Clearly, third-party informants should not automatically be handed the mantle of reliability. Family lawyers should ensure that MHP experts can describe why they used certain informants and how they accounted for potential third-party informant credibility problems. How MHPs answer these questions may either enhance or compromise the reliability of their testimony.

Psychological Testing

The third of three main elements in child custody evaluations involves psychological testing. Before proceeding, let us note the important distinction between psychological testing and an assessment or evaluation. Psychological testing is not synonymous with assessment or evaluation. Psychological tests systematically sample an examinee's behaviors, thoughts, and/or perceptions. However, assessment or evaluation is the professional application of several tools—among which are forensic interviewing and the gathering and review of third-party or collateral information—which may include and integrate testing, to address clinical or legal concerns.[137]

Two professional organizations that have developed guidelines for child custody/access evaluations—the Association of Family and Conciliation Courts (AFCC) and the American Academy of Child and Adolescent Psychiatry (AACAP)—indicate that psychological testing is not required in such evaluations, although they note that testing, at times, may be advisable.[138] The AFCC is a multidisciplinary organization of the various MHP disciplines, lawyers, and judges; psychologists are but one discipline represented in the organization. The AACAP is a psychiatric group. As a result, the testing stances of these organizations may reflect more guild concerns than good practice approaches because the use and interpretation of psychological testing is a particular expertise of psychologists.[139]

Nevertheless, psychological testing in child custody evaluations may be misused. For instance, testing may be overvalued when MHPs and lawyers treat it as the only important data source and inappropriately divine functional parenting behaviors from instruments not designed to measure those interactions. Or, testing may be undervalued when MHPs and lawyers fail to recognize that results, used properly, may add helpful and reliable research-based data and clinical information to the child custody puzzle.

No tests have been adequately validated to address specifically the best interest standard in child custody proceedings. Rather, the most widely accepted psychological tests were developed to address questions related to clinical diagnoses and treatment planning. Psychological testing, by itself, provides few specifics about parenting skills or abilities. Psychologists who offer opinions about custody/access matters based solely upon psychological tests overstep their professional bounds.[140] Instead, those tests, in such cases, must be integrated into comprehensive evaluations designed to address those matters and to provide a reliable basis for the offered opinions.

Survey research indicates that MHP evaluators primarily use one or more of three psychological tests in custody evaluations—the Minnesota Multiphasic Personality Inventory–2 (MMPI–2), the Millon Clinical Multiaxial Inventory–III (MCMI–III), and the Rorschach Inkblot Method.[141] In addition, some forensic evaluators may use the Personality Assessment Inventory (PAI) in place of the MMPI–2 or the MCMI–III because its questions are written at a lower reading level.[142]

These clinically oriented psychological tests often are placed in one of two categories: objective self-report tests and projective tests. Self-report psychological tests—such as the MMPI–2, the MCMI–III, and the PAI—compare an examinee's test performance with the performance of others from defined reference samples or gauge whether an examinee meets characteristics of defined criterion groups. Test responses are in dichotomous (such as true-false) or scale-range (such as four-point scales from false to very true) formats. From this information, psychologists may infer, with varying confidence levels, similarities between characteristics of test-takers and those of the reference samples or criterion groups.

The quality of those inferences may be affected by, among other factors, the test-taker's response set. Examinees sometimes adopt a response set other than accurately endorsing the test items.[143] For instance, examinees with low reading levels or reading comprehension disabilities may experience difficulties understanding the test questions and randomly respond to many questions because they are embarrassed to disclose their reading problems. Other examinees may resist taking the tests and decide then to respond randomly to the questions or endorse all items "true" or "false" or alternate "true" and "false" responses.[144] Still other examinees may seek to exaggerate their positive traits and underreport emotional problems in their test responses. When interpreting test profiles, evaluators must account for these possibilities. The MMPI–2, MCMI–III, and PAI each has scales that reflect examinees' response sets.

In sum, self-report psychological tests may be viewed as structured and standardized questionnaires that statistically compare the answers of examinees against those of other people in various carefully defined reference samples while also accounting for the examinee's approach to the test questions.

Projective tests are less structured than the self-report psychological tests just described. The responses to projective test stimuli are more open-ended; examinees report what they see in Rorschach Inkblot cards and tell stories of pictures they see in Thematic

Apperception Test cards. Projective test responses purport to reflect examinees' perceptual or thinking styles and personality concerns. The underlying theory is that examinees "project" their internal thinking, personality styles, and conflicts onto ambiguous-meaning stimuli—the inkblots or picture cards, for instance. Psychologists may also use projective tests or techniques to gauge examinees' abilities to organize and make adequate sense of less structured aspects of their experiences. For example, projective test responses of people with thought disorders may be more peculiar and idiosyncratic than responses of people with more normal thought processes.

The Rorschach Inkblot Method is the most frequently administered projective test in child custody evaluations.[145] Its proponents describe it as "a relatively unstructured, performance-based personality assessment instrument."[146] Exner's *Comprehensive System* for scoring the Rorschach is complex with reference group comparisons.[147] However, there has been vigorous debate among psychologists about the validity and utility of the Rorschach and other projective techniques in forensic cases.[148]

Nevertheless, Rorschach results may provide compelling information about the examinee's cognitive and emotional functioning if the results are adequately tied to research data, reflect consistent themes—confirmed by other data—or alert the examiner to key concerns. But test results, whether from self-report or projective tests or whether individually or computer scored, only suggest hypotheses (some stronger than others, depending on the test's reliability and validity) about individual examinees for evaluators to explore in the forensic evaluation process.[149] No test is an X-ray into the emotional state or functioning of any individual examinee.

Certain instruments purport to address parenting competency questions and targeted issues more directly than traditional clinically oriented tests. Examples are the ASPECT,[150] the Bricklin Scales,[151] the Child Abuse Potential Inventory,[152] the Parent-Child Relationship Inventory,[153] the Parenting Stress Index,[154] and the Custody Quotient.[155] Some child custody evaluators may use these instruments because they are more structured than clinical interviews, they claim to provide definitions of what constitutes effective parenting, and they employ content that is more specific to questions of parental capacity than traditional clinical psychological tests employ.[156] However, no instrument that only assesses parents meets basic scientific standards of reliability and validity for making judgments about "preferred parents," or for making comparisons between parents that would justify suggesting that one parent's abilities are more desirable than the other's.[157]

As noted earlier, child custody evaluators often interview collateral or third-party sources who are professionals—teachers, doctors, and day care personnel—to gain information from other perspectives about children's academic, emotional, and social functioning. Structured inventories may supplement those important contacts and often provide richer and more accurate descriptions of the children. Three sets of inventories offer evaluators such views of children's problem behaviors from the perspectives of significant adults in the children's lives: the Achenbach System of Empirically Based Assessment;[158] the Behavior Assessment System for Children, Second Edition (BASC-2);[159] and the Personality Inventory for Children, Second Edition (PIC-2).[160] Each of these inventory groups requires informants to rate children's behaviors. The ratings are then compared to those of normative groups of children upon which each inventory was developed in order to gauge whether the ratings on various syndromes rise to levels of clinical concerns for the rated child. Each of these sets of inventories provides forms for parents, teachers, and children to fill out, enabling evaluators to compare views of the child from each perspective.

Finally, certain instruments, such as the Warshak Parent Questionnaire, Second Edition (WPQ-2),[161] are extensive developmental inventories that parents complete on the child. In the WPQ-2, the parent describes the child's family and developmental information and rates health concerns, school adjustment, skills and abilities, a broad array of behavioral and emotional symptoms, and strengths. While these inventories give parents opportunities to provide information about their children in systematic ways, they do not measure the parents' response styles—whether parents are reporting accurately or trying to minimize or exaggerate the children's problems. Nevertheless—besides painting a broad yet specific survey of the child's development—differences in descriptions of a child when comparing the individual inventory report of each parent may provide an evaluator valuable information about how each parent recognizes and understands the child's needs.

Criteria for Choosing Psychological Tests

Given the immense number of psychological tests available and the range of quality of those tests, how should MHPs and lawyers decide whether certain tests should be used in a child custody evaluation? Otto, Edens, and Barcus offer several useful markers:[162]

1. Is the test commercially published? Commercial publication serves as a review process and ensures a reasonable level of availability and uniformity of test stimulus materials and protocols.[163]
2. Is a comprehensive test manual available? Test manuals are an authoritative resource that should fully describe the development, standardization, administration, scoring, and psychometric properties of the instrument—including its reliability and validity.[164]
3. Are adequate levels of the test's reliability demonstrated? MHPs should only use tests with known and adequate levels of reliability. Because the reliability of a measure limits its validity, tests with poor reliability are tests with poor validity, and tests with unknown reliability are tests with unknown validity.[165]
4. Have adequate levels of the test's validity been demonstrated? Does the test really assess what its authors claim? A test is not valid simply because it is published or because its authors purport it to be valid.[166]
5. Is the test valid for the purpose in which it will be used? In addition, evaluators must consider whether a test that is of proven validity for a specific purpose is valid with a particular examinee—issues of ethnicity, race, setting, and age may affect test results and test validity.[167]
6. Has the instrument been peer reviewed? Reliability and validity studies should be published in refereed journals because such studies allow for the most comprehensive examination of the test and its properties.[168]
7. What are the qualifications necessary to use this instrument? Even a valid and appropriate test can produce invalid results if it is administered, scored, or interpreted by a professional who lacks the requisite knowledge, training, and experience.[169]

Seven Keys to Understanding Tests

While the preceding markers help lawyers gauge the quality of tests used in child custody evaluations, lawyers may find the nature and theory of testing too confusing to cross-examine MHP experts effectively. But if lawyers do not effectively address testing issues, experts' uses and interpretations of the tests—even if incorrect—may stand unchallenged.

Unless lawyers find it essential to address the statistical structure of a particular psychological test—at which point an MHP consulting expert likely will be hired—they will be served well by focusing on seven key test issues. Understanding those issues will help make sense of test results and the experts' interpretations and uses of those results. Each issue will be explored using the MMPI-2 to illustrate the concepts—survey research notes that the MMPI-2 is the most frequently used adult psychological test administered in child custody evaluations.[170] Other tests will be noted when helpful.

The seven key test issues are:

- Response Styles of the Examinees
- Standardization Sample
- Reliability
- Standard Error of Measurement
- Validity
- Sensitivity and Specificity
- Computer-Based Test Interpretation (CBTI)

Response Styles of the Examinees

The examinee's response style while answering test questions during an evaluation is the first of seven key issues about testing that lawyers should understand. The MMPI-2, MCMI-III, and PAI are self-report inventories often administered in an evaluation. In these inventories, examinees respond to statements about their behaviors, emotional states, feelings, relationships, and history that will produce profiles describing the examinees along dimensions—mostly problem-oriented—the tests measure. As a result, one might expect that an examinee's response style, or approach, to the testing might be affected by the testing's context or setting. Testing standards note that it is important to assess the examinee's test-taking orientation in forensic evaluations, including response bias, to ensure that the examinee's test responses have not been overly affected by the legal context.[171] To illustrate, reports have documented incidents when an examinee's MMPI-2 profiles changed markedly over a three-year period depending on the testing context.[172] The first three MMPI-2 administrations occurred over a sixteen-month period during personal injury litigation; these profiles showed significant emotional distress. Seven months later, during a child custody evaluation, this same examinee produced a much more benign MMPI-2 profile. Fifteen months later another MMPI-2 administration in the personal injury litigation reflected the more seriously distressed profile. Context matters.

If examinees in child custody matters try to conform their test responses to a picture they want the examiner to see, they will likely present themselves in an overly favorable light. The MMPI-2 has the most developed series of validity indices to assess examinees' response styles of the tests psychologists commonly use in child custody evaluations. Some literature notes that the MMPI-2 can distinguish three different response styles by which examinees underreport emotional problems by presenting themselves in an overly favorable light: impression management, self-deception, or a combination of both.[173] Impression management refers to examinees' deliberate attempts to convey unrealistically favorable self-descriptions through their test responses, while self-deception refers to examinees' beliefs that the overly favorable picture presented through the test responses is actually accurate.[174] If the MMPI-2 profile is deemed invalid because the examinee's response style has indicated that the examinee may have presented himself or herself too favorably, the evaluator still should describe the examinee's response style and its possible causes.[175]

While professionals commonly presume that MMPI-2 profiles in child custody evaluations will more likely reflect a response style in which examinees present themselves in overly favorable ways, the research is not conclusive. Some studies found that MMPI-2 profiles of adults in child custody evaluations show well-established elevations on certain validity scales that reflect examinees' attempts to present themselves in overly favorable ways when compared with persons not undergoing custody evaluations.[176] But criticism of those studies distinguishes between statistical significance and clinical significance. That is, although validity scale elevations of child custody examinees may be significantly higher than those of persons not involved in these evaluations, the difference is inconsequential in a practical sense because the elevations still do not reach the level that would invalidate the MMPI-2 profile or otherwise significantly affect its interpretation.[177] As a result, one should not automatically expect overly favorable response styles from a child custody litigant administered the MMPI-2. Such a response style in an MMPI-2 profile may actually say more about the examinee than just an expected child custody profile.[178]

In sum, a psychological test's interpretation is not based just on the clinical scale profile. The examinee's response style, or approach to the testing task, is part of the interpretation's context that may directly impact the test's results.

Standardization Sample

Comparison of an examinee's raw test score to an appropriate standardization sample is an important second key to understanding test scores. Test norms are established using a sample developed to represent a larger population and, thus, provide a reference for test-takers' scores.[179] An examinee's score on any particular test is meaningless if not compared to appropriate reference or criterion groups. For example, to say, in the absence of additional interpretive data, that a person solved fifteen problems on a math test or defined twenty vocabulary words correctly conveys little or no information about that person's performances in those tasks.[180] Further, an adult's high score on an intelligence test is impressive if, for example, the score is compared to the test's reference group of similar-aged adults; the adult's score is spurious if the test's reference group comprises fifth-grade students.

While this principle seems elementary, MHPs may gloss over it when they use test results to develop their conclusions from tests that seem, at first glance, to apply reliably to the case. Consider the Parenting Stress Index (PSI), developed to assess stress within parent-child systems and presented as useful in evaluations of various problem family relationships that might arise in child-custody cases.[181] The PSI's normative sample included 2633 mothers (11 percent African American and 10 percent Hispanic) recruited, with no attempt to match census data, from "well-childcare" pediatric clinics in Virginia.[182] The sample also included 200 men—95 percent Caucasian—and a sample of 223 Hispanic New York City parents who completed a Spanish-language version of the PSI.[183] Apart from other concerns, attempts to apply PSI results to father-child relationships would be questionable given this normative sample. Clearly, one key limitation of the PSI is the standardization sample upon which it is based.[184] Individual test scores cannot be understood or meaningfully compared if the reference groups differ from the examinees; the primary requirement of reference groups is that they reflect the kinds of people for whom the tests are intended.[185]

The issue can be even more subtle. For example, test norms based on persons involved in counseling might be inappropriately compared to scores produced by persons who are not engaged in counseling. Some raise this concern about the use of the MCMI-III in child custody evaluations, although the MCMI-III is the second most frequently used adult psychological test in child custody evaluations.[186] Concern arises because the MCMI-III's reference groups are primarily composed of psychotherapy patients, and test results "are applicable only to individuals who evidence problematic emotional and interpersonal symptoms or who are undergoing professional psychotherapy or a psychodiagnostic evaluation."[187] Nevertheless, the MCMI-III manual points to the MCMI-III test as useful in child custody evaluations because "custody battles that reach the point of requiring psychological evaluation constitute such a degree of interpersonal difficulty that the evaluation becomes a clinical matter."[188]

The MMPI-2's reference group differs from the MCMI-III's primarily clinically oriented reference group. The MMPI-2 was standardized on a sample of 2600 people—contacted through a variety of methods, including advertisements and direct mail lists—who resided in seven different states to reflect national census parameters on age, marital status, ethnicity, education, and occupational status.[189] Thus, the MMPI-2 might be used in different contexts than the MCMI-III. For example, the MMPI-2 may be used as part of a preemployment test package to screen for psychopathology in certain sensitive occupations such as air traffic controllers, airline pilots, or police officers.[190] But administering the MCMI-III in personnel contexts or to assess personality traits among the general population "is to apply the instrument to settings and samples for which it is neither intended nor appropriate."[191] In some settings, both the MMPI-2 and the MCMI-III may be used appropriately in an evaluation testing package. An example might be a child custody evaluation. But other settings may require the examiner to choose one test or the other depending on whether the examinee's score may be appropriately compared to the test's reference group.

Reliability

Reliability is the third key test issue lawyers should understand. As pointed out earlier, reliability in the legal sense refers to evidentiary reliability or trustworthiness.[192] In psychological test theory, reliability refers to the extent to which test scores are consistent and free from measurement error.[193] Measurements are always subject to some error and variation. The objective of obtaining a "true" score on any measure is enhanced when the test produces consistent results with a minimum amount of error. For example, people trying to lose weight will not tolerate scales that yield inconsistent readings; rather, they look for scales that give as close to a true reading as possible to measure weight loss. In sum, the observed score on any measure equals the true score plus error; the less error, the closer the observed score is to the true score—really a theoretical concept.

Reliability in psychological testing may be considered in several ways. The most easily understood psychological test reliability concept is test-retest reliability. Simply, the test-retest reliability figure is the correlation between test scores that would be obtained by the same individual repeating the identical test on a second occasion.[194] Error relates to the random performance fluctuations from one test administration to the other.[195] Test reliability usually is figured under standard conditions of administration applied during the test's development and generally is reported in the test manual. But one always should note the time interval between test-retest administrations when considering the test manual's reported reliability figure. Understandably, retest correlations decrease as time intervals between test administrations increase.[196] For example, the MMPI-2 manual reports test-retest reliability figures for the basic validity and clinical scales of a selected group of the normative sample. But the time interval between test administrations in this group was only about one week.[197] For longer time intervals, the test-retest figures are lower.[198]

Lower test-retest figures over time are not surprising in personality testing where many emotional attributes or concerns (depression, anxiety, or other distress) being tested may change over short periods—in contrast, intelligence, aptitude, or interests are less likely to change over time. Nevertheless, MMPI-2 profiles are likely to be more stable when their scales are more elevated and when they are more elevated than other scales in the profile.[199]

Greene notes two important cautions about MMPI-2 profile stability or reliability that are relevant to the MMPI-2's use in court.[200] First, he cautions that psychologists should not readily make long-term predictions from a single administration of the MMPI-2—in a several-week child custody evaluation, the MMPI-2 typically is administered only once. Second, he warns that the literature is unclear about whether MMPI-2 profile shifts over time reflect meaningful changes in the examinee's behaviors, the psychometric instability of the MMPI-2, or a combination of both.

Finally, expanding from Greene's second caution, one should note that the quality of reliability, as applied to test scores, is not an absolute concept tied only to a number in the test manual. Errors that affect the reliability of test scores may arise from one or more of three sources: the context in which the testing takes place, the examinee, or the test itself.[201] Each of these sources may provide useful handles with which to organize cross-examination questions regarding the reliability of a test score offered in court.

The context in which the testing takes place is important to ensure that the examinee's obtained test score is reliable enough to be compared to the test's normative group. For example, standardized directions ensure that all examinees approach the test questions in the same ways and in the ways by which the normative group approached the test. Also, where the examinee takes the test may affect the obtained score's reliability. The MMPI-2 manual describes a typical testing situation as requiring "adequate space at a table . . . good lighting, a comfortable chair, and quiet surroundings free of intrusions and distractions."[202] Further, if the examinee asks the psychologist to clarify test questions or define words in the questions, the psychologist should only give simple definitions or rephrase colloquialisms or idioms; extended discussion of the test questions should be avoided.[203] In addition, the manual notes that the MMPI-2 should not be administered without proper supervision and should not be given to examinees to complete at home.[204] Lawyers should make sure that the "chain-of-custody" of the examinee's test responses is known and not muddled by the possibility that others helped the examinee answer the test questions.

The examinee is a second source of error that may affect the reliability of the test score. The two most common examinee characteristics that may affect the test score's reliability are the examinee's reading or language abilities and the examinee's response style discussed earlier. The MMPI-2 requires a sixth-grade reading level to comprehend and respond to the test items appropriately.[205] Therefore, adults who have not completed high school may not have the requisite reading skills to take the test. But even college graduates may have a reading learning disability that might prevent them from understanding the test questions adequately. If the examinee's reading ability is in doubt, the examiner should consider administering a reading test to establish the examinee's reading level or should administer a personality test with a lower required reading level, such as the Personality Assessment Inventory. Keep in mind that adults may feel defensive, even ashamed, if asked about how well they read. If the examiner wishes to administer the MMPI-2 despite the examinee's reading deficiencies, the examiner should utilize CDs or cassette tapes supplied by the MMPI-2 publisher that read the questions to the listener.[206] However, the examiner should not administer the MMPI-2 by reading the questions aloud to the examinee; this practice significantly departs from the standardized administration of the test, and the effects of such a practice are unknown.[207]

The test itself is a third source of error that may affect the reliability of the test score. How well the test is constructed psychometrically, the clarity of the test's questions, and the ease with which the examinee understands the test's instructions contribute to the test's reliability.

In sum, while the reliability figure in the test's manual is an important way to gauge the test's consistency and stability, other factors may also be sources of error that could affect the test score's reliability.

Standard Error of Measurement

In the preceding section, we noted that reliability refers to the extent to which test scores over test administrations are consistent and free from measurement error. It follows, then, that the objective of obtaining an examinee's true score on any measure is enhanced the more reliable that measure is. But because true scores, theoretically, can never be obtained—there always is some measurement error—the error that is part of any obtained score must be considered when interpreting the obtained score's meaning.

The Standard Error of Measurement (SEM), or standard error of a score, addresses this issue. The SEM reflects the confidence one may have in a particular test score by establishing the upper and lower limits within which the examinee's true score is likely to fall.[208] The size of the range within which an examinee's obtained test score falls depends on the probability range the examiner chooses and the test's reliability.[209] Each unit of an SEM figure represents a range around the examinee's obtained test score within which the true score may be found; obviously, the larger the confidence range, the less confidence the evaluator will have about what the particular obtained score means.

For example, suppose an examinee obtains an elevated T-score of 67 on the MMPI-2's Scale 2, which measures depression. While the MMPI-2 literature offers interpretations at various clinical scale levels, a T-score elevation of 65 generally is viewed as a level at which the interpretations take on greater clinical emphasis and is the level used in many clinical and research studies to denote depression. Does the examinee's T-score of 67 reflect the true score? Is the score statistically different than a T-score of 63? The MMPI-2 Manual notes that Scale 2's SEM, based on T-scores from the standardization sample, equals 4.59. Departing one SEM unit on either side of a particular score results in a range in which 68 percent of the total distribution is accounted for. Departing two SEM units on either side of a particular score accounts for 95 percent of the total distribution. Therefore, an obtained T-score of 67 on Scale 2 means that there is a 68 percent probability that the examinee's true score lies in the range of approximately 62 (67 − 4.59) through 72 (67 + 4.59). To heighten the probability to 95 percent that the true score would be captured, the examinee would have to consider a range of approximately 58 (67 − 9.18) through 76 (67 + 9.18).

In sum, understanding the SEM concept gives an important perspective to test score interpretation. Again, no measure is without error, and, as a result, no obtained test score, by itself, represents a true score. The SEM highlights the notion that one cannot unduly emphasize a single numerical test score. Interpreting test scores is a probability exercise—as is most scientific decision making. Psychologists who do not account for SEM risk misinterpretation of test results and profiles.

Validity

Validity is the fifth key issue lawyers should understand about testing. Traditionally, the validity of a test was defined as what the test measured and how well it did so.[210] The current definition fleshes out validity in a way that is more useful to lawyers examining the work of experts who use testing to support their conclusions. That is, validity is not a quality that characterizes a particular test or test data alone. Rather, validity relates to how test scores are used and the degree to which accumulated evidence supports the intended interpretation of test scores for the proposed purpose.[211]

For example, consider a child custody evaluation in which the psychologist administered the MMPI-2 to the parents. Questions about the validity of the profile should be raised if the psychologist used the profile as a direct measure to address the parents' child management skills. The MMPI-2 was not developed to address such issues, and, thus, there is no validity in the psychologist's application of MMPI-2 scores to those issues. Now, suppose the psychologist used the MMPI-2 profile as a direct measure to address the emotional "attachment" of each parent with the child. Again, the MMPI-2 was not developed to address this issue, and, again, there is no validity in the psychologist's application of MMPI-2 scores to emotional "attachment."

Alternatively, assume the psychologist administered the MMPI-2 to the parents to assess if either is experiencing personality or emotional problems and the father's profile shows a significant elevation on Scale 2, which measures depression. The notion that the father may be depressed is an interpretation that is supported by much literature comparing Scale 2 elevations with other test and behavioral measures of depression. This accumulated empirical support of the test result and the psychologist's interpretation that the father, therefore, may be depressed is what validity addresses. The psychologist may then take the notion that the father is depressed and address how that might affect his parenting sensitivity, but that is a step beyond concluding that the MMPI-2 result itself implicates the father's parenting. Lawyers should carefully question psychologists who stretch their inferences of test results beyond what the validity research for the particular inference allows.[212]

Also, keep in mind that MMPI-2 results are valid only for personality or emotional problems for which there is accumulated empirical support of the test results. For example, while an adult claiming PTSD may be quite anxious and hypervigilant—emotional and cognitive states that MMPI-2 results, based on validity research, may address—research has not supported the notion that MMPI-2 scales adequately differentiate people claiming to experience PTSD from other people experiencing generalized distress.[213] Therefore, the MMPI-2 would not be a valid measure for specifically identifying people with PTSD as it is for identifying people who are depressed or emotionally distressed.

Finally, note three more ideas about validity: validity as a relative concept; the relationship of validity to reliability; and the notion of face validity. First, validity is always a matter of degree rather than an all-or-none determination.[214] Validation of a particular test or measure for certain uses evolves as evidence is gathered to support certain propositions or interpretations of test results in particular contexts.[215]

Second, validity is related to reliability. Recall that reliability refers to the extent to which test scores are consistent and free from measurement error.[216] It makes sense, then, that inconsistent, unreliable test results cannot be tied usefully to research required for validity studies. If a test assessing depression produces inconsistent results over time due to measurement error, few meaningful conclusions may be drawn from comparing those results with other more reliable measures of depression or with research in depression.

Third, face validity refers to the notion that a test "looks valid" based on its content or title.[217] But, for example, just because a test says it measures depression or borderline personality disorder does not mean it does so. The test instead may be measuring general anxiety. While it would seem that this notion would be obvious in a *Frye-Daubert* evidentiary world, face validity is compelling to non-MHPs in court. So, lawyers should ask for the validity support that would justify the interpretation and application of test results to conclusions MHPs make in their evaluations.

In sum, a sound validity argument reflects "the degree to which existing evidence and theory support the intended interpretation of test scores for specific uses."[218] Listen carefully: Do you hear the echoes of *Frye-Daubert* principles?

Sensitivity and Specificity

The sensitivity and specificity issue is the sixth key that lawyers should understand about testing. As noted throughout this section, tests or other assessment techniques are not perfect measures of any construct. Because error is involved in any measure, the possibility exists that tests may miscategorize examinees by identifying the examinees with particular conditions they do not have, or not identifying the examinees with conditions they possess—the notions of false positives and false negatives. For example, consider a study in which the MMPI-2's Scale 2, measuring depression, is used to predict the diagnosis of depression: scores above 65 would classify the examinee as depressed, below 65 as not depressed.[219] Of those above 65 classified as depressed, many will be depressed; these are true positives. Of those below 65 and classified as not depressed, many will not be depressed; these are true negatives. But some classified as depressed may not actually be depressed—false positives. And those classified as not depressed may actually be depressed—false negatives.

Sensitivity and specificity address these classification issues. Sensitivity asks: What are the chances that a person who is depressed will be identified by the MMPI-2's Scale 2 as having the disorder?—true positives. In contrast, specificity asks: What are the chances that a person who is not depressed will be identified by Scale 2 as not being depressed?—true negatives.

MHPs may neglect these concepts when testifying about test results or opinions resulting from clinical interviews. Greene illustrates the problem with the PK and PS supplementary scales of the MMPI-2—these scales purport to measure Posttraumatic Stress Disorder.[220] While there is abundant research on these scales, there is question about whether these scales truly discriminate between people with the disorder and those without it. That is, while the PK and the PS scales may tap into the distress PTSD patients experience (sensitivity), the scales do not adequately exclude examinees with non-PTSD distress (specificity). Generalized distress is a significant factor common to all MMPI-2 clinical scale elevations. Therefore, the PK and PS cannot be relied upon to distinguish PTSD patients from non-PTSD patients who are otherwise distressed. In sum, testimony solely on the sensitivity side of the equation presents an inaccurate picture of what the scales actually measure.

The sensitivity/specificity issue may show itself in any expert testimony—test-related or not—in which MHPs categorize people. For example, consider the MHP who testifies that a four-year-old child has been sexually abused because that child has nightmares, does not want to visit the accused parent, and frequently touches her own genitals. While these characteristics may result from abuse, they also are common characteristics of anxious children who have not been abused.[221] Similar analysis may apply when MHPs testify about an abuser's profile—psychological research has not identified a specific abuser profile. Abuse-related issues will be addressed later in Chapter 8.

In sum, lawyers should always be ready to look at the other side (specificity) of an MHP's testimony when tests or clinical interviews are used to classify a person. That is, to what extent do the characteristics attributed to the person differ from characteristics attributed to people without that classification?

Computer-Based Test Interpretation (CBTI)

CBTI is the final key issue lawyers should understand about psychological tests. The computer—as an information gathering, storing, and sorting device—has significantly affected psychological testing. Test scoring and interpretation programs now are available for the most frequently used psychological tests in child custody evaluations. Even less-formal inventories or questionnaires use computer programs to organize examinee responses and produce profiles or narratives that summarize those responses.

Computer use in test scoring and interpretation has several benefits. For example, computer scoring minimizes the possibility of hand-scoring errors by examiners or technicians[222]—the MMPI-2 has 567 True-False statements that when scored are sorted into several validity scales, eight clinical scales, and over 100 content and supplementary scales. Also, computer databases make use of a significant amount of research information on profiles that test responses generate to produce richer and more descriptive interpretive narratives than MHPs may produce on their own.[223] In addition, some argue that computer interpretation of test scores and profiles is more reliable than an MHP's interpretation because the computer will always provide the same interpretation of a given test profile or pattern of scores.[224]

Despite these benefits, many psychologists resist using computer-based test interpretation narratives in forensic evaluations for several reasons:

- Because CBTIs are written to generate a maximum number of clinical hypotheses about examinees rather than to focus on case-specific, clearly delineated issues, experts who use the interpretive narratives find themselves having to defend even slight contradictions between their testimony and the narrative report.[225]
- Generally, the algorithms, or problem decision rules, used by testing services to produce CBTIs are proprietary information and unavailable for examiners to review. The examiner, then, is unable to testify about how CBTI narrative statements were derived and how research used to support the narrative statements is weighed in the algorithms[226]—potentially, a key *Frye-Daubert* problem. Twenty years ago, Matarazzo expressed the concern that CBTIs present as "pages and pages of neatly-typed, valid-sounding narrative interpretations that are products, for the most part, of secretly developed disks."[227] Greene, Brown et al.'s *MMPI-2 Adult Interpretive System Version 3* distinguishes itself by providing explicit documentation for every interpretive report statement.[228]

  Courts' treatment of the Abel Assessment of Sexual Interest (AASI) test illustrates the issue. In a Texas appellate case, *In the Interest of CDK, JLK, and BJK*,[229] an expert in a termination of parental rights trial "all but labeled (the father) a pedophile" based on interpretation of the father's Abel Assessment results. The appeals court reversed the trial court's judgment terminating the parents' parental rights because, in part, of the expert's reliance on the Abel Assessment results. The court noted that the expert sent the father's raw data to Dr. Abel who later returned the assessment's findings to the expert. But the expert was unable to describe the "formulas" that Dr. Abel applied to the raw data that subsequently resulted in the conclusions about the father. The court wrote that the expert did not testify about the formulas applied by Abel, how those formulas were derived, and whether those formulas have ever been subjected to analysis or testing. The expert simply interpreted the "information" he received from Dr. Abel. The court noted: "How that undeniably pivotal 'information' was contrived or applied by those in Atlanta remains a mystery, given the record before us and the trial court."[230]
- Given their seeming validity and extensive psychological descriptions—written with reference to groups of individuals, not to a specific examinee—CBTIs may be erroneously equated with full and responsible psychological assessments[231] and foster an aura of scientific precision that cannot be supported by the particular tests or instruments.[232] As a related concern, CBTIs may increase the risk of test use by professionals who do not understand the given test or test theory and are unqualified to administer or interpret the given test.[233]
- Because computer programs have no knowledge of important moderator variables or examinees' historical information, CBTIs do not account adequately for examinees as individuals[234]—profiles showing depression have different implications for people with histories of suicide attempts as opposed to people going through the emotional throes of a divorce. Using CBTIs apart from other important information such as personal history, biographical data, interview observations, and previous records is inappropriate and not recommended by the CBTI developers.[235]

Clearly, while computers have made test scoring easier and, often, more accurate, significant questions remain about how MHPs might use narrative CBTIs when developing and supporting their conclusions and opinions. Butcher et al. describe CBTIs as largely performing "look up and list out" functions; that is, "a broad range of interpretations are stored in the computer for various test indexes, and the computer simply lists out the stored information for appropriate scale score levels."[236] It follows, then, that just because a report comes from a computer does not necessarily make it valid, particularly when applied to an individual. Consequently, the CBTI should be viewed as a valuable aid to professional clinical judgment that comprises a series of research-based hypotheses or tentative judgments about the examinee rather than as a substitute for a skilled evaluator.[237]

Professional codes and testing standards wrestle with the responsibilities of psychologists who utilize computer-based testing procedures. The *APA Ethics Code* addresses the issue of test scoring and interpretation services.[238] The *Code* states that test scoring services are required to describe "the purpose, norms, validity, reliability, and applications" of the tests to be used, and that psychologists are to "select scoring and interpretation services (including automated services) on the basis of evidence of validity of the program and procedures as well as on other appropriate considerations."[239] The forensic psychologist, as well as the lawyer, may legitimately ask if much of the bases of what test scoring services are required to provide is claimed to be proprietary—and, therefore, not to be distributed—on what basis may the forensic psychologist use the CBTI of a given test in a court-related evaluation? Can the use of hidden methodology—the decision algorithms—that produces the CBTI pass muster in a *Daubert*-oriented hearing? The Abel Assessment case example discussed earlier is a useful caution.

However, the *APA Ethics Code* is clear on the issue of psychologists' responsibilities if they use CBTIs. Standard 9.09(c) asserts: "Psychologists retain responsibility for the appropriate application, interpretation, and use of assessment instruments, whether they score and interpret such tests themselves or use automated or other services." This directive strongly implies that psychologists who use CBTIs must be competent in the use of the particular test.[240]

The *Standards for Educational and Psychological Testing* also caution that CBTIs should be used with care because "they may not take into account other information about the individual test-taker, such as age, gender, education, prior employment, and medical history that provide context for the test results."[241] In addition, these standards note that professionals who use CBTIs "should evaluate the quality of the interpretations and, when possible, the relevance and appropriateness of the norms upon which the interpretations are made."[242]

STEP THREE—DRAWING CONCLUSIONS FROM DATA AND THE PSYCHOLOGICAL PERSPECTIVE

In the previous section, we looked at the methods MHPs bring to family law matters and stressed that understanding the MHP's approach to methodology is vital when addressing *Step Two*—the methods step—of our *Frye-Daubert* legal analysis model. *Step Three* focuses on the empirical and logical connections MHPs make between the data generated from their methods and the conclusions that will inform their expert opinions. Recall *Joiner*: "[C]onclusions and methodology are not entirely distinct from one another." As noted earlier, the tie between data and conclusions needs to make sense and is required under a *Frye-Daubert* analysis. Lawyers should raise serious questions about whether the expert's opinion is reliable if the tie is too attenuated—that is, if the "analytical gap" is too large—and consider whether to challenge the admission of the testimony.

How should lawyers evaluate the quality of MHP expert conclusions? The key is recognizing that experts link data to conclusions by interpretation and synthesis—products of their knowledge, experiences, and training. At times, the links are not as tight as experts try to present. Lawyers should explore the links and examine the resulting "analytical gaps." And, as we noted earlier, examine whether the expert "employs in the courtroom the same level of intellectual rigor that characterizes the practice of an expert in the relevant field."[243] The greater the empirical and logical gaps between the expert's data—drawn from the methods—and conclusions, the less trustworthy those conclusions will likely be.

Lawyers may evaluate the quality of MHPs' conclusions by focusing on three issues: first, how judgment biases may compromise inferences MHPs draw from their data and how MHPs guard—or don't guard—against those biases; second, how MHPs use research and the professional literature to support their inferences and conclusions; and, finally, how MHPs organize their data and present their conclusions. Understanding these three issues will allow lawyers to gauge the reliability of MHPs' conclusions and, ultimately, the expert opinions that flow from those conclusions. Let us look at each issue in the following sections.

Judgment Biases

Cognitive psychology research demonstrates that people will rely on a limited number of heuristic principles, or decision-rule shortcuts, when weighing complex problems or incomplete information.[244] Usually, these principles are efficient and useful: they help categorize information we encounter and reduce complex decision making to simpler judgments. But applying these principles may also lead to systematic and predictable errors that bias and, thereby, compromise the quality of those judgments.[245] MHPs are not immune from judgment biases, especially in complicated, emotionally charged family law cases. But before discussing how MHP experts may counter the effects of judgment biases, let us identify some common biases and consider their effects.

- *Overconfidence Bias.* Overconfidence bias is the tendency for people to hold unwarranted beliefs that their answers or judgments are correct.[246] People's confidence estimates about their own judgments tend to be too high, at least for tasks that offer moderate to high levels of difficulty, and particularly when viable alternatives to the favored hypotheses are neglected or ignored.[247]

  EXAMPLE: An MHP evaluator with several years' experience believes so strongly in her ability to understand problems of custody disputes that in a difficult relocation case she dismisses the need to consider possible alternative explanations for her belief that the mother's involvement with the children has been lacking. She has seen the fact pattern and emotional dynamics in other cases, and she has "gotten it right" in those cases—and in this case.

- *Confirmatory Bias.* Confirmatory bias is the tendency to seek, favor, or remember evidence that supports one's view of the problem while discounting or ignoring evidence that is inconsistent with one's view.[248] Confirmatory strategies also may lead to beliefs in nonexistent relations, or "illusory correlations," because people, uncomfortable with notions of chance in events, feel compelled to provide "reasonable" explanations and to believe that those events are associated.[249] Illusory correlations may occur if people notice when events are paired but fail to notice situations in which they are not.[250]

EXAMPLE: An MHP evaluator settles early in the belief offered by the father that the mother—who has spent the most time with the child as the father traveled for work throughout the marriage—lacks discipline skills with their school-age son. As the evaluation proceeds, the evaluator readily notes information that seems to confirm the father's contentions and labels the mother as an incompetent disciplinarian. Later in the evaluation, the evaluator dismisses compelling information that suggests the boy has an untreated attention deficit disorder and that the boy's misbehaviors may be more attributable to the disorder than to the mother's lack of discipline skills.

• *Hindsight Bias.* Hindsight bias is the tendency for people with knowledge of the outcome of an event to believe falsely that they would have predicted the outcome while also denying that the outcome information influenced their prediction.[251] Such people claim that they "would have known it all along."[252] Contrary to conventional wisdom, hindsight is not always twenty-twenty. Social psychology research on hindsight bias indicates that people tend to be overly deterministic when they explain causes of past events.[253] Likewise, when MHPs describe patient behaviors and symptoms, they already know the outcome (the behavior or symptom); if hindsight bias is present, the MHPs are likely to overestimate the probability that their causal notions are correct.[254] As a result, these MHPs may be overly deterministic, looking at situations as a series of linear, logically connected steps—a process unlike foresight, "where information is limited, and indeterminate, occasional surprises and resulting failures are inevitable."[255] Notions of chance and the vicissitudes of everyday life are less likely to be factored into explanations colored by hindsight bias. The result leads to a tendency to blame people unfairly for events that have elements beyond their control.[256] Also, hindsight bias reduces what the evaluator can learn from the outcome information because the evaluator thinks the outcome is already so obvious.[257]

EXAMPLE: An MHP learns during an evaluation that a child got hurt while playing in the front yard and believes that the mother neglected the child and should have prevented the child from being injured. After reaching this conclusion, the MHP minimizes the mother's account of the incident. The mother said that the child's injury resulted from an accident on a hot summer day when she left the child for a moment to answer a ringing telephone. The mother had been waiting for four hours for the call, which she expected to be the technician who would come to fix her broken air conditioner. Other than this incident, the mother has no record of neglecting her child's care.

• *Discounting Base Rates Bias.* The base rate of a particular behavior refers to the prevalence of that behavior in a particular population. The discounting base rates bias occurs when a person neglects to account for the base rate of a particular behavior when making decisions about that behavior. The base rates for certain behaviors in a particular population may be higher or lower than in the general population.[258] As a result, considering base rates has important implications. Age, gender, education level, or social factors are among variables that may affect base rates, depending on the behavior of interest.[259] The more common the behavior in a particular group—high base rate—the less likely that the behavior will be able to distinguish people accurately who show that behavior. Likewise, failure to consider base rates when making judgments and predictions about low base rate behaviors—for example, the number of suicides in a given population—may result in overprediction of those behaviors, giving rise to false positives.[260]

EXAMPLE: An MHP concludes that a young child has been abused by a noncustodial parent based largely on reports that the child has nightmares, shows anxiety when leaving the custodial parent to visit the noncustodial parent, has made vague statements about being uncomfortable during bath time at the noncustodial parent's home, and has produced drawings that show more enjoyable activities at the custodial parent's home. While abused children might show some of these behaviors, so may nonabused, anxious children. The base rate for these behaviors is high among all anxious young children—including many children experiencing anxiety as a result of the marital separation—and, therefore, cannot adequately distinguish children who have been abused from other anxious children.[261] Issues in this example will be discussed more fully in a later chapter.

- *Availability Bias.* The availability bias refers to the tendency to make a judgment based on how easily instances or occurrences can be brought to mind;[262] salient or memorable instances that easily come to mind are judged as more likely than instances that do not easily come to mind.[263] In addition, the decision maker may be more influenced by salient or dramatic news than by routine information or by recent rather than older events. People may also make events and their related outcomes mentally available merely by imagining them and, thereby, be influenced to make judgments based on whether they view those imagined events with positive or negative outcomes.[264] Finally, *primacy and recency effects* predict that information near the beginning or the end of a series or task will be more available to the decision maker and, therefore, likely to influence judgments more than other information considered.[265]

EXAMPLE: An MHP begins a child custody evaluation intending to include both parents and the children. But because of the father's unavailability for several weeks due to work-related travel, the MHP interviews the mother several times and sees the mother with the child before interviewing the father. The mother's initial information, particularly if it is vivid and/or laced with emotional concerns, may be especially remembered by the MHP during the evaluation. In addition, the primacy effect—the MHP's receiving the mother's information first, therefore making it more easily "available" or remembered—may invoke the availability bias. But if the MHP conducts the father's later sessions without interviewing the mother during the same period, the father's contentions may become more easily remembered—the recency effect—particularly if the father's statements are more vivid and/or emotional.

- *Anchoring and Adjustment.* Anchoring errors are evident when people presented with the same critical information at different points in a process reach different conclusions about the import of that information.[266] One interesting study showed a bias among clinicians to minimize or dismiss data of a patient that indicated emotional disturbance when that patient was seen initially as less disturbed.[267] One explanation for this bias may be that people hold to their initial judgments to reduce dissonance stirred by the new critical information and to maintain consistency in their thinking.[268] Anchoring and adjustment also may occur when a person bases a decision on incomplete information.[269]

EXAMPLE: An evaluator's judgment about a parent accused of child abuse might differ depending on whether the evaluator learns of the allegation early or later in the evaluation. The evaluator's judgment may be anchored to the time when that salient information was received—perhaps more likely to believe the abuse allegation if it is aired early in the evaluation process—and other evaluation information then may be adjusted to the previously anchored judgment. Anchoring and adjustment may also occur when the parent or child in an evaluation presents with problems different than those with which the evaluator has experience. The range of problems with which the evaluator is experienced may become the anchor from which the evaluator structures views and judgments about the parent or child rather than the parent's or child's actual concerns.[270]

- *Fundamental Attribution Error.* The Fundamental Attribution Error, or Correspondence Bias, refers to the tendency to attribute the behaviors of others to stable personality traits rather than to situational factors.[271] That is, people will often decide that a person who performed a particular behavior was predisposed to do so and will minimize situational factors that may have contributed to the behavior. But when explaining their own behaviors, people will emphasize situational factors.[272]

  EXAMPLE: In a child custody evaluation, each parent accuses the other of problems with anger control. When explaining his view during an interview, dad says that mom gets angry easily because she is hot-tempered—a stable personality-trait explanation. Dad attributes times when he has gotten angry to the pressures of balancing significant work responsibilities and of being involved in a divorce he did not want—a situational factors explanation.

Countering Judgment Biases

MHPs will assert that they check their biases when conducting evaluations. But because judgment biases are inherent cognitive strategies by which we organize information, these biases may insidiously compromise the conclusions MHPs draw from their data. Even experienced researchers are prone to these biases when they think intuitively;[273] judgment shortcomings and biases of MHPs are not distinctively different from those of other professional decision makers.[274] Consequently, MHPs may convey greater confidence in their conclusions than an unbiased consideration of the data would justify. Overconfidence, then, may lead to premature conclusions and insufficient consideration of alternate explanations of the evaluation data.[275]

How should MHPs address these critical concerns in their evaluations? Research in hindsight bias suggests that merely warning people what the thinking bias is and urging them to prevent its occurrence is ineffective.[276] Also, just considering implausible alternative or opposite outcomes is ineffective.[277] Rather, people improve the accuracy of their judgments when they actively generate and consider a plausible alternative explanation for the event supporting a different outcome.[278] Such a debiasing strategy "breaks the inertia" that sets in if the evaluator is pulled by a particular view of the case.[279] For evaluators, such a strategy should heighten appreciation of the difficulty of a case, the plausibility of other conclusions, and the information value of the conclusion upon which the evaluator settles.[280] The *Forensic Specialty Guidelines* echo this research: "[T]he forensic psychologist maintains professional integrity by examining the issue at hand from all reasonable perspectives, actively seeking information that will differentially test plausible rival hypotheses."[281]

MHP Use of Research and Professional Literature

Applying Social Science Research in Court

Lawyers should examine how MHPs use research and the professional literature to support their conclusions and opinions. Experienced forensic MHPs know that citing research and professional literature will invoke the *Frye-Daubert* factors of general acceptance in the relevant scientific community and of peer review and publication. But just citing research studies does not support reliable expert testimony. If those studies do not support MHPs' methods or conclusions because of inadequate designs or unsupported claims, MHPs' resulting opinions could be characterized as subjective, unconnected to the disciplines MHPs claim to represent. Increasingly, MHPs and lawyers have raised concerns about the inappropriate use of social science research in court.[282] MHPs who cite research to support their conclusions and opinions bear responsibility for assuring the accuracy of their claims. As a result, lawyers should look critically at research MHPs invoke in their testimony.

When considering research, lawyers should recognize a key concept: most medical and social science research involves comparing differences between groups of people; in contrast, the specific behavior of individual parents and children in particular circumstances are at issue in court.[283] The reasoning task of MHPs who cite research in their testimony is to apply that group-oriented research to the person at issue in court. The chain that links group-oriented research to individuals in a case is made of inferences and probabilities, scientifically reasoned from the professional literature. That chain's links in the expert testimony should be clear. The poorer the supporting research, the less adequately MHPs will be able to link their opinions—empirically or logically derived—with bodies of knowledge in the relevant scientific and professional field.

Because social science and medical research designs and statistics may be quite elaborate and complicated, lawyers will be wise to consult with MHP experts for help in understanding the strengths and weaknesses of relevant studies. Nevertheless, certain basic principles underlie research studies that will help lawyers examine and cross-examine MHPs when MHPs invoke research to support their opinions.

Social science research is presented in various forms, including in journal articles or at conferences and workshops. But not all published research receives the same level of prior scrutiny by other professionals. For example, peer reviewed journal articles are published only after the initial manuscript submissions are, purportedly, reviewed by professionals with expertise in the subject matter. Manuscripts may be returned to the author after initial review to clarify issues or revise sections. This process is intended to ensure that the author's research methods and conclusions account for biases and fairly consider the field's knowledge base, and that the quality of published research is maintained.

However, peer review processes are not standardized or equivalent. Some are more stringent than others. For instance, the rejection rate of submitted manuscripts to the APA's primary and special journals is high—73 percent in 2006; that is, only 27 percent of submitted manuscripts have a chance to be accepted.[284] Also, not all peer review is conducted in the same way. For example, in the most prestigious journals, the reviewer is unaware of the manuscript's author. Other journals' peer review methods are more lax, and peer review in some journals may be in name only. In addition, conferences and workshops often do not scrutinize a presenter's ideas or methodology before the program.[285] Finally, *Daubert* does not define the nature or type of peer review that courts should find reliable.[286] In sum, having one's work vetted is really the critical component of peer review, not whether the research appeared in a peer-reviewed journal or whether the findings were presented at a conference or workshop.[287] Consequently, lawyers faced with MHPs invoking research, particularly that drawn from obscure sources or from journals representing questionable procedures, should question the MHPs about the quality of vetting involved in the purported peer review of that research.

Research and Its Elements: Deconstructing the Journal Article

APA journal articles typically are of three types: reports of empirical studies, review articles, and theoretical articles.[288] Reports of empirical studies include original research; review articles are critical evaluations of material that has already been published; and theoretical articles draw on existing research to advance theory in an area of psychology.[289] Understanding key issues in reports of empirical studies will help lawyers appreciate basic principles that underlie psychological research. Let us examine the sections of an empirical study report or article in an APA journal and highlight issues to which lawyers should attend as they assess the study's quality.

Abstract   The Abstract, found on the article's front page just below the title and listing of authors, is a brief, comprehensive summary of the article's contents.[290] The Abstract orients readers to the components, conclusions, and implications of the study.[291]

Introduction   The Introduction begins the article by describing the study's purpose.[292] It then reviews relevant prior theory and research studies to provide context to the study's topic. Finally, the section discusses the study's implications in light of previous research.[293] A well-written Introduction will give the reader a synopsis of the topic and the topic's background, and may provide lawyers with a broader understanding of the theoretical and research background of the study.

Method   The Method section of the article is critical because it describes how the study was conceptualized and details how the study was designed and conducted. This three-component section describes the study's participants or subjects, the materials (testing or otherwise) used to measure variables to be addressed, and the study's procedures—the heart of the methods section.[294] Weaknesses that compromise the study's internal validity—how sound the study's conclusions are—will be most evident in this section. These concerns directly implicate *Frye-Daubert* because reliable data and conclusions cannot flow from flawed methodology. Lawyers should consider the following questions when reviewing the three Methods section components:

Study Participants or Subjects

- How are the study participants characterized as to gender, age, race, social class? Are the characteristics similar enough to the parent, child, or grandparent evaluated or testified about by the MHP in the legal case?
- Do the study samples correspond to the legal issues and case before the court? For example, if the MHP uses the study to support directly an opinion about the adjustment of children of divorce, do the study samples contain children of divorce?
- How many participants are in the study? Too few may not allow the study's results to be generalized to a larger population or to the family in court. On the other hand, a very large sample size may produce statistically significant results that have little meaning in an individual case.[295]

- How were the study participants chosen? For example:

    Was the sample limited to a self-selected group of people who read a particular news-paper or listen to a particular radio program?

    Was the sample haphazardly drawn from people congregating in a public place such as a laundromat or an airport? Such a selection process makes it difficult to replicate the study because these people may differ systematically from people who do not use laundromats or fly regularly.[296]

    Was the sample one of convenience? For example, was the sample drawn from college sophomores in the university where the researcher teaches, from psychotherapy patients in the researcher's private practice, or from criminals in the prison where the researcher works? It may be inappropriate to generalize results from these special samples to other people.[297]

    Was the sample developed by networking? Asking the few initial participants to rec-ommend family members, friends, or fellow car pool drivers may make the sample too homogeneous.[298]

    Was the sample composed of volunteers? If so, how were the volunteers attracted to the study? Volunteers may range from people who are indifferent in their participation in the study to people who are eager to be involved and who are prepared to go well out of their way to participate, even to the point of expending considerable time and tolerating much inconvenience.[299] Volunteers, in contrast to nonvolunteers, are better educated, higher in social class, more intelligent, more approval-motivated, and more sociable.[300] Also, a study with college students found that the benefit of extra course credit increases participation rates for studies versus conditions when no rewards for participation were offered. In addition, volunteer students offered credit were more motivated in the studies.[301]

Materials or Apparatus

- How were the study's variables defined? This section is key because prior to designing the study the researcher will have had to define, or *operationalize*, the variables to be examined to allow those variables to be measured—vague and abstract definitions resist meaningful measurement.
- What materials—checklists, questionnaires, surveys, inventories—or tests were used to measure the variables of interest in the study? Look at three issues: First, do the materials or tests purport to measure the variable as the researcher defines the variable? Second, are the materials or tests constructed well enough to provide results that are reliable and valid in the study's context? Third, do the materials or tests provide response style indices that are sensitive to whether examinees are trying to exaggerate problems or attempting to present themselves in an overly favorable light? Self-report checklists without response style indices—for example, some depression, anxiety, or self-esteem "checklist" inven-tories—used as "tests" to select study participants or measure variables examined by the study may cloud the study's results.

Procedures

- The researcher places study participants in various groups. Were the participants allo-cated among the groups in a random manner? Random selection requires that partici-pants have an equal chance of being assigned to any of the study groups. When samples are not random, the possibility of selection bias or error exists.[302]

But, in social science research, for ethical reasons, pure random allocation of study participants cannot always be done. For example, in a study on the emotional effects of physical abuse on children, a researcher cannot randomly assign children to abuse and nonabuse groups and then subject the children in the abuse group to physical abuse to carry out the experiment. Rather, the researcher will seek out children who already have been physically abused—perhaps from Child Protective Services clients—and assign those children to the abuse group. That assignment is not a true random assignment because the allocations of the participants to the two groups did not originate from the same population. As a result, more variables are introduced into the study—because the children come from different "populations," the differences between abused and non-abused children may be due to more than just the abuse variable.[303] Researchers would try to control for some of the other variables by how they design the research study. But because full experimental control is unattainable and all variables cannot be accounted for, every experiment is imperfect,[304] and experimental results are framed as probabilities, not certainties—useful concepts for lawyers to keep in mind and to remind experts of.

- Does the sample that is claimed to have been randomly selected come from a population in which that kind of selection could be made? For example, a researcher may select a random sample from the roster of the American Bar Association, but would be unlikely to be able to select a random sample of the entire population of people who have taken some law school classes. Be sensitive to unsubstantiated claims of random selection.

- Does the study employ control or comparison groups? Control groups help researchers draw more valid conclusions and eliminate rival explanations to the study results by serving as comparisons to the experimental groups.[305] While experimental groups receive treatments or experimental interventions, control groups may be given placebos, alternate treatments, or nothing at all; researchers then compare results to ensure that the treatments or interventions are responsible for the measured results.[306] Beware of research that employs inappropriate or no control groups. For example, research on the effects of divorce on children that examines only children whose parents are in the midst of a divorce may provide useful hypotheses about those children. But absent control group comparisons with children whose parents have not been divorced, the researcher will be unable to conclude that the emotional effects experienced by children-of-divorce in the study are unique to those children or, perhaps, are emotional concerns shared by children in general. Of course, other variables also may require other control groups or experiments to answer the research question more fully. For instance, if unique emotional effects are found with children in the midst of a divorce, might those effects be more prevalent or primarily identified with such children who live in high-conflict families versus children whose parents are divorcing but who relate to each other civilly in the children's presence?

- Do the study participants who do not respond in the study or drop out reflect a random distribution of the participants' groups? Nonresponse in studies often is not random.[307] For example, in U.S. Census Bureau surveys, people who are single typically have three times the "not at home" rate of family members.[308] These nonresponding participants could distort study results intended to be based on random assignment of participants to the study groups.

These Procedure section issues highlight the probabilistic nature of social science research findings. Rarely are findings conclusive. And the less conclusive the findings are in the group research, the more imperfect will be the fit to a particular family member in court.

Results The Results section will seem the densest part of the study. This section pulls together the study's data and presents the statistical treatment of that data.[309] If you question whether appropriate statistics were applied to the data, consider retaining an expert consultant.

There are two kinds of statistics: descriptive and inferential. Descriptive statistics help to organize data into more manageable groups and to describe the nature of those groups. For example, central values include the mean, which is the group's average score; the median, the group's middle score; and the mode, the group's most frequent score. The standard deviation of the scores measures the variability of the scores within a particular group; variability measures help describe individual differences in a group by gauging how far from the group's mean an individual score lies.[310]

Correlation, the relationship or association between variables, is a descriptive statistic that often is misinterpreted. Don't confuse correlation with causation. High correlation between two variables does not mean one variable caused the other—even if the relationship is statistically significant. For example, when two factors are associated, such as fathers' uninvolvement with no opportunities for overnights with their children, either factor may be the cause, or a third factor might link the two—rather than overnights ensuring father involvement, fathers who, initially, are more committed to remaining involved with their children may be more likely to seek and gain overnights with them.[311]

In contrast to descriptive statistics, inferential statistics help researchers make educated guesses from relatively small data samples. The researcher usually is unable to include the entire population in the study, so smaller samples of that population are utilized; inferential statistics allow the researcher to gauge differences between groups in a study.[312] Whether differences between groups in a study are acceptable is indicated by the significance level of those differences. The significance level is "the level of confidence that a difference or relationship of the same size or larger could have occurred by chance,"[313] "rather than the fact that the relationship actually exists in the population."[314] For example, conventionally, the highest level of chance that a psychologist researcher may accept and still infer that the compared groups in the study are significantly different is 5 percent, expressed as $p = .05$—that is, one assumes that the possibility that differences between the groups are attributable to chance is 5 percent. A significance level of $p = .08$—or the possibility that differences between the groups are attributable to chance is 8 percent—for example, is deemed to reflect insignificant differences between the groups. Take care that the researcher does not characterize the $p = .08$ significance level as a "trend" to shoehorn significance into a result that does not reach the significance level ($p = .05$) accepted as the field's standard; rather, it might be more appropriate to refer to p values that fall between .05 and 1.0 as "equivocal" or "indeterminate."[315]

Discussion The Discussion section is used to evaluate and interpret the study's results and draw implications in light of the study's hypothesis.[316] Authors also seek to integrate their findings into or distinguish them from the work of others on the topic. Commonly, authors also will discuss the limitations of their studies in this section to temper overgeneralization of the results and to give directions for further research in the area.

Lawyers may feel confused when evaluating MHPs' uses of research and the professional literature. But with the trial court's emphasis on the reliability of expert testimony, how

MHPs use research and the professional literature to support their conclusions may determine whether the testimony will be admitted into evidence. As a result, lawyers should not shy from trying to understand relevant studies' strengths and weaknesses. Most important, lawyers should track the reasoning process of MHPs who invoke research in their testimony. Remember, the chain from group research to individuals in the legal case is composed of inferences and probabilities. Make sure that the chain's links are clear.

Organizing Data and Presenting Conclusions

A Functional Approach

After MHPs account for judgment biases when drawing inferences from their data and ensure that the research upon which their conclusions lie is applicable and valid, MHPs must organize their conclusions in ways that address legal concerns at issue. Generally, the conclusions about people's capacities should be framed in functional, behavior terms—what people can do as well as the knowledge necessary to accomplish those tasks.[317] Functioning may be related to, but is distinct from, psychiatric diagnoses, which are abstract constructs presumed to influence functioning.[318] For example, in child custody or child welfare cases, statutes and case law look to parents' functional abilities, not psychiatric or psychological diagnoses, to meet their children's needs and their understanding about how to meet those needs, although strong beliefs exist that poor parenting is inherent in a diagnosis.[319] Good witness preparation or cross-examination will focus MHPs on defining how parenting strengths and weaknesses identified from their data actually impact the parent-child relationships at issue in court. If the expert is unable to make such connections, the testimony will mostly amount to abstract notions about parenting traits. Such notions invite value-oriented testimony—unhinged from research or professional consensus—about what defines adequate or competent parenting in a particular case.

The *APA Child Custody Guidelines* emphasize the functional nature of child custody evaluations. In sum, the focus is three-part: the adults' parenting capacities, "including whatever knowledge, attributes, skills, and abilities, or lack thereof, are present"; the child's psychological functioning and developmental needs; and "the functional ability of each parent to meet these needs, including an evaluation of the interaction between each adult and child."[320] Further, the *Guidelines* note that psychopathology of the parents is relevant but not the primary focus in a child custody evaluation except to the extent that the psychopathology impacts the child or compromises the adult's parenting capacities;[321] mental disorder diagnoses alone are insufficient to support MHPs' conclusions and opinions without tying evaluation data to specific parenting abilities and capacities.[322]

DSM-IV and the Functional Approach

What, then, is the place of DSM-IV mental disorder diagnoses in family law cases? Can diagnoses help MHPs adequately communicate problems of parents or children in family law cases? Do diagnoses present their own evidentiary problems? Before addressing these questions, it may be helpful to consider what DSM-IV is, how MHPs use it, and what it states about its own use in court.

The *Diagnostic and Statistical Manual of Mental Disorders* (DSM) is a diagnostic system, developed under the direction of the American Psychiatric Association, that classifies mental disorders. It is the primary diagnostic system for mental disorders used in the United States.[323]

Since its inception, DSM has been through five editions. DSM-IV, the current general edition, was published in 1994; the DSM-IV Text Revision (DSM-IV-TR) was released in 2000 to update the research support for some of the diagnostic criteria, although most of the original DSM-IV text remained up-to-date and unchanged in the revision, and no substantive changes to the diagnostic criteria were considered.[324] Previous DSM editions included DSM-I (published in 1952), DSM-II (published in 1987), DSM-III (published in 1980), and DSM-III-R (published in 1987). Each DSM edition was expanded from the previous edition, with more diagnostic categories and changed or new criteria for various disorders with each revision. DSM-III marked a significant change from previous DSMs. DSM-I and DSM-II were not empirically based, relying mainly on a consensus reached by the small number of senior academic psychiatrists who drafted them.[325] DSM-III grew out of psychiatric research in the 1970s that identified diagnostic criteria for certain mental disorders. Consequently, DSM-III developed explicit criteria to describe mental disorders.[326] In addition, DSM-III introduced a new method for reporting mental disorders, requiring MHPs to classify the patient's disorders on five dimensions, or axes.[327] DSM-IV's development involved a substantially larger and more diverse group of MHPs and is more empirically based than its predecessors.

DSM-IV-TR is used for at least three primary purposes. First, mental health clinicians, researchers, and educators use DSM-IV-TR to communicate about diagnostic issues related to mental disorders. Second, clinicians use DSM-IV-TR to plan mental health treatment of patients and to anticipate treatment outcomes.[328] Finally, the health care and insurance industries use DSM-IV-TR to reimburse mental health treatment costs.

A full DSM-IV-TR diagnosis is arranged on five axes, each of which refers to a different domain of information about the patient. The prerequisite to a DSM-IV-TR diagnosis is that the patient is experiencing clinically significant impairment or distress in social, occupational, or other important areas of functioning[329]—sometimes it is difficult to distinguish "clinically significant impairment or distress" from normal psychological functioning.[330] While the full diagnosis is intended to provide an overall context for the patient's mental disorders, the mental disorders themselves are classified on the first two axes; often, MHPs report only information from the first two axes. Axis I includes clinical disorders such as depressions, anxiety conditions, psychotic conditions, and adjustment disorders—all disorders or conditions except for Axis II disorders are listed on Axis I.[331] Axis II classifies personality disorders and mental retardation. Personality disorders are long-term patterns of characteristics that organize a person's emotional and perceptual experiences and interpretations of others, self, and events in a manner that is pervasive and inflexible across a broad range of personal and social situations.[332] Axis III classifies medical conditions that are relevant to the patient's mental disorder,[333] Axis IV identifies psychosocial and environmental problems that may affect the mental disorder,[334] and Axis V is an impression-based numerical rating of the patient's level of functioning.[335]

DSM-IV-TR's use in court may be supported or criticized. On the support side of the ledger, DSM-IV-TR, as noted earlier, is the generally accepted diagnostic system for mental disorders in the United States.[336] Also, DSM-IV-TR claims to "be supported by an extensive empirical foundation."[337] In addition, because DSM-IV-TR is a product of a task force and thirteen work groups staffed by mental health experts in the various disorders who reviewed and incorporated empirical findings in the professional literature, it was subjected to extensive peer review.[338]

Nevertheless, DSM-IV's use in court can be criticized on several counts. Most important: DSM-IV-TR cautions that for forensic purposes "there are significant risks that diagnostic information will be misused or misunderstood," and that "these dangers arise because of the imperfect fit between the questions of ultimate concern to the law and the information contained in a clinical diagnosis."[339]

Among other issues, two reliability problems for DSM-IV-TR arise from the lack of an empirical base for the specific criteria cutoffs for many of the diagnoses,[340] and from strong reliance on the professional's "clinical judgment" on which to base the diagnosis.[341] Regarding the former problem, while general definitions and specific characteristics of many DSM-IV-TR diagnoses are supported by the psychological and psychiatric literature, the number of specific criteria needed to define many diagnoses was not arrived at empirically—this is particularly evident for the personality disorders.[342] Consequently, with other information, MHPs may assign a specific diagnosis even if the patient does not meet all the required criteria of that diagnosis. While this may be useful for treatment planning in a professional's office—a primary purpose for DSM-IV's development—this raises reliability questions about DSM-IV diagnoses in court. In addition, even within a DSM-IV-TR disorder, patients may differ considerably.[343] Also, the boundaries between disorders often are fuzzy; that is, many patients manifest combinations of symptoms that "fall through the diagnostic cracks" and cannot fit into any of the DSM-IV-TR categories.[344]

A final criticism of DSM-IV-TR's use in family law cases brings us back to a basic theme of this section: MHP expert testimony in family law cases is expected to be functional-oriented, not diagnosis-oriented. Insanity and civil commitment cases require diagnosis as an essential element of a claim or defense; for example, most insanity defense statutes require the presence of a severe mental disease or defect and exclude personality disorders. But family law statutes and case law involving parents and children concern themselves with impairment or capacity without regard to diagnosis.[345] The fact finder is to assess each parent's abilities to perform functions that will best meet a child's needs; a DSM-IV-TR diagnosis does not measure those abilities. For example, a child with conduct problems may benefit best from a parent who values structure, while an emotionally reserved child might do better with a creative and affirming parent; diagnoses do not speak directly to these functional concerns.[346] And parents with diagnosable disorders may still be able to meet a child's needs.[347] Recall, again, the *APA Child Custody Guidelines* injunction that "psychopathology may be relevant to such an assessment, insofar as it has impact on the child or the ability to parent, but it is not the primary focus."[348]

In sum, a DSM-IV-TR diagnosis does not, by itself, substitute for a functional-oriented psychiatric or psychological evaluation, nor is a DSM-IV-TR diagnosis a legal conclusion. And, importantly, DSM-IV-TR warns about the "significant risks" of its use in court for fear that the diagnostic "information will be misused or misunderstood."[349] These caveats make it incumbent on MHP experts, if they use DSM-IV-TR to inform their opinions, to articulate how DSM-IV-TR diagnoses relate to the issues about which they are offering opinions.[350]

Syndrome Testimony

While lawyers should note how MHPs use DSM-IV-TR diagnoses in their conclusions, lawyers should become particularly vigilant when MHPs invoke syndromes in their reports or testimony. A syndrome is a pattern of symptoms that tend to appear together in particular clinical presentations.[351] In fact, in DSM-IV-TR, "each of the mental disorders is conceptualized as a clinically significant behavioral or psychological syndrome or pattern that occurs in an individual . . . ."[352] Nevertheless, many purported syndromes and their theories upon which some MHPs have based their expert testimony have not been incorporated into the DSM system.

As a result, syndromes and their theories have bred much controversy in the social science literature. Judge Marvin O. Teague—in his dissent in a 1990 Texas Court of Criminal Appeals case in which a certified social worker expert for the prosecution used the Child Sexual Abuse Syndrome to describe phases through which an abuse victim passes during the period of the abuse and after—wrote that "at the present time, there are too many 'syndromes' and no consensus in the mental health community as to what they actually mean or are meant to mean."[353] In a previous dissent, Judge Teague listed several syndromes that had appeared in legal cases and in the psychiatric literature. Among the syndromes listed were: The Battered Wife Syndrome; The Battered Husband Syndrome; The Battered Child Syndrome; The Rape Trauma Syndrome; The Vietnam Post-Traumatic Stress Syndrome; The Organic Delusional Syndrome; and The Love Fear Syndrome. Judge Teague suggested that the future might see "The Appellate Court Judge Syndrome."[354]

Besides the controversies surrounding various syndromes that might be offered by forensic MHPs, some research demonstrates that judges continue to rely on the traditional general acceptance and expert qualifications standards when determining whether to admit psychological syndrome and profile evidence.[355] In other words, judges will more likely accept the MHP expert's word that the syndrome is generally accepted rather than ask key *Daubert*-like questions that would scrutinize more carefully the scientific basis of the syndrome.[356]

Despite the appeal of syndrome theories as explanatory constructs, the supporting empirical research of many is not rigorous. Often, syndrome testimony has been proffered in court when proponents have tried to prove an event, with symptoms exhibited by the alleged victim that could have arisen by other means, giving rise to "syndrome error."[357]

Nevertheless, not every so-called syndrome is defined by syndrome error; some syndromes are more certain or reliable than others.[358] John E.B. Myers notes the fallacy that all syndromes point clearly and convincingly to a particular cause, leading "to unwarranted inflation of the probative value of particular syndromes."[359] Myers notes that syndromes lie on a "continuum of certainty." For example, he says that battered child syndrome has greater certainty; the syndrome has high diagnostic and, thereby, probative value because it points directly to child physical abuse—certain multiple injuries in various stages of healing and skin bruising are among specific signs that identify battered child syndrome.[360] Myers says, in contrast, that rape trauma syndrome offers less certainty because the syndrome consists of symptoms that are caused by a number of events including, but not limited to, rape.[361] Courts also have used this scheme to classify the probative value of syndrome testimony.[362]

Another way to test the reliability of syndrome testimony is to deconstruct and test the syndrome's elements.[363] If elements of the proposed syndrome can be supported sufficiently by research, they should pass muster under a *Frye-Daubert* analysis. But the lawyer should analyze each element to build the case or to impeach the opponent's case.[364] Remember, "it is not so simply because an expert says it is so."[365]

STEP FOUR—THE EXPERT OPINION AND THE PSYCHOLOGICAL PERSPECTIVE

In *Step Three* of our *Frye-Daubert* Analysis Model, we looked at the processes by which MHPs develop their conclusions from the data they gathered or considered. We noted that MHP experts link their data to their conclusions by interpretation and synthesis—products of their knowledge, experiences, and training. In particular, we focused on three issues in this process: first, the judgment biases that may color or compromise the inferences MHPs draw from their data and how MHPs guard—or do not guard—against those biases; then, how MHPs use research and the professional literature to support their inferences and conclusions; and finally, the functional approach with which MHPs should organize their data and present their conclusions. Until this point in our analysis, the first three of four steps for MHPs in our *Frye-Daubert* Analysis Model have been based in the social science research and professional literature.

But the focus changes in *Step Four* of our model when MHPs offer their expert opinions: MHPs now apply their psychology-based conclusions to legal standards applicable to the case in court. Here, the two basic tests of our model merge. First, the *Applicable Professional Standards Test*: "[T]he [district] court should ensure that the opinion comports with *applicable professional standards* [emphasis added] outside the courtroom, and that it will have a reliable basis in the knowledge and experience of the discipline."[366] Second, the *Analytical Gap Test* of *Joiner*: "A court may conclude that there is simply too great an *analytical gap* [emphasis added] between the data and the opinion proffered."[367] It is up to the lawyer to question whether the expert's opinion has a reliable basis in the knowledge and experience of the discipline and then to gauge whether the gap between the psychologically based conclusions and the opinion is too attenuated. Questions on either count may provide the lawyer a basis for challenging the admissibility of the expert's testimony or, at least, for gauging the quality of the expert's testimony.

As noted earlier, there is some debate among forensic psychologists about whether psychologists serving as experts should offer opinions on the legal question or ultimate issue before the court—notwithstanding Federal Rule of Evidence 704(a), which states that "testimony in the form of an opinion or inference otherwise admissible is not objectionable because it embraces an ultimate issue to be decided by the trier of fact."[368] And it seems logical that a child custody evaluation would conclude with recommendations to the court about the specific referral questions that gave rise to the evaluation—for example, which custody arrangement is in the child's best interests, or whether the court should terminate the parent's parental rights. However, the MHP disciplines see the issue differently: The *AFCC Child Custody Standards* and the *Psychiatry Parameters* clearly view recommendations as the product of a child custody evaluation.[369] But while the *APA Child Custody Guidelines* allow psychologists to offer recommendations to the

court, the *Guidelines* note the professional debate on the issue and then obligate psychologists to know the arguments on both sides of the issue and be able to explain the
logic of the position they hold.[370]

The professional psychology literature reflects and fleshes out the ultimate issue testimony debate.[371] Yet, practically, psychologists who object to offering recommendations
and ultimate opinion testimony find themselves caught in an uncomfortable bind when
trying to explain in court why such testimony is inappropriate.[372]

Psychologists who oppose offering recommendations and ultimate opinion testimony
in family law matters argue several concerns. First, they contend that it is not psychologists' role to offer such recommendations because MHPs have not been authorized by
society to make such decisions—those decisions are solely for the fact finder to make.[373]

Second, proponents of this view assert that testifying to the ultimate legal issue raises
standard-of-practice concerns for psychologists.[374] For example, the best interests of the
child or provisions for termination of parental rights are legal constructs established
by statutes through the legislative process or by case law, not psychological constructs
developed and supported by psychological theory or research. Consequently, when psychologists testify to the ultimate issue, they testify outside their area of competence and,
thus, make inferences that exceed their data and for which little supporting research is
available.[375] As a result, those inferences and recommendations can only be based on
personal value and moral judgments.[376]

Instead, MHPs who oppose ultimate issue testimony would offer the court information about the evaluated family that falls in their areas of expertise and is empirically
supported—parenting skills and styles, specific needs of a child, the effects of a parent's
depression on caretaking abilities. Psychological testing and application of research findings may, in many cases, construct a picture of the family that reflects the needs and
abilities of the family members. Then, the court would use these empirically and professionally based conclusions to inform its ultimate issue decision.

Practically, most family courts expect recommendation-based opinions from MHP
experts. Indeed, as noted earlier, Federal Rule of Evidence 704(a) allows expert opinions
that embrace the ultimate issue except in federal criminal prosecutions on the issue of
the defendant's mental state. The arguments against ultimate issue testimony have come
from forensic psychologists intent on clarifying their professional roles, not from the law.

Other psychologists offer arguments to support ultimate issue testimony. One argument is that psychologists opposed to ultimate issue testimony engage in "semantic
brinksmanship" when they testify "up to the line," while hinting, with "close approxi-
mations," at the ultimate issue.[377] In addition, supporters of ultimate issue testimony
assert that experts' misuse or miscasting of data is more related to whether those experts
can support their conclusions and opinions rather than casting the problem in the ultimate versus nonultimate issue framework.[378]

Another justification for MHPs' offering recommendations and ultimate issue testimony in family law cases is the notion that MHPs have a responsibility to the court and
to the family to make sensible and defensible recommendations that reflect the knowledge base of developmental and family psychologies and also provide some direction to
the court and to the family about how the dispute may be resolved.[379] These psychologists refer to a twenty-five-year history of research related to the effects of divorce on
children, the effects of high conflict on children, parenting skills and styles that benefit

children, domestic violence, and children's resiliency and coping abilities.[380] Other psychologists note—in light of the research—that not providing recommendations to the court may cause even more harm to families, and that judges benefit from input about what is considered to be "in the best interests of the child."[381]

The *APA Child Custody Guidelines* articulate a firm rationale—supported by the Rules of Evidence and the model proposed in this book—for MHPs who choose to offer recommendations and ultimate issue testimony:

> If the psychologist chooses to make custody recommendations, those recommendations should be derived from sound psychological data and must be based on the best interests of the child. Recommendations are based on articulated assumptions, data, interpretations, and inferences based upon established professional and scientific standards.[382]

In sum, the rules—and our model—still apply. Look to the Applicable Professional Standards Test to ensure that the MHP's expert opinion has "a reliable basis in the knowledge and experience of the discipline," and then apply the Analytical Gap Test to gauge whether the gap between the MHP's psychologically based conclusions and the opinion is too attenuated.

FAMILY EVALUATIONS AND THE FUNCTIONAL APPROACH: ORGANIZING PRINCIPLES

In the earlier discussion of *Step Two* of our *Frye-Daubert* Analysis Model, a generally accepted set of procedures for child custody evaluations was presented. These procedures included individual interviews of the parents; individual interviews of the children; interviews with significant others, including stepparents, teachers, health care providers, and counselors, among others; observations of the child jointly with each parent; some psychological testing; and review of the children's school records.

But structuring an evaluation by generally accepted procedures will not, by itself, address the court's concerns about what parenting arrangement is in the child's best interest. After all, lawyers seek child custody evaluations to address a broad range of difficult questions, including parental fitness concerns, sexual or physical abuse allegations, child alienation issues, and parent relocation cases.[383] Consequently, MHP experts will assist the court by evaluating the child's various needs, each parent's capacity to meet those needs, and the resulting parent-child fits. As discussed earlier, this functional approach is different than looking primarily for parents' psychopathology or psychiatric-psychological diagnoses.

The functional approach also provides a useful structure by which lawyers may organize MHPs' case and evaluation data and conclusions in child custody cases. "How do you know what you say you know?" then becomes a tool in service of insisting that MHPs address the court's goal to remain focused on the particular child custody question(s) rather than on concerns less relevant to the parents' capacities to care adequately for their children.

The Functional Assessment Model

The Functional Assessment Model draws largely from a model proposed and developed by psychologist Thomas Grisso to assess various competencies in criminal law and civil law cases.[384] Competencies assessed in criminal cases might include defendants' competency to stand trial, criminal responsibility, or capacity to waive Miranda rights.[385]

Competencies assessed in civil cases might include competence to care for self or property, competence to consent to treatment, or competence to execute a will.[386]

In a child custody case, the court generally focuses on parental competence to determine which parent would provide the best prospects for meeting the child's developmental needs and general welfare.[387] Parental competence may also be a focus in adoption cases or in assessing the abilities of adults to serve as foster parents.[388] The functional assessment model adapted from Grisso centers MHPs' attentions on children's needs, parents' behaviors, and family interactions of concern to the court rather than just on abstract, ill-defined psychological constructs that convey little useful information. In addition, the model helps courts see the links that tie experts' data to their conclusions and opinions—the more empirically and rationally supported the links, the narrower the analytical gaps will be.

The model comprises four questions:

1. What are the child's developmental needs?
2. What are the functional parenting abilities of each parent?
3. What causal factors explain parenting deficits noted in either parent?
4. How do each parent's abilities and deficits compare with the demands required to meet each child's developmental needs?

What Are the Child's Developmental Needs?

Because the child's best interest is the court's primary concern in child custody or termination of parental rights cases, addressing the child's needs should be an important component of MHPs' expert testimony. Lawyers should look at four key areas of the child's life to organize their understanding of this step: the child's *school performance, emotional development, social development,* and *parent-child relationship.*

School Performance School performance gives valuable information about the child's intellectual abilities, task-orientation and task-completion skills, self-confidence, skills relating to peers, capacity to follow directions, and general maturity level. School for a child is like a job for an adult; the child will spend more waking hours in school-related activities than at home. In addition, the child's abilities and adjustment are rated up to six times within a nine-month period. Finally, in the younger grades, one or two teachers who spend the majority of school time with the child will have a wealth of knowledge about the child. Clearly, school is a significant source of information about the child and should be a focus of child-related information gathering.

One key school performance issue is the child's capacity to do grade-level work. Of course, problems in this area may have many causes, including family disruptions and open parental conflict witnessed by the child. For some children, developmental delays, learning disabilities, and attention disorders may interfere with their learning process; these children may have been assessed at school to determine eligibility for special education services. But besides the obvious ways they compromise the learning process, these problems also frustrate the school experience for these children. A child with developmental delays may experience difficulties relating with peers and feel socially isolated. A child with a reading disability may come to dislike reading strongly and become bored with school as the amount of reading intensifies through the upper grades. And a child with attention problems may get in trouble as a result of not following instructions or by not staying focused on the classroom task at hand.

Emotional Development While an in-depth treatment of children's emotional development is beyond this book's scope, some helpful concepts will help lawyers address with MHPs this element of understanding the child in family law cases.

- Two general principles are useful for differentiating normal from abnormal development in children: The Principle of Age-Appropriateness, and the Principle of Future Implications.[389] The Principle of Age-Appropriateness refers to the notion that children at all ages must deal with certain developmental tasks.[390] For example, children five and six years old adjust to the transition from home to school, and early adolescents must accept and emotionally manage their physical changes.[391] This principle maintains that ways in which children and adolescents can be expected to behave as they cope with the developmental challenges of their age group are normal ways of thinking, feeling, and acting.[392] In contrast, behaviors uncharacteristic of a child's or adolescent's peers or that continue beyond the age at which they might be expected to occur may reflect emerging emotional problems.

    The Principle of Future Implications holds that problem behaviors that can be expected to lead to psychopathology are more likely to reflect abnormal development than problem behaviors that disappear of their own accord and do not result in later disturbance.[393] For instance, some depressed and anxious children whose parents are divorcing may have a history of these problems. These children are more likely to continue with these problems after the divorce in comparison to children who became depressed and anxious as a reaction to their parents' divorce.

- One line of research indicates that children may be characterized by certain biologically based temperaments that reflect distinctive behavior styles.[394] The "easy child" is regular in routines and typically approaches unfamiliar people and situations with minimum fear.[395] The "slow-to-warm-up" child typically reacts to unfamiliar situations with withdrawal, timidity, and fear.[396] The "difficult child," the smallest group, is irregular in routines, often irritable, may have difficulty easily adapting to changes, and often withdraws from unfamiliar situations;[397] this group was more likely than the others to develop emotional problems in childhood.[398]

    These differences in children suggest parenting implications. The more difficult the child, the more challenging the parenting task with the potential for quicker negative and mutually coercive parent-child interactions.[399] In such situations, the child's temperament influences the parents' behavior and attitude, just as the parents influence their children.[400] Moreover, the stress of a divorce may magnify problems of a difficult temperament child in an already difficult parent-child relationship. Conversely, that same stress may draw together a parent and an easy temperament child[401]—sometimes in age-inappropriate ways.

- Children with the ability to control and regulate their emotional reactions demonstrate greater social and psychological adjustments.[402] These children manifest less anxiety or acting-out behaviors than children without this ability, and they are high in social competence, prosocial behavior, compliance, and sympathetic responses.[403] These children are able to control their attention and behavior as needed.[404]

- By themselves, traditional clinical methods to evaluate children's emotional development—including intellectual and extensive personality testing—will not adequately provide the court the feedback necessary to address the child's best interest in a custody dispute.

Rather, focused data-gathering and interviewing are useful ways to collect information that will reliably inform experts' conclusions and opinions. These methods include interviewing both family members and collateral interested others as well as reviewing appropriate records—school and medical records, mental health records, police reports, and Child Protective Services records among others.[405]

Well-chosen behavior rating scales offer other means of gathering information from people who have spent much time with the child.[406] While such scales can provide a wealth of information, most are limited by being subject to biases and opinions, and few have adequate validity checks to gauge whether the respondent is completing the task honestly. Nevertheless, if evaluators consider and apply the results appropriately, they will be well served by using these instruments.

An example of a useful set of instruments is the *Achenbach System of Empirically Based Assessment*. Among other forms, this system contains the *Child Behavior Checklist* (CBC), the *Teacher's Report Form*, and the *Youth Self-Report*.[407] These instruments are supported by a good deal of research.[408] Use of all the instruments enables evaluators to obtain standardized ratings and descriptive details of children's functioning as seen by parents, parent surrogates, and teachers, and the *Youth Self-Report* enables eleven- to eighteen-year-olds to rate their own functioning.[409] Results reflect internalizing problems, such as anxiety, depression, and somatic complaints, and externalizing concerns, such as conflicts with other people and with expectations.[410] Social problems, thought problems, and attention problems are also measured.[411] In addition, competence scales compare children's involvement in activities, social relations, and school.[412]

An additional inventory such as the *Warshak Parent Questionnaire–2* (WPQ-2), which asks parents to provide developmental information about the child, to rate children's problem behaviors, and to provide additional information by elaborating concerns, will yield useful information about the child.[413]

Social Development Essentially, the child's social development emerges from countless exchanges between the child and family members over a period of many years.[414] The goal is for children to function adequately when they reach adulthood.[415] To do so, children must acquire habits, skills, values, and motives that will enable them, among other things, to avoid self-centered behaviors that burden others, to form and sustain close relationships with others, and to regulate their behaviors, desires, and impulses with respect to social norms.[416] A critical aspect of adequate social development is the child's ability to comply with adult requests.[417] In contrast, noncompliant children do not follow explicit rules even when adults are present. Nor will such children follow implicit rules; noncompliant children must be constantly reminded to mind.[418]

How parents manage their marital struggles may affect their children's social development, particularly if the children witnessed inappropriate arguments that included raised voices, derogatory name-calling, and physical altercations. In addition, children's social development may be compromised if a parent passively condones or overtly encourages the children to verbally denigrate and misbehave with the other parent in ways that would not be tolerated toward any other adult.

Parent-Child Relationship The quality of parent-child relationships also is a key index of children's adjustment. While children may do well in the other three adjustment areas just discussed, their overall development may be hampered by difficulties in their relationships with their parents. Lawyers should ensure that MHPs have attended to this important factor. The court will.[419]

Kelly and Johnston note that children's relationships with their parents after separation and divorce may depend on many factors.[420] Some children maintain positive relationships with both parents and clearly value both.[421] Other children value their relationships with each parent but have an affinity for one parent while still desiring continuity and contact with both.[422] Such children may feel more identified with one parent because of similar interests, personalities, or activities or because that parent may be more directly involved in those children's daily lives.

In addition, some children develop a strong alliance with one parent. They demonstrate a consistent preference for one parent and may wish for only limited contact with the nonpreferred parent.[423] These alliances may have arisen when children were encouraged to take sides during the pre-and post-separation conflicts or when the children morally judged the nonpreferred parent's behaviors deemed responsible for the divorce.[424] Despite the alliance, these children do not completely reject the other parent.[425] Other children with a strong alliance with one parent become estranged from the nonpreferred parent because of that parent's history of family violence, emotional abuse, or other severe parenting deficits.[426] The anger or fear of these children toward the nonpreferred parent is realistic;[427] they may or may not reject the nonpreferred parent.[428]

A small group of children, whose rejection of a parent is not warranted by that parent's behavior, stridently and patently reject the nonpreferred parent without guilt or ambivalence and strongly resist any contact with that parent. Such rejection of the nonpreferred parent is irrational, exaggerated, and distorted and bears little resemblance to the prior history of the child's relationship with that parent.[429] This emotionally unhealthy parent-child relationship dynamic occurs most often in high-conflict custody disputes.[430]

But as the quality of parent-child relationships varies, how much weight should be given to children's voices in child custody evaluations? The UMDA notes that one of five factors judges should consider when making child custody determinations is "the wishes of the child as to his or her custodian."[431] Listening to children's wishes is important; doing so may give important insights into the children's relationships with their parents. But summarily accommodating children's custody wishes presents two problems: it equates the children's thoughts and feelings with expressions of their true best interests, and it places them in the middle of their parents' disputes.[432] And while older children's preferences might be accorded greater deference than younger children's wishes, even older children might be enticed toward one parent by promises of greater freedom. Or, they may feel compelled to "fix" their parents' disputes by balancing time in both homes, even if contrary to their best interests. Careful evaluation is required to place children's custody wishes in the family context and to invoke research that may address such issues in a particular case. Lawyers should ensure that MHP experts properly listen to the child and appropriately incorporate the child's wishes into the evaluation's findings and recommendations.

What Are the Functional Parenting Abilities of Each Parent?

Functional parenting abilities are the behaviors, knowledge, understanding, and beliefs that are necessary for adequate parenting.[433] There are many ways to address this concern:

statutes and case law provide some guidance, albeit with narrow or vague requirements. The psychology literature provides more wide-ranging notions of parenting skills that reflect some empirical support for parenting behaviors that may help or harm a child's development. While a full discussion of theoretical and empirical support in the parenting literature is beyond this book's scope, the following list highlights parenting skills and responsibilities that impact children's development.

- *Meet basic material needs*—food, shelter, clothing—of the child.
- *Advocate for the child's needs outside the home.* For example, if a child experiences reading problems, will the parent advocate for the child at school to ensure that those problems are addressed appropriately?
- *Monitor the child's behaviors and activities appropriately*—at home and school.[434] Parental monitoring is essential to ensure the child's safety and to train the child to develop better self-control. Monitoring implies a general awareness of the child's whereabouts.[435] Social development matures as children adopt acceptable standards for good and bad behavior. As children expand their social worlds and activities, they must be willing to inform their parents of their activities outside their parents' presence; methods will vary with the child's age.[436] Ineffective parental monitoring is linked to antisocial behaviors throughout childhood.[437]
- *Empathize with and adapt to the child's thinking, capacities, and emotional states.* Empathic parents are able to view the child's experiences from the child's perspective and be attentive to the child's needs and emotional signals.[438] Also, parents' empathy is evident when they are able to adjust occasionally to children's plans and concerns rather than consistently expecting children to adjust to their plans.[439]
- *Appropriately arrange situations and events* so that the demands of a particular situation are within the child's developmental abilities and do not overly frustrate or tax the child's abilities.[440]
- *Employ an authoritative rather than an authoritarian or permissive parenting style.*[441] Authoritarian parents use harsh and rigid discipline at the expense of empathy and understanding to control the child's behaviors.[442] Permissive parents emphasize affection and caring while imposing few guidelines or restrictions in their interactions with the child.[443] *Authoritative* parenting balances control and empathy, is consistent and respectful, and teaches the child self-control and other prosocial behaviors.[444] Authoritative parenting has a significant protective effect against the stresses children encounter in all types of families but, unfortunately, is found less often in families during the first year post-divorce.[445]
- *Employ appropriate, consistent discipline.* Appropriate, consistent discipline is a key aspect of an authoritative parenting style. Discipline is a significant aspect of family life that strongly influences child adjustment.[446] Inadequate discipline includes: *inconsistent discipline*, which serves to strengthen the child's difficult behaviors; *irritable explosive discipline*, which is characterized by frequent and harsh behaviors such as hitting, yelling, and threatening; *low supervision and lack of involvement by the parent*, which results in little monitoring or engagement with the child and his or her activities; and *inflexible rigid discipline*, which does not adjust to the infraction's severity, does not give the child rationales for the discipline, and relies on a single or limited range of discipline style for all transgressions.[447]
- *Understand and competently control emotional reactions while parenting.*[448] Parents whose emotional reactions interfere with measured responses to their children are less than effective—their own needs interfere with meeting their children's needs.[449] In contrast,

parents whose emotions are too subdued do not actively engage their children or respond adequately to their children's needs.[450] Aroused emotions in parenting situations engage and organize parents' actions toward their children.[451]

What Causal Factors Explain Parenting Deficits Noted in Either Parent?

Deficits in parents' abilities to manage their children effectively may point to reasons why their children are experiencing academic, emotional, and social development difficulties. But before using such information to fashion post-divorce child custody arrangements, MHPs must examine the reasons for those deficits. For example, deficits that are distinct reactions to a divorce or that may be remedied within a relatively short time by education or treatment should be viewed differently than long-standing deficits. A depression resulting from the marital separation that has made a parent less attuned to the children's needs may be very different from a depression of several years that has compromised that parent's attentions to the children throughout their lives. Thus, research that has documented the less responsive styles of depressed mothers to their children[452] might be more important to consider in a case of the mother depressed for several years rather than that of the mother depressed because of the marital breakup. The latter mother may be more amenable to treatment, and the depression may be time limited rather than characteristic of that mother's life approach. The inquiry revolves around parents' functional abilities, not psychiatric diagnoses.

One or more of the following causes may have led to parenting deficits that might compromise the child's best interests and about which the court should be concerned:[453]

- *Life situational stress*: As in the preceding example, are the parenting deficits related to normal or adjustment reactions to stressful life situations that might be remedied by treatment, education, or time? Or, are the deficits due to more long-standing problems that have compromised the parent's care and responsiveness to the child for a longer period?
- *Evaluation-related stress*: Some parents may become quite anxious about submitting themselves to a child custody evaluation that they perceive will decide whether their children will be "taken" from them. This discomfort may translate into poorly articulated or rationalized responses to evaluators' questions as well as marked test anxiety. These parents may seem self-conscious, even awkward when interacting with their children in the evaluator's office.
- *Ambivalence*: Some parents may feel ambivalence about gaining primary custody of their children and may appear to have more parenting skills deficits than what might be expected given the history of their parenting during the marriage.
- *Lack of information*: Some parents lack certain parenting skills or knowledge of key developmental aspects because they have not learned those skills or information. Many of these parents might improve their skills with instruction or education—one-on-one or in a group or classroom setting.
- *Mental disorder or disability*: While a parent may have been assigned a DSM-IV-TR diagnosis by the evaluator or a prior MHP, such a diagnosis, by itself, says nothing directly about the parent's functional parenting abilities. No statute or case law predicates child custody or termination of parental rights decisions on a psychiatric diagnosis. Some parents with psychiatric diagnoses may be unable to manage their children's development competently as primary parents. But other parents, with the same diagnoses, may be able to use education or appropriate treatment or both to meet parenting challenges adequately.

How Do Each Parent's Abilities and Deficits Compare with the Demands Required to Meet Each Child's Developmental Needs?

This step highlights the Functional Assessment Model's approach to evaluating parent and child relationships for family courts. In previous steps, key concerns have been assessed: the child's academic, emotional, and social development needs; the parents' parenting abilities and understanding of parenting concepts; and reasons for any deficits in abilities and understanding shown by either parent. Now, matching parents' strengths and children's needs is required.

But this endeavor is no cookie-cutter exercise. It parallels the highly individualized best-interest-of-the-child standard that guides courts' ultimate dispositions of child custody cases. This step requires comparing *this* parent's abilities to the particular needs of *this* child.[454] However, not every parent-child match is perfect. In addition, deficiencies in certain parenting abilities may have greater or lesser significance in various cases, depending on the needs of the specific child in question.[455] Nevertheless, in child custody cases, the universe of choices is restricted to two parents for whom the court must fashion a parenting plan if the parents are unable to resolve the issue themselves.

It is at this point that analytical gaps in MHPs' reasoning may become most exposed. For example, assume that the MHP has determined that the child has an attention deficit/hyperactivity disorder. Such children do best with parents who employ a structured parenting style, tolerate frustration, and advocate for the child in school. Further assume that one parent is more structured than the other, but the other provides a more emotionally warm and tolerant home environment. In this situation, the MHP might recommend that either parent remedy the deficits, if either parent is open to such remediation. Certainly, a temperamental, difficult child will require structure and tighter monitoring of his or her behaviors, especially when not in the presence of the parent. Can the parent without the ability to manage that child's behavior effectively learn new parenting techniques that reduce that child's noncompliance with and inappropriate challenges to that parent's rules? And, of course, parenting lapses with a temperamentally easy child are quite forgiving; this child is unlikely to act out inappropriately if needs for parental support are not met adequately—recall that such children are able to regulate their emotional expressions and seek to follow parental rules. But the development of even these children may be compromised if their general compliance is taken for granted when the parent is forced to deal with the problems of siblings who wrestle with the parent for control of the relationship. Questioning how MHPs address this step—based on findings from the previous three steps—and reach their conclusions will expose analytical gaps in the reasoning process and allow lawyers and the court to gauge the quality of the MHPs' expert opinions.

SUMMARY

The psychological perspective addressed in this chapter is the third of three critical areas family lawyers should consider when they organize and manage mental health materials and critique mental health testimony. This perspective focuses on the methods and mind-sets MHPs bring to family law cases and provides substance to the *Frye-Daubert* Analysis Model presented in Chapter 3.

Part I, Chapters 2–4, presented three critical perspectives that family lawyers should consider when they organize and manage mental health materials and critique mental health testimony. The emotional perspective focused lawyers on personal and intimate concerns of the spouses that may significantly impact the legal divorce and modification actions. The legal perspective introduced a *Frye-Daubert* Analysis Model to help lawyers organize mental health materials, structure questions for expert witnesses, and present arguments to the court. The psychological perspective provided substance to our legal model.

Part 2, the next four chapters, will help lawyers use the Analytical Gap test to recognize and expose MHPs who hide deficiencies in the reasoning they use to support their conclusions and expert opinions. "How do you know what you say you know?", our main challenge to MHPs, will continue to be our touchstone.

NOTES

1. http://www.psychologymatters.org/glossary.html#p.
2. Education Directorate, *Specialties and Proficiencies in Professional Psychology* (2006), http://www.apa.org/crsppp/rsp.html. (Specialties include: Clinical Neuropsychology; Clinical Health Psychology; Psychoanalysis Psychology; School Psychology; Clinical Psychology; Clinical Child Psychology; Counseling Psychology; Industrial-Organizational Psychology; Behavioral Psychology; Forensic Psychology; and Family Psychology.)
3. Russell J. Bent et al., *The American Board of Professional Psychology, 1947 to 1997: A Historical Perspective*, 30 PROF'L PSYCHOL: RES. & PRAC. 65, 65 (1999).
4. ABPP, *ABPP General Brochure*, http://www.abpp.org/brochures/general_brochure.htm (As of September 25, 2007, there are thirteen member Specialty Boards under ABPP. They include: The American Board of: Clinical Child and Adolescent Psychology; Clinical Health Psychology; Clinical Neuropsychology; Clinical Psychology; Cognitive and Behavioral Psychology; Counseling Psychology; Family Psychology; Forensic Psychology; Group Psychology; Organizational and Business Consulting Psychology; Psychoanalysis in Psychology; Rehabilitation Psychology; and School Psychology.
5. Bernard S. Brucker, *CPPSA Report*, 25 THE SPECIALIST 5 (Winter 2006).
6. American Board of Professional Psychology, http://www.abpp.org/abpp_public_about.htm.
7. American Board of Forensic Psychology Brochure, http://www.abfp.com/brochure.asp.
8. *Id.*
9. Mark Hansen, *See the Cat? See the Credentials? Psychologist's Scam Gets His Pet Board Certified*, ABA JOURNAL REPORT (October 25, 2002).
10. American Board of Psychiatry and Neurology, *2007 Information for Applicants: Initial Certification in Psychiatry and the Subspecialties* (2006).
11. *Id.*
12. *Id.* at 36. "Training programs approved by the Residency Review Committees and accredited by the ACGME can be found in the current edition of the *Graduate Medical Education Directory* published by the American Medical Association. This directory includes the program requirements for residency education."
13. *Id.* at 39.
14. *Id.* at 28–29.
15. Beyond the board certification in psychiatry, the ABPN certifies eight subspecialties: Addiction Psychiatry, Child and Adolescent Psychiatry, Clinical Neurophysiology, Forensic Psychiatry, Geriatric Psychiatry, Pain Medicine, Sleep Medicine, and Vascular Neurology. *Id.* at 3–4.
16. American Academy of Psychiatry and the Law, *Ethical Guidelines for the Practice of Forensic Psychiatry* 1 (last revised 1995).

17.   American Board of Psychiatry and Neurology, *2007 Information for Applicants: Initial Certification in Psychiatry and the Subspecialties* (2006), 45–46.

18.   *Id.* at 44.

19.   *See* http://www.socialworkers.org/credentials/default.asp.

20.   http://www.socialworkers.org/nasw/default.asp.

21.   *See, e.g.,* 22 TEX. ADMIN. CODE § 781.418, *Provision of Court Ordered Home Studies, Adoption Studies, or Custody Evaluations.*

22.   Carolyn I. Polowy & Joel Gilbertson, *Social Workers as Expert Witnesses* (1997).

23.   *Cf.* Texas State Board of Examiners of Professional Counselors website, *About the Profession—Scope of Practice.*

24.   In Texas, "counseling-related field" is defined as "[a] mental health discipline utilizing human development, psychotherapeutic, and mental health principles, including, but not limited to, psychology, psychiatry, social work, marriage and family therapy, and guidance and counseling. Non-counseling fields include, but are not limited to, sociology, education, administration, and theology." http://www.dshs.state.tx.us/counselor/lpc_scope.shtm.

25.   http://www.nbcc.org/home/national-counselor-certification-and-exam-information.

26.   http://www.nbcc.org/certmain2.

27.   *What Is Marriage and Family Therapy,* http://www.aamft.org/about/index_nm.asp (follow to FAQs on MFTs).

28.   *Directory of MFT Licensure and Certification Boards,* http://www.aamft.org/resources/Online_Directories/boardcontacts.asp. (In the United States, the number of states regulating marriage and family therapy has grown rapidly—from eleven in 1986 to forty-eight in 2005 plus the District of Columbia.)

29.   http://www.aamft.org/about/index_nm.asp (follow to FAQs on MFTs).

30.   Randy K. Otto & Kirk Heilbrun, *The Practice of Forensic Psychology: A Look Toward the Future in Light of the Past,* 57 AM. PSYCHOL. 5, 13 (2002).

31.   *See supra* note 4.

32.   *See supra* note 15.

33.   *See* Frank M. Dattilio, *Board Certification in Psychology: Is It Really Necessary?,* 33 PROF'L PSYCHOL.: RES. & PRAC. 54 (2002).

34.   American Psychological Association, *Guidelines for Child Custody Evaluations in Divorce Proceedings,* 47 AM. PSYCHOL. 677, 678 (1994) [hereinafter *APA Child Custody Guidelines*].

35.   *Id.*

36.   American Psychological Association, *Ethical Principles of Psychologists and Code of Conduct,* 57 AM. PSYCHOL. 1597 (2002) [hereinafter *APA Ethics Code*].

37.   *See, e.g.,* FED. R. CIV. PROC. 26(b)(4)(A) and (B) (an expert who will testify at trial may be deposed, but an expert "retained or specifically employed . . . in anticipation of litigation or preparation for trial" who will not testify at trial may not be deposed except as provided in Rule 35(b) (Order of Physical and Mental Examinations of Persons) or upon showing of exceptional circumstances).

38.   Gammill v. Jack Williams Chevrolet, 972 S.W.2d 713, 719 (Tex. 1998), *quoting* Broders v. Heise, 924 S.W.2d 148, 152 (Tex. 1996). *Broders* also notes, "[O]ur holding does not mean that only a neurosurgeon can testify about the cause in fact of death from an injury to the brain, or even that an emergency room physician could never so testify. What is required is that the expert has 'knowledge, skill, experience, training, or education' regarding the specific issue before the court which would qualify the expert to give an opinion on that particular subject." *Broders,* 924 S.W.2d at 153.

39.   *See* Kumho Tire Co., Ltd. v. Carmichael, 526 U.S. 137, 152 (1999).

40.   General Electric Co. v. Joiner, 522 U.S. 136, 146 (1997).

41.   Committee on Ethical Guidelines for Forensic Psychologists, *Specialty Guidelines for Forensic Psychologists*, 15 Law & Hum. Behav. 655, 661 (1991) [hereinafter *Forensic Specialty Guidelines*].

42.   Karen Hirschman, *Selecting, Preparing, and Cross-Examining Expert Witnesses (with Form)*, The Prac. Litigator 47, 51 (July 2005).

43.   *Id.*

44.   Marcus T. Boccaccini, *What Do We Really Know About Witness Preparation?*, 20 Behav. Sci. & L. 161, 169 (2002).

45.   *Id.* at 173–74.

46.   Steven Lubet, Expert Testimony: A Guide for Expert Witnesses and the Lawyers Who Examine Them 26 (1998).

47.   Boccaccini, *supra* note 44, at 181.

48.   *See* Fed. R. Civ. Proc. 26(b)(4)(A) and (B), *supra* note 37.

49.   *See, e.g., APA Ethics Code, supra* note 36, at 1073.

50.   Kirk Heilbrun, Principles of Forensic Mental Health Assessment 65 (2001).

51.   *APA Ethics Code, supra* note 36, at 1065.

52.   Heilbrun, *supra* note 50, at 65–66.

53.   Daniel W. Shuman & Stuart A. Greenberg, *The Expert Witness, the Adversary System, and the Voice of Reason: Reconciling Impartiality and Advocacy*, 34 Prof'l Psychol.: Res. & Prac. 219 (2003).

54.   *Id.* at 220. *See also APA Child Custody Guidelines, supra* note 34, at 678.

55.   *Forensic Specialty Guidelines, supra* note 41, at 664.

56.   *See, e.g.,* American Bar Association, ABA Criminal Justice Mental Health Standards 5, 146 (1989) (Standards 7-1.1 and 7-3.13 discuss a scientific role for MHP experts who will testify on matters of present scientific or clinical knowledge) [hereinafter ABA MH Standards].

57.   *APA Ethics Code, supra* note 36, at 1065.

58.   *See* Trigon Ins. Co. v. United States, 204 F.R.D. 277, 290 (E.D. Va. 2001); *see also* ABA MH Standards, *supra* note 56, at 9; Eric Y. Drogin, *Utilizing Forensic Psychological Consultation: A Jurisprudent Therapy Analysis*, 25 Mental & Physical Disability Rep. 17, 17 (2001); Forensic Specialty Guidelines, *supra* note 41, at 207 (when testifying, forensic psychologists have an obligation to all parties to a legal proceeding to present their findings, conclusions, evidence, or other professional products in a fair manner).

59.   ABA MH Standards, *supra* note 56, at 11–12; *see also Trigon Ins. Co.*, 204 F.R.D. at 290.

60.   Drogin, *supra* note 58, at 18.

61.   ABA MH Standards, *supra* note 56, at 11–12.

62.   Heilbrun, *supra* note 50, at 75.

63.   *Id.* at 81.

64.   Shuman & Greenberg, *supra* note 53, at 219; *see also Trigon Ins. Co.*, 204 F.R.D. at 290.

65.   *Id.* at 221.

66.   Drogin, *supra* note 58, at 17–18.

67.   Shuman & Greenberg, *supra* note 53, at 219.

68.   *Id.* at 221.

69.   *Id.*

70.   *APA Ethics Code, supra* note 36, at 1063.

71.   Shuman & Greenberg, *supra* note 53, at 219, 221.

72.   *Id.*

73.   *Gammill*, 972 S.W.2d at 719, *quoting Broders*, 924 S.W.2d at 152.

74.   Shuman & Greenberg, *supra* note 53, at 219, 222.

75.   *Id.*

76.   *Forensic Specialty Guidelines, supra* note 41, at 662.

77.   *Id.*

78.   *Id.*

79.   Shuman & Greenberg, *supra* note 53, at 223.

80.   *Id.* at 223.

81.   *Id.* at 223.

82.   *Id.* at 223.

83.   Watkins v. Telsmith, Inc., 121 F.3d 984, 991 (5th Cir. 1997) (emphasis added).

84.   *Trigon Ins. Co.,* 204 F.R.D. at 290.

85.   Shuman & Greenberg, *supra* note 53, at 224.

86.   *Id.*

87.   Stuart A. Greenberg & Daniel W. Shuman, *Irreconcilable Conflict Between Therapeutic and Forensic Roles,* 28 PROF'L PSYCHOL.: RES. & PRAC. 50, 56 (1997).

88.   *Id.*

89.   *Id.* at 52.

90.   *Id.*

91.   *Id.*

92.   *Id. See also* HEILBRUN, *supra* note 50, at 9 for other, but related, differences between treatment and forensic roles for mental health professionals.

93.   *APA Child Custody Guidelines, supra* note 34, at 678.

94.   *Forensic Specialty Guidelines, supra* note 41, at 659.

95.   American Academy of Child and Adolescent Psychiatry, *Practice Parameters for Child Custody Evaluation,* 4 (1997).

96.   American Academy of Psychiatry and the Law, *Ethics Guidelines for the Practice of Forensic Psychiatry* (Adopted May 2005).

97.   Larry H. Strasburger, Thomas G. Gutheil & Archie Brodsky, *On Wearing Two Hats: Role Conflict in Serving as Both Psychotherapist and Expert Witness,* 154 AM. J. PSYCHIATRY 448 (1997).

98.   Lyn R. Greenberg & Jonathan W. Gould, *The Treating Expert: A Hybrid Role with Firm Boundaries,* 32 PROF'L PSYCHOL.: RES. & PRAC. 469, 473 (2001).

99.   *Id.*

100.   *Id.*

101.   *Id.* at 477.

102.   *Kumho Tire,* 526 U.S. at 152.

103.   *Daubert,* 509 U.S. at 592.

104.   Nancy E. Walker, *Forensic Interviews of Children: The Components of Scientific Validity and Legal Admissibility,* 65 LAW & CONTEMP. PROBS. 148, 163, 169–70 (2002); Y. Orbach et al., *Assessing the Value of Structured Protocols for Forensic Interviews of Alleged Child Abuse Victims,* 24 CHILD ABUSE & NEGLECT 733 (2000).

105.   *See* Walker, *supra* note 104, at 170 n.154.

106.   *See* Black v. Food Lion, 171 F.3d 308 (5th Cir. 1999).

107.   *See id.*

108.   *Id.*

109.   David A. Martindale, *Play Therapy Doesn't Play in Court,* 3 J. CHILD CUSTODY 77, 81 (2006), noting L. Handler, *The Clinical Use of Drawings: Draw-A-Person, House-Tree-Person, and Kinetic Family Drawings, in* MAJOR PSYCHOLOGICAL ASSESSMENT INSTRUMENTS, 206 (C.S. Newmark ed., 2d ed. 1996).

110.   ANNE ANASTASI, PSYCHOLOGICAL TESTING 614 (6th ed. 1988).

111.   Kyle D. Pruett & Albert J. Solnit, *Psychological and Ethical Considerations in the Preparation of the Mental Health Professional as Expert Witness, in* EXPERT WITNESSES IN CHILD ABUSE

CASES 123, 126 (Stephen J. Ceci & Helene Hembrooke eds., 1998). *See also* Daniel W. Shuman, *The Use of Empathy in Forensic Examinations,* 3 ETHICS & BEHAV. 289 (1993).

112. Greenberg & Shuman, *supra* note 87, at 52; *see also* American Academy of Child and Adolescent Psychiatry, *Practice Parameters for Child Custody Evaluation* (1997).

113. *See* Christopher W. Williams, Paul R. Lees-Haley & Stacy E. Djanogly, *Clinical Scrutiny of Litigants' Self-Reports,* 30 PROF'L PSYCHOL.: RES. & PRAC. 361 (1999) (The authors note that there is evidence to show that the behavior of patients in litigation differs from that of nonlitigating patients in ways that substantially affect the data on which psychologists rely for decision making).

114. *Forensic Specialty Guidelines, supra* note 41, at 661.

115. HOWARD N. GARB, STUDYING THE CLINICIAN: JUDGMENT RESEARCH AND PSYCHOLOGICAL ASSESSMENT 237 (1998).

116. *APA Child Custody Guidelines, supra* note 34, at 678.

117. *Id.*

118. *See* THOMAS GRISSO, EVALUATING COMPETENCIES: FORENSIC ASSESSMENTS AND INSTRUMENTS (1986).

119. DEBRA A. POOLE & MICHAEL E. LAMB, INVESTIGATIVE INTERVIEWS OF CHILDREN 69 (1998).

120. Kathryn Kuehnle, Lyn R. Greenberg & Michael C. Gottlieb, *Incorporating the Principles of Scientifically Based Child Interviews into Family Law Cases,* 1 J. CHILD CUSTODY 97, 102 (2004).

121. *See* Michael E. Lamb, Kathleen J. Sternberg & Philip W. Esplin, *Effects of Age and Delay on the Amount of Information Provided by Alleged Sex Abuse Victims in Investigative Interviews,* 71 CHILD DEV. 1586 (2000).

122. M.D. Leichtman & Stephen J. Ceci, *The Effects of Stereotypes and Suggestions on Preschoolers' Reports,* 31 DEV. PSYCHOL. 568 (1995).

123. POOLE & LAMB, *supra* note 119, at 64.

124. Debra A. Poole & D. Stephen Lindsay, *Children's Eyewitness Reports After Exposure to Misinformation from Parents,* 7 J. EXPERIMENTAL PSYCHOL.: APPLIED 27 (2001).

125. *See* STEPHEN J. CECI & MAGGIE BRUCK, JEOPARDY IN THE COURTROOM 78 (1995) for discussion of this issue.

126. POOLE & LAMB, *supra* note 119, at 120.

127. *Id.* at 67.

128. CECI & BRUCK, *supra* note 125, at 79.

129. POOLE & LAMB, *supra* note 119, at 67.

130. Kuehnle et al., *supra* note 120, at 109.

131. JONATHAN W. GOULD & DAVID A. MARTINDALE, THE ART AND SCIENCE OF CHILD CUSTODY EVALUATIONS 108 (2007); *see also* HEILBRUN, *supra* note 50, at 167.

132. Kirk Heilbrun, Janet Warren & Kim Picarello, *Third Party Information in Forensic Assessment, in* 11 HANDBOOK OF PSYCHOLOGY: FORENSIC PSYCHOLOGY 69, 71 (Alan M. Goldstein ed., 2003).

133. *See* William G. Austin, *Guidelines for Utilizing Collateral Sources of Information in Child Custody Evaluations,* 40 FAM. CT. REV. 177, 182 (2002).

134. HEILBRUN, *supra* note 50, at 174–75.

135. *Id.*

136. Kathleen J. Sternberg, Michael E. Lamb & S. Dawud-Noursi, *Using Multiple Informants to Understand Domestic Violence and Its Effects, in* CHILDREN EXPOSED TO MARITAL VIOLENCE, 121, 136–37 (G.W. Holden et al. eds., 1998). *See also* T.M. Achenbach, S. McConaughy & C.T. Howell, *Child/Adolescent Behavioral and Emotional Problems: Implications of Cross-Informant Correlations for Situational Specificity,* 87 PSYCHOL. BULL. 213 (1987).

137. Joseph D. Matarazzo, *Computerized Clinical Psychological Test Interpretations: Unvalidated Plus All Mean and No Sigma,* 41 AM. PSYCHOL. 14, 18 (1986).

138.   Association of Family and Conciliation Courts, *Model Standards of Practice for Child Custody Evaluation*, 45 Fam. Ct. Rev. 70, 82–83 (2007) [hereinafter *AFCC Child Custody Standards*] ("[T]he use of formal assessment instruments is not always necessary," and "[I]f testing is advisable and if the evaluator does not have sufficient education, training, and/or experience, s/he should refer the testing portion of the evaluation to a case consultant who has sufficient training and experience . . . ."); American Academy of Child and Adolescent Psychiatry, *Practice Parameters for Child Custody Evaluation*, 36 J. Am. Acad. Child & Adolescent Psychiatry 65S (1997) [hereinafter *Psychiatry Parameters*] ("[I]n most cases, psychological testing of the parents is not required. . . . When the psychiatric health of a parent or child is a legitimate issue, the evaluator may request psychological testing of each parent to help support an opinion and provide relevant data. This may add to the degree of certainty of the parenting assessment").

139.   *See* Randy K. Otto, Jaqueline K. Buffington-Vollum & John F. Edens, *Child Custody Evaluation, in* 11 Handbook of Psychology: Forensic Psychology 179, 184 (2003).

140.   *See* Society for Personality Assessment, *The Status of the Rorschach in Clinical and Forensic Practice: An Official Statement by the Board of Trustees of the Society for Personality Assessment*, 85 J. Personality Assessment 219, 220 (2005) [hereinafter *Status of the Rorschach*] (the practice of using findings of a personality test to draw a legal conclusion or to determine if a historical event occurred, such as trauma or childhood sexual abuse, is indefensible).

141.   James N. Bow, *Review of Empirical Research on Child Custody Practice*, 3910 J. Child Custody 23, 29 (2006).

142.   Leslie C. Moray & Christopher J. Hopwood, *The Personality Assessment Inventory, in* Forensic Uses of Clinical Assessment Instruments 89, 94 (Robert Archer ed., 2006) (reading-level analysis of the PAI test items indicated that reading ability at the fourth-grade level was necessary to complete the inventory); Martin Sellbom & Yossef S. Ben-Porath, *The Minnesota Multiphasic Personality Inventory-2, in* Archer 19, 19 (individuals with less than sixth-grade reading level should not be administered the MMPI-2 in the standard format); Robert J. Craig, *The Millon Clinical Multiaxial Inventory-III, in* Archer 121 (the MCMI-III was designed for use with adults with at least an eighth-grade education).

143.   Roger L. Greene, The MMPI-2: An Interpretive Manual 122 (2d ed. 2000).

144.   *Id.*

145.   *See* Bow, *supra* note 141, at 29.

146.   Irving B. Weiner, *The Rorschach Inkblot Method, in* Forensic Uses of Clinical Assessment Instruments 181, 181 (Robert Archer ed., 2006).

147.   *See* John E. Exner, 1 The Rorschach: A Comprehensive System: Basic Formulations and Principles of Interpretation (4th ed. 2003).

148.   *See* John Hunsley, Catherine M. Lee & James M. Wood, *Controversial and Questionable Assessment Techniques, in* Science and Pseudoscience in Clinical Psychology 39 (Scott O. Lilienfeld et al. eds., 2003); *Status of the Rorschach, supra* note 140, at 219; Weiner, *supra* note 146, at 181.

149.   Kenneth S. Pope, James N. Butcher & Joyce Seelen, The MMPI, MMPI-2 and MMPI-A 27 (1993).

150.   *See* Randy K. Otto & John F. Edens, *Parenting Capacity, in* Evaluating Competencies: Forensic Assessments and Instruments 258–68 (Thomas Grisso, 2d ed. 2003).

151.   *Id.* at 274–81.

152.   *Id.* at 281–92.

153.   *Id.* at 298–307.

154.   *Id.* at 292–98.

155.   Randy K. Otto, John F. Edens & Elizabeth H. Barcus, *The Use of Psychological Testing in Child Custody Evaluations*, 38 Fam. Conciliation Cts. Rev. 312, 331–33 (2000).

156. M.C. Heinze & Thomas Grisso, *Review of Instruments Assessing Parenting Capacities Used in Child Custody Evaluations,* 14 Beh. Sci. & L. 293, 309 (1996).

157. *Id.* at 310. *See also* Otto et al., *supra* note 155, at 312.

158. *See* Thomas M. Achenbach & Leslie A. Rescorla, *The Achenbach System of Empirically Based Assessment, in* Forensic Uses of Clinical Assessment Instruments 229 (Robert P. Archer ed., 2006).

159. Cecil R. Reynolds & Randy Kamphaus, BASC-2: Behavior Assessment System for Children, Second Edition (1996).

160. *See* David Lachar, Byron A. Hammer & Jill Hayes Hammer, *The Personality Inventory for Youth, the Personality Inventory for Children, Second Edition, and the Student Behavior Survey, in* Forensic Uses of Clinical Assessment Instruments 263 (Robert P. Archer ed., 2006).

161. Richard A. Warshak, Warshak Parent Questionnaire-2, http://www.wpqonline .com/.

162. Otto et al., *supra* note 155, at 333–35.

163. *Id.* at 333.

164. *Id.*

165. *Id.* at 333–34.

166. *Id.* at 334.

167. *Id.* at 334–35.

168. *Id.* at 335.

169. *Id.*

170. Bow, *supra* note 141, at 29; Margaret A. Hagan & Nicole Castagna, *The Real Numbers: Psychological Testing in Custody Evaluations,* 32 Prof. Psychol. 269 (2001).

171. American Educational Research Association et al., Standards for Educational and Psychological Testing 129 (1999) [hereinafter Testing Standards].

172. Roger L. Greene, Forensic Applications of the MMPI-2 32–34 (Workshop of the American Academy of Forensic Psychology, Dallas, TX), Feb. 10, 2005.

173. Greene, *supra* note 143, at 89.

174. *Id.* at 89.

175. *Id.* at 107.

176. R. Michael Bagby et al., *Defensive Responding on the MMPI-2 in Family Custody and Access Evaluations,* 11 Psychol. Assessment 24, 26 (1999); Kay Bathurst et al., *Normative Data for the MMPI-2 in Child Custody Litigation,* 9 Psychol. Assessment 205, 209 (1997).

177. David Medoff, *MMPI-2 Validity Scales in Child Custody Evaluations: Clinical Versus Statistical Significance,* 17 Behav. Sci. & L. 409, 410 (1999).

178. *Id.* at 411.

179. *See* Susana Urbina, Essentials of Psychological Testing 78 (2004).

180. Anastasi, *supra* note 110, at 71.

181. Richard R. Abidin, Parenting Stress Index: Professional Manual 36–51 (3d ed. 1995).

182. *Id.* at 25.

183. *Id.*

184. Otto & Edens, *supra* note 150, at 295.

185. Urbina, *supra* note 179, at 83.

186. Francella A. Quinnell & James N. Bow, *Psychological Tests Used in Child Custody Evaluations,* 19 Behav. Sci. & L. 491, 498 (2001).

187. Theodore Millon et al., MCMI-III Manual 6 (2d ed. 1997).

188. *Id.* at 144.

189. Greene, *supra* note 143, at 20.

190. John R. Graham, MMPI-2: Assessing Personality and Psychopathology 197 (1990).

191.   MILLON ET AL., *supra* note 187, at 6.

192.   *Daubert,* 509 U.S. at 591 n.9.

193.   URBINA, *supra* note 179, at 117.

194.   ANASTASI, *supra* note 110, at 116.

195.   *Id.*

196.   *Id.* at 117.

197.   JAMES N. BUTCHER ET AL., MMPI-2: MANUAL FOR ADMINISTRATION, SCORING, AND INTERPRETATION: REVISED EDITION 30 (2001).

198.   GRAHAM, *supra* note 190, at 174.

199.   *Id.* at 177.

200.   GREENE, *supra* note 143, at 312.

201.   URBINA, *supra* note 179, at 121.

202.   BUTCHER ET AL., *supra* note 197, at 9.

203.   *Id.*

204.   *Id.* at 8.

205.   *Id.* at 9.

206.   GREENE, *supra* note 143, at 29; *see also* BUTCHER ET AL., *supra* note 197, at 10.

207.   GREENE, *supra* note 143, at 29.

208.   URBINA, *supra* note 179, at 140.

209.   *Id.* at 141.

210.   ANNE ANASTASI & SUSANA URBINA, PSYCHOLOGICAL TESTING 113 (7th ed. 1997).

211.   *Id.* at 11.

212.   *See* TESTING STANDARDS, *supra* note 171, at 15.

213.   GREENE, *supra* note 143, at 253.

214.   URBINA, *supra* note 179, at 151.

215.   TESTING STANDARDS, *supra* note 171, at 10.

216.   URBINA, *supra* note 179, at 117.

217.   ANASTASI, *supra* note 110, at 144; URBINA, *supra* note 179, at 168.

218.   TESTING STANDARDS, *supra* note 171, at 17.

219.   *See* GREENE, *supra* note 143, at 365 (for a detailed analysis of decision making using sensitivity and specificity, and positive predictive power (PPP) and negative predictive power (NPP)).

220.   GREENE, *supra* note 143, at 253.

221.   *See* THOMAS M. ACHENBACH, MANUAL FOR THE CHILD BEHAVIOR CHECKLIST/4–18 AND 1991 PROFILE 128–47 (1991); *see also* William N. Friedrich et al., *Normative Sexual Behavior in Children: A Contemporary Sample,* 101 PEDIATRICS e9 (1998), http://www.pediatrics.org/cgi/content/full101/4/e9.

222.   *See* Gregory Allard, Julian Butler, David Faust & M. Tracie Shea, *Errors in Hand Scoring Objective Personality Tests: The Case of the Personality Diagnostic Questionnaire–Revised (PDQ-R),* 26 PROF'L PSYCHOL.: RES. & PRAC. 304 (1995).

223.   Randy K. Otto & James N. Butcher, *Computer-Assisted Psychological Assessment in Child Custody Evaluations,* 29 FAM. L.Q. 79, 85 (1995).

224.   *Id.*

225.   Frank J. Dyer, *Application of the Millon Inventories in Forensic Psychology, in* THE MILLON INVENTORIES 124, 134 (Theodore Millon ed., 1997).

226.   James R. Flens, *The Responsible Use of Psychological Testing in Child Custody Evaluations: Selection of Tests,* 2 J. CHILD CUSTODY 3, 17 (2005).

227.   Joseph D. Matarazzo, *Computerized Clinical Psychological Test Interpretations,* 41 AM. PSYCHOL. 14, 15 (1986).

228. Roger L. Greene, Robert C. Brown et al., MMPI-2 Adult Interpretive System Version 3 (2005), http://www3.parinc.com/products/ (type in product search: MMPI-2 AIS V3).
229. *In the Interest of CDK, JLK, and BJK, Minor Children,* 64 S.W.3d 679 (2002).
230. *Id.*
231. *Id.*
232. Otto & Butcher, *supra* note 223, at 89.
233. *Id.* at 87.
234. Millon et al., *supra* note 187, at 134.
235. Pope et al., *supra* note 149, at 27.
236. James N. Butcher, Julia N. Perry & Mera M. Atlis, *Validity and Utility of Computer-Based Test Interpretation,* 12 Psychol. Assessment 6, 15 (2000).
237. *Id.;* Theodore Millon & Carrie Millon, *History, Theory, and Validation of the MCMI, in* The Millon Inventories 35 (Theodore Millon ed., 1997).
238. *APA Ethics Code, supra* note 36, at 1072 (Standard 9.09—Test Scoring and Interpretation Services. The standard notes: "(a) Psychologists who offer assessment or scoring services to other professionals accurately describe the purpose, norms, validity, reliability, and applications of the procedures and any special qualifications applicable to their use; (b) Psychologists select scoring and interpretation services (including automated services) on the basis of evidence of validity of the program and procedures as well as on other appropriate considerations; (c) Psychologists retain responsibility for the appropriate application, interpretation, and use of assessment instruments, whether they score and interpret such tests themselves or use automated or other services").
239. *Id.*
240. Stephen Behnke, *Test-Scoring and Interpretation Services,* 35 Monitor on Psychol. 58 (Mar. 2004).
241. Testing Standards, *supra* note 171, at 65.
242. *Id.* at 134.
243. *Kumho Tire,* 526 U.S. at 152.
244. Amos Tversky & Daniel Kahneman, *Judgment and Uncertainty: Heuristics and Biases,* 185 Science 1124 (1974).
245. *Id.*
246. Asher Koriat, Sarah Lichtenstein & Baruch Fischhoff, *Reasons for Confidence,* 6 J. Experimental Psychol.: Hum. Learning & Memory 107, 108 (1980).
247. Derek J. Koehler, *Hypothesis Generation and Confidence in Judgment,* 20 J. Experimental Psychol.: Learning, Memory & Cognition 461 (1994).
248. Poole & Lamb, *supra* note 119, at 225.
249. *See* Jonathan Sandoval, *Critical Thinking in Test Interpretation, in* Test Interpretation and Diversity: Achieving Equity in Assessment 31, 39 (Jonathan H. Sandoval et al. eds., 1998).
250. Poole & Lamb, *supra* note 119, at 229.
251. Scott A. Hawkins & Reid Hastie, *Hindsight: Biased Judgments of Past Events After the Outcomes Are Known,* 107 Psychol. Bull. 311, 311 (1990).
252. *Id.;* Baruch Fischhoff, *Hindsight ≠ Foresight: The Effect of Outcome Knowledge on Judgment Under Uncertainty,* 1 J. Experimental Psychol.: Hum. Perception & Performance 288, 297 (1975).
253. Hawkins & Hastie, *supra* note 251, at 313.
254. Howard N. Garb, Studying the Clinician: Judgment Research and Psychological Assessment 190 (1998).
255. Fischhoff, *supra* note 252, at 298.

256.   Aaron Robb, *Strategies to Address Clinical Bias in the Child Custody Evaluation Process*, 3(2) J. CHILD CUSTODY 45, 56 (2006).

257.   Hal R. Arkes, Thomas J. Guilmette, David Faust & Kathleen Hart, *Eliminating Hindsight Bias*, 73 J. APPLIED PSYCHOL. 305, 307 (1988).

258.   Sandoval, *supra* note 249, at 36.

259.   Randy Borem et al., *Improved Clinical Judgment and Decision Making in Forensic Evaluation*, 21 J. PSYCHIATRY & L. 35, 45 (1993).

260.   *Id.*

261.   *See* Kathleen A. Kendall-Tackett et al., *Impact of Sexual Abuse on Children: A Review and Synthesis of Recent Empirical Studies*, 113 PSYCHOL. BULL. 164 (1993).

262.   Tversky & Kahneman, *supra* note 244, at 1127.

263.   Edward R. Hirt & Keith D. Markman, *Multiple Explanation: A Consider-an-Alternative Strategy for Debiasing Judgments*, 69 J. PERS. & SOC. PSYCHOL. 1069, 1070 (1995).

264.   Tversky & Kahneman, *supra* note 244, at 1127–28; *see also* John S. Carroll, *The Effect of Imagining an Event on Expectations for the Event: An Interpretation in Terms of the Availability Heuristic*, 14 J. EXPERIMENTAL SOC. PSYCHOL. 88 (1978).

265.   GARB, *supra* note 254, at 184.

266.   Myrna L. Friedlander & Susan D. Phillips, *Preventing Anchoring Errors in Clinical Judgment*, 52 J. CONSULTING & CLINICAL PSYCHOL. 366 (1984); Tversky & Kahneman, *supra* note 244, at 1128.

267.   Myrna L. Friedlander & Susan J. Stockman, *Anchoring and Publicity Effects in Clinical Judgment*, 39 J. CLINICAL PSYCHOL. 637 (1983).

268.   Friedlander & Phillips, *supra* note 266, at 367 citing D.J. Bem, *Self-Perception Theory, in* 6 ADVANCES IN EXPERIMENTAL SOCIAL PSYCHOLOGY 2 (L. Berkowitz ed., 1976) and N. Cantor & Walter Mischel, *Prototypes in Person Perception, in* 9 ADVANCES IN EXPERIMENTAL SOCIAL PSYCHOLOGY 4 (L. Berkowitz ed., 1979).

269.   Tversky & Kahneman, *supra* note 244, at 1128.

270.   GARB, *supra* note 254, at 185.

271.   Daniel T. Gilbert & Patrick S. Malone, *The Correspondence Bias*, 117 PSYCHOL. BULL. 21 (1995).

272.   *See* Gordon Wood, *Research Methodology: A Decision-Making Perspective, in* 4 THE G. STANLEY HALL LECTURE SERIES 211 (A. Rogers & C. James Scheier eds., 1984).

273.   David Faust, *Research on Human Judgment and Its Application to Clinical Practice*, 17 PROF'L PSYCHOL.: RES. & PRAC. 420, 424 (1986).

274.   J. Wiggins, *Clinical and Statistical Prediction: Where Are We and Where Do We Go from Here?*, 1 CLINICAL PSYCHOL. REV. 3, 14 (1984).

275.   Arkes et al., *supra* note 257, at 307.

276.   Baruch Fischhoff, *Perceived Informativeness of Facts*, 3 J. EXPERIMENTAL PSYCHOL.: HUM. PERCEPTION & PERFORMANCE 349 (1977).

277.   Hirt & Markman, *supra* note 263, at 1084.

278.   *Id.*; Koehler, *supra* note 247, at 468; Koriat et al., *supra* note 246, at 116.

279.   Hirt & Markman, *supra* note 263, at 1070; Koehler, *supra* note 247.

280.   Arkes et al., *supra* note 257, at 307.

281.   *Forensic Specialty Guidelines, supra* note 41, at 661.

282.   Janet R. Johnston, *Introducing Perspectives in Family Law and Social Science Research*, 45 FAM. CT. REV. 15 (2007).

283.   HEILBRUN, *supra* note 50, at 189.

284.   American Psychological Association, *Summary Report of Journal Operations, 2006*, 62 AM. PSYCHOL. 543 (2007).

285.   BRUCE D. SALES & DANIEL W. SHUMAN, EXPERTS IN COURT: RECONCILING LAW, SCIENCE, AND PROFESSIONAL KNOWLEDGE 59 (2005).

286. *Id.* at 58–60.

287. *Id.* at 58.

288. AMERICAN PSYCHOLOGICAL ASSOCIATION, PUBLICATION MANUAL OF THE AMERICAN PSYCHOLOGICAL ASSOCIATION 4–5 (4th ed. 1994) [hereinafter APA PUBLICATION MANUAL].

289. *Id.*

290. *Id.* at 9.

291. *Id.* at 10.

292. *Id.* at 11–12.

293. *See id.* at 11.

294. PAUL J. SILVA, HOW TO WRITE A LOT 84 (2007).

295. Larry G. Daniel, *Statistical Significance Testing: A Historical Overview of Misuse and Misinterpretation with Implications for the Editorial Policies of Educational Journals,* 5 RES. IN SCH. 23, 26 (1998).

296. JULIAN MELTZOFF, CRITICAL THINKING ABOUT RESEARCH: PSYCHOLOGY AND RELATED FIELDS 51 (1998).

297. *Id.* at 52.

298. *Id.* at 53.

299. *Id.* at 57.

300. *Id.* at 58 citing R. ROSENTHAL & R.L. ROSNOW, ESSENTIALS OF BEHAVIORAL RESEARCH (2d ed. 1991).

301. Elizabeth C. Sharp, Luc G. Pelletier & Chantal Levesque, *The Double-Edged Sword of Rewards for Participation in Psychology Experiments,* 38 CAN. J. BEHAV. SCI. 269, 275 (2006).

302. MELTZOFF, *supra* note 296, at 60–61.

303. *See* CAMPBELL & STANLEY, EXPERIMENTAL AND QUASI-EXPERIMENTAL DESIGNS FOR RESEARCH 34 (1963).

304. *Id.*

305. STEPHEN H. GEHLBACH, INTERPRETING THE MEDICAL LITERATURE 87 (3d ed. 1993).

306. *Id.*

307. Shari Seidman Diamond, *Reference Guide on Survey Research, in* REFERENCE MANUAL ON SCIENTIFIC EVIDENCE, SECOND EDITION 229, 245 (Federal Judicial Center ed., 2000), http://www.fjc.gov/library/fjc_catalog.nsf (type Diamond in search, follow to REFERENCE MANUAL ON SCIENTIFIC EVIDENCE, SECOND ED., follow to *Reference Guide on Survey Research*).

308. *See id.*

309. APA PUBLICATION MANUAL, *supra* note 288, at 15.

310. NEIL McK. AGNEW & SANDRA W. PYKE, THE SCIENCE GAME 137–44 (2d ed. 1978).

311. Richard A. Warshak, *Blanket Restrictions: Overnight Contact Between Parents and Young Children,* 38 FAM. & CONCILIATION CTS. REV. 422, 437 (2000).

312. AGNEW & PYKE, *supra* note 310, at 137.

313. MELTZOFF, *supra* note 296, at 287.

314. Robert F. Kelly & Sarah H. Ramsey, *Assessing and Communicating Social Science Information in Family and Child Judicial Settings: Standards for Judges and Allied Professionals,* 45 FAM. CT. REV. 22, 31 (2007).

315. MELTZOFF, *supra* note 296, at 136.

316. APA PUBLICATION MANUAL, *supra* note 288, at 18.

317. THOMAS GRISSO, EVALUATING COMPETENCIES: FORENSIC ASSESSMENTS AND INSTRUMENTS 23–24 (2d ed. 2003).

318. *Id.* at 24.

319. *See* Corina Benjet, Sandra T. Azar & Regina Kuersten-Hogan, *Evaluating the Parental Fitness of Psychiatrically Diagnosed Individuals: Advocating a Functional-Contextual Analysis of Parenting,* 17 J. FAM. PSYCHOL. 238, 241 (2003).

320. *APA Child Custody Guidelines, supra* note 34, at 678.

321. *Id.*

322. GRISSO, *supra* note 317, at 13.

323. *See* Peter E. Nathan, *In the Final Analysis, It's the Data that Counts,* 4 CLINICAL PSYCHOL.: SCI. & PRAC. 282 (1997). Dr. Nathan asserted that more than 500,000 MHPs use the DSM-IV in their practices.

324. AMERICAN PSYCHIATRIC ASSOCIATION, DIAGNOSTIC AND STATISTICAL MANUAL OF MENTAL DISORDERS (4th ed., Text Revision xxix, 2000) [hereinafter DSM-IV-TR].

325. Peter E. Nathan, *The DSM-IV and Its Antecedents: Enhancing Syndromal Diagnosis, in* MAKING DIAGNOSIS MEANINGFUL 3, 6 (J.W. Barron ed., 1998).

326. ALLEN FRANCES, MICHAEL B. FIRST & HAROLD A. PINCUS, DSM-IV GUIDEBOOK 34 (1995).

327. *Id.*

328. Joseph R. Scotti, Tracy L. Morris, Cheryl B. McNeil & Robert P. Hawkins, *Can Structural Criteria Be Functional?,* 64 J. CONSULTING & CLINICAL PSYCHOL. 1177 (1996).

329. DSM-IV-TR, *supra* note 324, at 7.

330. Thomas A. Widiger & Timothy J. Trull, *Plate Tectonics in the Classification of Personality Disorder,* 62 AM. PSYCHOL. 71, 73 (2007).

331. DSM-IV-TR, *supra* note 324, at 25.

332. *Id.* at 629.

333. *Id.* at 27.

334. *Id.* at 29–30.

335. *Id.* at 32–33.

336. *See* Nathan, *supra* note 325.

337. DSM-IV-TR, *supra* note 324, at xxiii.

338. *Id.* at xxiii.

339. *Id.* at xxxii–xxxiii.

340. FRANCES ET AL., *supra* note 326, at 60.

341. DSM-IV-TR, *supra* note 324, at xxxii.

342. Widiger & Trull, *supra* note 330, at 73.

343. FRANCES ET AL., *supra* note 326, at 19; Widiger & Trull, *supra* note 330, at 73.

344. FRANCES ET AL., *supra* note 326, at 19; Widiger & Trull, *supra* note 330, at 72.

345. Stuart A. Greenberg, Daniel W. Shuman & Robert G. Meyer, *Unmasking Forensic Diagnosis,* 27 INT'L J.L. & PSYCHIATRY 1, 1 (2004).

346. *Id.*

347. *Id.* at 13.

348. *APA Child Custody Guidelines, supra* note 34, at 678.

349. DSM-IV-TR, *supra* note 324, at xxxii–xxxiii.

350. *See* Tope v. America West Airlines 935 S.W.2d 908, 918 (Tex. App. El Paso 1996, no writ) where the social worker's testimony was excluded because her opinion relied solely on a DSM-IV diagnosis that was arrived at subjectively and was based solely on asking the plaintiff about his symptoms. The social worker offered no objective, or other, evidence, by testing or even interview notes, to support her opinion.

351. FRANCES ET AL., *supra* note 326, at 16–17.

352. DSM-IV-TR, *supra* note 324, at xxxi.

353. Duckett v. State, 797 S.W.2d 906, 927 (Tex. Crim. App. 1990) (Teague, J., dissenting).

354. Werner v. State, 711 S.W.2d 639, 649 (Tex. Crim. App. 1986) (Teague, J., dissenting).

355. Veronica B. Dahir et al., *Judicial Application of* Daubert *to Psychological Syndrome and Profile Evidence,* 11 PSYCHOL. PUB. POL'Y & L. 62, 74 (2005).

356. *Id.*

357. John A. Zervopoulos, Robinson/Daubert *and Mental Health Testimony: The Sky Is Not Falling*, 64 Tex. B.J. 350, 359 (2001).

358. John E.B. Myers, *Expert Testimony Describing Psychological Syndromes*, 24 Pac. L.J. 1449, 1453 (1993).

359. *Id.* at 1455.

360. *Id.* at 1454.

361. *Id.*

362. *See* Commonwealth v. Dunkle, 602 A.2d 830 (Pa. 1992).

363. Zervopoulos, *supra* note 357, at 359.

364. *Id.*

365. *Gammill*, 972 S.W.2d at 726.

366. *Watkins*, 121 F.3d at 991.

367. *Joiner*, 522 U.S. at 146.

368. Federal Rule of Evidence 704(b) provides an exception to (a): "No expert witness testifying with respect to the mental state or condition of a defendant in a criminal case may state an opinion or inference as to whether the defendant did or did not have the mental state or condition constituting an element of the crime charged or of a defense thereto. Such ultimate issues are matters for the trier of fact alone."

369. *AFCC Child Custody Standards, supra* note 138, at 89 ("[E]valuators shall only offer opinions to the court in those areas where they are competent to do so, based on adequate knowledge, skill, experience, and education"); *Psychiatry Parameters, supra* note 138, at 66S ("A 'Conclusions and Recommendations' section should contain the formulation of the case with specific and detailed recommendations for custody, visitation (if that is an issue), and any other comments or recommendations").

370. *APA Child Custody Guidelines, supra* note 34, at 679.

371. *Id.* (noting that the psychology profession has not reached consensus about whether psychologists ought to make recommendations about the final custody determination to the courts).

372. *See* Norman G. Poythress, *Concerning Reform in Expert Testimony: An Open Letter from a Practicing Psychologist*, 6 Law & Hum. Beh. 39 (1982) (a humorous yet realistic account of a forensic psychologist trying to convince a court that ultimate issue testimony is inappropriate).

373. Chad Tillbrook, Denise Mumley & Thomas Grisso, *Avoiding Expert Opinions on the Ultimate Legal Question: The Case for Integrity*, 3 J. Forensic Psychol. Prac. 77, 84; Timothy M. Tippins & Jeffrey P. Wittmann, *Empirical and Ethical Problems with Custody Recommendations: A Call for Clinical Humility and Judicial Vigilance*, 43 Fam. Ct. Rev. 193, 215 (2005).

374. Tillbrook et al., *supra* note 373, at 85.

375. *Id.; see* Tippins & Wittmann, *supra* note 373, at 215.

376. *Id.;* William O'Donohue & A.R. Bradley, *Conceptual and Empirical Issues in Child Custody Evaluations*, 6 Clinical Psychol.: Sci. & Prac. 310 (1999).

377. Richard Rogers & Charles P. Ewing, *The Prohibition of Ultimate Opinions: A Misguided Enterprise*, 3 J. Forensic Psychol. Prac. 65, 71–72 (2003).

378. Richard Rogers & Daniel W. Shuman, Conducting Insanity Evaluations 46 (2d ed. 2000).

379. Philip M. Stahl, Conducting Child Custody Evaluations (1994).

380. Philip M. Stahl, *The Benefits and Risks of Child Custody Evaluators Making Recommendations to the Court: A Response to Tippins and Wittmann*, 43 Fam. Ct. Rev. 260 (2005).

381. Joan B. Kelly & Janet R. Johnston, *Commentary on Tippins and Wittmann's "Empirical and Ethical Problems with Custody Recommendations,"* 43 Fam. Ct. Rev. 233, 237 (2005).

382. *APA Child Custody Guidelines, supra* note 34, at 679.

383. Erika M. Waller & Anasseril E. Daniel, *Purpose and Utility of Child Custody Evaluations: The Attorney's Perspective*, 33 J. AM. ACAD. PSYCHIATRY & L. 199, 203 (2005).
384. *See* GRISSO, *supra* note 317, at 21–40.
385. *Id.* at 3–5.
386. *Id.* at 8–9.
387. *Id.* at 7–8.
388. *Id.* at 8.
389. IRVING B. WEINER, CHILD AND ADOLESCENT PSYCHOPATHOLGY 8 (1982).
390. *Id.*
391. *Id.*
392. *Id.*
393. *Id.*
394. Jerome Kagan, *Temperament, in* 8 ENCYCLOPEDIA OF PSYCHOLOGY 34 (Alan E. Kazdin ed., 2000).
395. *Id.*
396. *Id.*
397. *Id.*
398. *Id.*
399. Ann Sanson & Mary K. Rothbart, *Child Temperament and Parenting, in* 4 HANDBOOK OF PARENTING: APPLIED AND PRACTICAL PARENTING 313 (Marc H. Bornstein ed., 1995).
400. Stella Chase, *Foreword* to STANLEY TURECKI & LESLIE TONNER, THE DIFFICULT CHILD (1985).
401. E. MAVIS HETHERINGTON & JOHN KELLY, FOR BETTER OR FOR WORSE: DIVORCE RECONSIDERED 148 (2002).
402. Carlos Valiente & Nancy Eisenberg, *Parenting and Children's Adjustment: The Role of Children's Emotion Regulation, in* EMOTION REGULATION IN COUPLES AND FAMILIES: PATHWAYS TO DYSFUNCTION AND HEALTH 129 (Douglas K. Snyder, Jeffrey Simpson & Jan N. Hughes eds., 2006).
403. *Id.*
404. *Id.* at 126.
405. HEILBRUN, *supra* note 50, at 176 (the principle of using and reviewing third-party collateral information is an established methodology when conducting forensic mental health assessments).
406. RUSSELL A. BARKLEY, DEFIANT CHILDREN: A CLINICIAN'S MANUAL FOR ASSESSMENT AND PARENT TRAINING 57 (2d ed. 1997).
407. *See* THOMAS M. ACHENBACH & LESLIE A. RESCORLA, MANUAL FOR THE ASEBA SCHOOL-AGE FORMS AND PROFILES (2001).
408. *Id.* at 16.
409. *Id.* at 17.
410. *Id.* at 93.
411. *Id.* at 22.
412. *Id.* at 18.
413. *See* Richard A. Warshak, *Parent Questionnaires in Psychological and Custody Evaluations*, 58 TEX. PSYCHOL. 21 (Summer 2007) (the online description is found at http://www.wpqonline.com/).
414. Patricia Chamberlain & Gerald R. Patterson, *Discipline and Child Compliance in Parenting, in* 4 HANDBOOK OF PARENTING: APPLIED AND PRACTICAL PARENTING 211 (Marc H. Bornstein ed., 1995).
415. Eleanor Maccoby, *The Role of Parents in the Socialization of Children: An Historical Overview*, 22 DEV. PSYCHOL. 1006 (1992).
416. *Id.*
417. *See* Chamberlain & Patterson, *supra* note 414, at 213 (citing Eleanor E. Maccoby & J. Martin, *Socialization in the Context of the Family: Parent-Child Interaction, in* 4 HANDBOOK OF

CHILD PSYCHOLOGY: SOCIALIZATION, PERSONALITY, AND SOCIAL DEVELOPMENT 1 (E. Mavis Hetherington ed., 2d ed. 1983).

418.　Chamberlain & Patterson, *supra* note 414, at 213.

419.　*See, e.g.,* Uniform Marriage and Divorce Act (1973), 402 9A U.L.A. 561 (1988) [hereinafter UMDA] (one of the five factors a judge should consider when making child custody determinations is "the interaction and interrelationships of the child with the parent or parents . . . .").

420.　*See* Joan B. Kelly & Janet R. Johnston, *The Alienated Child: A Reformulation of Parental Alienation Syndrome,* 39 FAM. CT. REV. 249, 251 (2001).

421.　*Id.*

422.　*Id.* at 252.

423.　*Id.*

424.　*Id.*

425.　*Id.*

426.　*Id.* at 253.

427.　*Id.*

428.　*Id.*

429.　*Id.* at 254; *see also* Richard A. Warshak, *Bringing Sense to Parental Alienation: A Look at the Disputes and the Evidence,* 37 FAM. L.Q. 273, 274 (2003).

430.　Kelly & Johnston, *supra* note 420, at 254.

431.　UMDA, *supra* note 419.

432.　*See* Richard A. Warshak, *Payoffs and Pitfalls of Listening to Children,* 52 FAM. REL. 373, 374–75 (2003).

433.　*See* GRISSO, *supra* note 317, at 23–24.

434.　W. Andrew Collins, Michael L. Harris & Amy Susman, *Parenting During Middle Childhood, in* 4 HANDBOOK OF PARENTING: APPLIED AND PRACTICAL PARENTING 65, 72 (Marc H. Bornstein ed., 1995).

435.　GERALD R. PATTERSON, COERCIVE FAMILY PROCESSES 222 (1982).

436.　Collins et al., *supra* note 434, at 72.

437.　PATTERSON, *supra* note 435, at 223.

438.　Maccoby, *supra* note 415, at 1015.

439.　Theodore Dix, *The Affective Organization of Parenting: Adaptive and Maladaptive Processes,* 110 PSYCHOL. BULL. 3, 10 (1991).

440.　Maccoby, *supra* note 415, at 1015.

441.　*See* D. Baumrind, *The Development of Instrumental Competence Through Socialization, in* 7 MINNESOTA SYMPOSIUM ON CHILD PSYCHOLOGY 3 (A.D. Pick ed., 1973).

442.　HETHERINGTON & KELLY, *supra* note 401, at 131.

443.　*Id.* at 130.

444.　*Id.* at 130–31.

445.　*Id.* at 127.

446.　Chamberlain & Patterson, *supra* note 414, at 209.

447.　*Id.* at 206–9.

448.　*See* Dix, *supra* note 439, at 8.

449　*Id.* at 9.

450.　*Id.* at 8.

451.　*Id.* at 13.

452.　*See id.* at 12.

453.　Otto & Edens, *supra* note 150, at 253.

454.　*Id.* at 254.

455.　*Id.* at 255.

Exposing the Analytical Gaps: Applying a Scientific–Critical Thinking Mind-Set

CHAPTER 5

Scientific–Critical Thinking

Lawyers face special challenges when considering MHP expert conclusions and opinions in reports or testimony, even when they persistently apply the "How do you know what you say you know?" standard. In Part 1, we explored a four-step *Frye-Daubert* Analysis Model to address this key question of experts and their materials and showed how to apply that model, step-by-step, to gauge the reliability of experts' opinions. We noted that a failing at any one of the four steps could trigger a *Frye-Daubert* motion to exclude parts or all of the testimony or, at least, provide useful fodder for the expert's cross-examination.

Although addressing each of the four steps of the model is important, the last two—gauging the analytical gaps between experts' data and conclusions and between their conclusions and opinions—may be the lawyer's most difficult challenge. The first step, exploring experts' qualifications, is fairly straightforward if one is aware of the various MHP disciplines and training requirements, and if one is able to track experts' experiences and training—formal and continuing education—in the areas the testimony covers. For example, should an evaluator, licensed as a psychologist but with little training or experience with preschool children, offer expert opinions on sexual abuse allegations involving a three-year-old child? In sum, those who purport to be experts must have expertise concerning the actual subject about which they offer an opinion.[1] The second step, examining whether experts' methods comport with accepted methodology outside the courtroom, may present more challenges, even serious ones.[2] But lawyers may access many resources to determine whether testifying experts' methods pass muster in the applicable scientific community. Then, in the model's third and fourth steps, experts, once they derive their data from reliable methods, must use their judgments and experiences—also informed by the professional literature—to reach their conclusions and opinions about relevant case issues. These last steps require lawyers to apply the Analytical Gap Test to weigh the quality of experts' conclusions and opinions.

Recall *Joiner*'s assertion that "a court may conclude that there is simply too great an analytical gap between the data and the opinion proffered."[3] Note that the language is relative, not absolute. Because expert opinions are judgments, there always will be some gap between the considered data and conclusions and the conclusions and proffered opinions. The lawyer's task, then, is to gauge whether the breadth of those gaps is "too great."

The task is difficult on two counts. First, in most jurisdictions, the primary legal standard in family law cases, the best interest of the child, is not defined specifically by statutes or case law. And even jurisdictions that give some definition burden their best interest factors with abstract psychological terms.[4] Applying ill-defined legal standards provides opportunities for courts to accept opinions with wide analytical gaps—the trial court has much discretion in defining "best interest of the child" in a particular case,[5] and the appellate review standard for trial courts' decisions to admit or exclude expert evidence is abuse of discretion.[6]

Second, the task of determining whether the analytical gap in the expert's opinion is adequate or too large is complicated by experts' tendencies to hide the gaps in their empirical and logical reasoning in ways that are not often evident to lawyers or courts. Sometimes, experts hide the reasoning gaps intentionally. Other times, biases unintentionally keep experts from properly applying the required scientific–critical thinking mind-set to the ways they gather their data (methodology) or to how they interpret the data they collect. Or, MHPs may, by habit, use overly abstract psychological jargon without adequate definitions to communicate their conclusions and opinions.

Finding the analytical gaps in expert testimony, uncovering them, and prying them open are key tasks for lawyers attempting to gauge the reliability of expert testimony in their cases. This section will help lawyers use a scientific–critical thinking mind-set to expose analytical gaps MHP experts hide in their testimony. Trial courts are expected to adopt this mind-set when they weigh whether to admit or exclude proffered expert testimony. But even if the court does not exclude testimony based on analytical gap arguments, focusing on the gaps provides fertile ground for direct- or cross-examination: how lawyers choose to use their experts or cross-examine their opponents' experts will govern whether they should seek to narrow the gap in their questions or open it up as far as will be allowed.

To illustrate how lawyers may use the scientific–critical thinking mind-set to expose experts' analytical gaps, we will first explore this essential mind-set—an approach that our theme—"How do you know what you say you know?"—typifies.

THE SCIENTIFIC–CRITICAL THINKING MIND-SET

The most useful way to expose analytical gaps in expert testimony is to employ the same mind-set the *Frye-Daubert* cases demand of the trial judge—that of a scientist. Recall that the *Frye* reliability inquiry is neither "scientific nose-counting"[7] nor "a simple numerical majority" of expert opinion.[8] Rather, courts should consider the quality, as well as the quantity, of the scientific literature and opinion supporting or opposing the technique.[9] And *Daubert* notes that "the adjective 'scientific' (in Rule 702) implies a grounding in the methods and procedures of science."[10] Of course, the trial court should consider the specific *Daubert* factors "where they are reasonable measures of reliability."[11] But the *Daubert* reliability standard applies to all expert testimony[12]—the objective is for expert testimony to be reliable, or trustworthy.[13]

If, then, the reliability analysis is to flow from a scientific mind-set, how does one apply that mind-set to analyze expert testimony? Some view science primarily as an application of a "scientific method"—and *Daubert* notes that "'scientific knowledge' ... must be derived by the scientific method."[14] However, no single scientific method adequately describes the work of all scientists:[15] some scientists conduct controlled experiments; some, like astronomers, must rely instead on rigorous observations to test their ideas.[16] In addition, some people view science merely as an accumulated body of research-derived facts. But this notion is lacking because science does not traffic in certainty; a key task in science is to seek hypotheses that may falsify previous experimental findings or accepted theories.[17] Instead, the scientific mind-set is a way of viewing the world,[18] an attempt to understand the world with a special, systematic effort to ensure that things said about it are accurate[19]—in *Frye-Daubert* parlance, reliable or trustworthy. The key to valid science is a convergence of well-reasoned explanation with supporting observations or experimental results.[20]

The scientific mind-set is a way to conduct critical thinking[21]—the ability and willingness to assess claims and make objective judgments based on well-supported reasons and evidence and to resist claims with no supporting evidence.[22] This mind-set guides one to assess systematically which ideas are reasonable by seeking to rule out competing hypotheses until the hypothesis entertained is the likeliest explanation within the smallest margin of error.[23]

Critical Thinking Elements

Professors Wade and Tavris identified several critical thinking elements.[24] For example, consider an MHP who offers an opinion that the child in a custody dispute should be allowed to choose which parent she will primarily live with after the divorce. The lawyer might use those critical thinking elements to assess the MHP's level of critical thinking in the case:[25]

- *Define terms of the question:* What is the child's age? How will the child express her choice? What schedule defines a "primary" living arrangement for the child as opposed to a schedule in which neither home merits the designation "primary"?
- *Examine the evidence about the question:* While the MHP is confident that the opinion is correct, did she or he consider psychological research and literature noting that children's feelings change easily during their parents' divorces,[26] and that children's strong preferences may represent reactions to a recent crisis rather than the long-term quality of the relationships with each parent?[27]
- *Analyze assumptions and biases:* Does the MHP have a bias toward the notion that children have a right to choose between parents in a divorce? If so, how did the MHP account for that bias when forming conclusions and opinions in this case?
- *Avoid emotional reasoning:* Does the MHP's professional background reflect involvement in advocacy causes that emotionally and intellectually predispose the MHP to the position that children's custody wishes should be followed? If so, do the case facts contradict the MHP's opinion?
- *Don't oversimplify arguments:* Does the MHP believe that children's self-worth will be disrespected if they are not allowed to choose their post-divorce primary custody home?
- *Consider alternate explanations:* Did the MHP consider that the child's primary custody choice may have been influenced by greater freedom at the preferred parent's home, by an age-inappropriate attempt to "care" for the parent perceived to be hurt most emotionally by the divorce, or by promises for a bright red Miata?

- *Tolerate uncertainty:* Is the MHP able to say "I don't know" to questions that ask for certainty regarding the future effects on the child of having openly taken sides in the parents' dispute? Or to questions that ask about the likely stability of the child's expressed preferences?

In sum, experts think critically when they actively evaluate how they reach conclusions—the underlying reasoning and the factors that informed those conclusions.[28] The critical thinker's underlying question? "How reliable is the evidence that supports or refutes the argument?"[29] Or, "How do you know what you say you know?" In contrast, experts think uncritically when they reach ill-informed conclusions with little thought of alternative ways to consider the data or issues before the court.

Benefits of the Scientific–Critical Thinking Mind-Set

Adopting the scientific–critical thinking mind-set helps lawyers on three counts. First, this mind-set enables lawyers to focus on case facts and issues without being drawn into the strong emotions that attend these cases. Second, this mind-set gives lawyers the proper conceptual approach to wrestle with the disputes among professionals about how literature and research apply to problems inherent in these cases. Finally, this mind-set prepares lawyers to evaluate effectively the reasoning threads in expert testimony and to organize their evidentiary arguments to the court when the Daubert reliability factors do not apply to particular expert testimony.[30]

As noted earlier, however, the empirical and logical connections that experts make between their evaluation data and conclusions in their testimony may not be as tight as those experts try to present. Experts may hide the analytical gaps in their reports or testimony, sometimes in ways not easily uncovered by lawyers or the court. In the remainder of this section, we will highlight six methods by which experts hide analytical gaps in their thinking and testimony, illustrate how each might be manifested in particular issues that arise in family law cases, and then offer ways that lawyers may use the scientific–critical thinking mind-set to expose those hidden analytical gaps. Hints that experts are hiding the gaps may be evident when they do the following:

1. use overly abstract psychological concepts in their reports and testimony
2. invoke "common sense" to support conclusions and opinions
3. make "ipse dixit" assertions to support conclusions and opinions
4. resort to "general acceptance" arguments to support conclusions and opinions
5. misapply and misrepresent professional literature in their reports and testimony
6. succumb to confirmatory bias when forming their conclusions and opinions

Let's explore each gap-hiding method. The first four methods will be discussed in the next chapter. The last two will follow in Chapter 7 and Chapter 8, respectively.

NOTES

1. *See* Broders v. Heise, 924 S.W.2d 148, 152 (Tex. 1996).

2. Recall that the case issues in both *Frye* and *Daubert* focused on methodology, not on the experts' qualifications.

3. General Electric Co. v. Joiner, 522 U.S. 136, 146 (1997); *see also* du Pont v. Robinson, 923 S.W.2d 549, 557 (Tex. 1995) (This Texas Supreme Court case, Texas's complement to *Daubert*, lists, like *Daubert*, several nonlimited factors the court may use to test the reliability of expert testimony and methodology. One listed factor is "the extent to which the technique relies upon the subjective interpretation of the expert.").

4. *See* MICH. COMP. LAWS § 722.23 (There are no guidelines available to define "love," "affection," "other emotional ties," and "moral fitness.").

5. *See* Gillespie v. Gillespie, 644 S.W.2d 449 (Tex. 1982).

6. *Joiner*, 522 U.S. at 138–39.

7. Logerquist v. McVey, 1 P.3d 113 (Ariz. 2000).

8. People v. Leahy, 882 P.2d 321, 336–37 (Cal. 1994).

9. *Id.* at 336.

10. Daubert v. Merrell Dow Pharmaceuticals, 509 U.S. 579, 590 (1993).

11. Kumho Tire Co., Ltd. v. Carmichael, 526 U.S. 137, 152 (1999).

12. *Id.* at 149.

13. *Daubert*, 509 U.S. at 590 n.9.

14. *Daubert*, 509 U.S. at 590.

15. D. Allan Bromley, *Science and the Law, in* SCIENCE AND TECHNOLOGY POLICY YEARBOOK (American Association for the Advancement of Science, 1999), http://www.aaas.org/spp/yearbook/chap10.htm.

16. *Id.*

17. *See Daubert*, 509 U.S. at 593 (one of *Daubert*'s factors to gauge whether a theory or technique is scientific is whether it can be, and has been, tested and falsified. *Daubert* at 590 also notes that "arguably, there are no certainties in science").

18. NATALIE ANGIER, THE CANON 19 (2007); Daubert, 509 U.S. at 590 ("[S]cience is not an encyclopedic body of knowledge about the universe. Instead, it represents a *process* for proposing and refining theoretical explanations about the world that are subject to further testing and refinement (emphasis added in original) (citing Brief for the American Association for the Advancement of Science and the National Academy of Sciences as Amici Curiae in Support of Respondent, Daubert v. Merrell Dow Pharmaceuticals, Inc. 509 U.S. 579 (1993) (No. 92-102) 7–8 [hereinafter AAAS Brief]).

19. Stephen Pinker, *The Known World*, N.Y. TIMES, May 27, 2007.

20. AAAS Brief, *supra* note 18.

21. *See* ANGIER, *supra* note 18, at 19; *see also* CAROLE WADE & CAROL TAVRIS, PSYCHOLOGY 8 (7th ed. 2003) (critical thinking is fundamental to all science).

22. WADE & TAVRIS, *supra* note 21, at 7.

23. ANGIER, *supra* note 18, at 19; *see also* CAMPBELL & STANLEY, EXPERIMENTAL AND QUASI-EXPERIMENTAL DESIGNS FOR RESEARCH (1963), at 36 ("[V]arying degrees of 'confirmation' are conferred upon a theory through the number of *plausible rival hypotheses* available to account for the data. The fewer such plausible rival hypotheses remaining, the greater the degree of 'confirmation.'").

24. WADE & TAVRIS, *supra* note 21, at 7.

25. *Id.* at 14 (critical thinking elements from WADE & TAVRIS).

26.   *See, e.g.,* JUDITH S. WALLERSTEIN & JOAN B. KELLY, SURVIVING THE BREAKUP (1980).

27.   Richard A. Warshak, *Payoffs and Pitfalls of Listening to Children,* 52 FAM. REL. 373, 374 (2003).

28.   Diane F. Halpern, *Teaching Critical Thinking for Transfer Across Domains,* 53 AM. PSY-CHOL. 449, 451 (1998); *see also* Sharon Begley, *Critical Thinking: Part Skill, Part Mindset, and Totally Up to You,* WALL ST. J., October 20, 2006, at B1 ("You have to want to think critically. If you have good critical-thinking skills but for some reason are not motivated to deploy them, you will reach conclusions and make decisions no more rationally than someone without those skills.").

29.   WADE & TAVRIS, *supra* note 21, at 9.

30.   *Kumho Tire* 526 U.S. at 151 (*Daubert*'s "helpful" factors "do not all necessarily apply even in every instance in which the reliability of scientific testimony is challenged").

CHAPTER 6

Exposing the Analytical Gaps

EXPOSING OVERLY ABSTRACT PSYCHOLOGICAL CONCEPTS

Overly abstract psychological concepts are the bane of expert testimony. MHPs often hide analytical gaps in their reasoning by using abstract psychological concepts to support and communicate their opinions. Consider these assertions:

- The child's *attachment* to the parent is affected by the quality of the parent's responsiveness to that child.
- The child's *self-esteem* has been affected by witnessing the parents' physical altercations with each other.
- The infant will not be *emotionally damaged* by sleeping overnight regularly at the other parent's house.

When one considers, after short reflection, the psychological concepts in the preceding statements, one realizes that the statements may be very meaningful or may relate little, if any, information. These concepts, when unpackaged, reveal useful psychological constructs, richly discussed and empirically supported in the professional literature. But people who are not MHPs also commonly use these terms in daily conversations. For example, ask MHPs familiar with the professional literature about the meaning of a child's *attachment* to parents. The response might include findings from infant-parent studies, longitudinal day-care studies, the different attachment capacities of infants, and implications of attachment patterns in adult relationships. In contrast, MHPs unfamiliar with the attachment literature may only refer to a child's "close relationship" with the parent—a response reflecting little difference from a lay definition. Yet, those MHPs may hide wide gaps in the connecting links of their opinions, implying a fuller understanding of the attachment concept than the lay understanding that actually informed the opinion. In this simple example, the "How do you know what you say you know?" inquiry should quickly expose the wide analytical gaps in the latter MHPs' thinking and testimony.

Professor S.I. Hayakawa's "abstraction ladder" metaphor[1] is a tool lawyers may use to deconstruct experts' uses of abstract psychological concepts. If you will, visualize a stepladder. Hayakawa maintained that descriptors of a concept on higher ladder rungs are more abstract and inclusive; descriptors of a concept on lower ladder rungs are more concrete and differentiated.[2] Actually, concepts identified at any ladder rung are abstractions; that is, any concept can be defined by more particular lower level elements.

Therefore, the key to understanding a concept is not whether it is a "high level" or "low level" abstraction, but whether the concept can point to lower levels or be explained more fully.[3] For example, consider the concept "house" on an "abstraction ladder" rung.[4] Moving a rung higher on the ladder could invoke the concept of "building." But with "house," the "building" concept may also include a store, a church, or a courthouse. Not much is learned about "house" moving up the ladder. But if one moves down the ladder from the "house" rung, one might note several structures of which "house" is a more abstract concept—a bungalow, a cottage, a guest home, a mansion. The common characteristics of these structures and the characteristics that distinguish these structures from one another help to define "house."

In sum, from a certain rung on the abstraction ladder, moving up the ladder hides the "house" concept in the midst of other concepts. If one stays only at the "house" ladder rung or abstraction level, little will be learned about what "house" means.[5] But moving down the ladder helps to define "house."

Let us now use the abstraction ladder to consider an opinion that an MHP expert might offer in a child custody case: "Tim is a noncompliant, defiant twelve-year-old boy when he is with his father." The parents' lawyers may decide to walk the expert higher up on the ladder or walk the expert down. For instance, the father's lawyer might take the expert one rung higher and ask whether most twelve-year-old boys may occasionally be noncompliant or defiant with their fathers—note that Tim's behaviors are not really defined but rather become incorporated into more normal twelve-year-old boy behaviors. Mother's lawyer, on the other hand, may decide to walk the expert down the ladder to bring more definition to the expert's label of noncompliant, defiant behavior. Mother's lawyer might ask the expert to describe what Tim does that characterizes the noncompliant, defiant label: Is Tim just occasionally disobedient? Is he aggressive toward others? Does Tim lie and steal? Does Tim have an attention deficit/hyperactivity disorder diagnosis? Mother's lawyer may then try to walk the expert farther down the ladder and assert that Tim's problems arise from the father's poor parenting skills.

Note that the mother's lawyer forces the expert to unpackage the initial opinion by walking the expert down the abstraction ladder. If the expert is unable to step to a lower ladder rung from the rung to which the opinion is tacked, the expert will offer little information about Tim's noncompliant, defiant behavior with his father—the opinion will remain nothing more than an abstract, unsupported judgment that will be easily exposed if pressed. Concepts are understood when they can point to lower levels.[6]

In this instance, however, the father's lawyer may not have to be resigned to just moving up the ladder to mitigate the expert's opinion about Tim and Tim's father, particularly if Tim's misbehaviors clearly are more serious than those of normal twelve-year-old boys. Father's lawyer then may decide to try walking the expert down the ladder by asking if the expert explored the possibility that Tim's noncompliant, defiant behaviors might be explained by an attention deficit/hyperactivity disorder, the behavioral effects of which could be moderated by medication. If so, Tim's misbehaviors may be less likely due primarily to the father's alleged lack of parenting skills. Or, the father may volunteer to attend parenting classes to learn how to manage Tim's misbehaviors more effectively.

In sum, lawyers can use the abstraction ladder to expose analytical gaps in expert testimony that lean on abstract psychological concepts and to frame their examinations of the expert. Simply visualize the abstraction ladder, tack the expert to a particular ladder rung, and force the expert to walk down the ladder using "How do you know what you say you know?"–related questions to make that happen. Of course, if the expert gets stuck at a certain rung and cannot climb down farther, the expert's thinking level will be exposed, and the lawyer then can assess whether the expert's analysis and reasoning are sufficient or lacking—and at what level.

EXPOSING "COMMON SENSE" NOTIONS USED TO SUPPORT EXPERT OPINIONS

Most people—including lawyers, judges, jurors, and MHPs—have grown up in families and are a part of at least one family as adults. As a result, "common sense" notions abound about how families should work and what family relationships should be like. At times, such notions attain the status of conventional wisdom, gain acceptance among professionals, and may find their way into courts to support expert opinions.

But while "common sense" may provide a useful standard for making some daily decisions, the courts' approach to the reliability of expert opinions requires a different metric than "societal general acceptance," particularly for common sense notions that do not stand up under empirical scrutiny. Rather, courts view reliable, trustworthy analysis and opinions as flowing from the scientific–critical thinking mind-set upon which the *Frye* and *Daubert* cases require courts to rely.[7]

Problems with common sense notions in court arise when experts lack a scientific–critical thinking mind-set as they link their data to their conclusions and opinions. Unfortunately, the attempt to invoke common sense—overtly or by unexamined values or biases—to support expert opinions may have significant implications in family court.

An example of such a common sense notion has been use of the term *psychological parent*. The term, first introduced by Goldstein, Freud, and Solnit in their influential writings of the late 1970s, highlighted their beliefs that children have one psychological parent to whom they have primary emotional attachments and from whom they should not be separated.[8] To these authors, continuity of care is of primary importance for the child; it is through that continuity that children gain the perception of parental competence and protection for their well-being and growth.[9] Goldstein et al. also emphasized that permanency was the child's paramount developmental need.

In custody matters, Goldstein et al. asserted that the child's needs are best served by maintaining a continuous, unconditional, and permanent relationship with at least one adult who is or will become the child's psychological parent.[10] They wrote that the state should not disrupt the relationship between a wanted child and a psychological parent except in the gravest circumstances. Children, according to Goldstein et al., have only one psychological parent, and that parent should be given custody in a divorce dispute[11]—the "least detrimental alternative" is the child placement option that matches the particular child with his or her psychological parent.[12]

Although the views of Goldstein et al. influenced courts and policy makers, those views were challenged as lacking empirical support. Goldstein et al. based their "primary parent" notions in psychoanalytic theory, and they cited little supporting empirical evidence to support even their assumptions.[13] In contrast, contrary to widespread "common sense,"[14] contemporary theory, supported by much empirical research, holds that infants normally develop close attachments to both of their parents and that infants do best when they have the opportunity to establish and maintain such attachments.[15]

Past acceptance of the notion that children have one psychological parent to whom they have primary emotional attachments and from whom they should not be separated led to another "common sense" assumption: that infants of divorced parents would become emotionally damaged if they slept overnight in the residence of the noncustodial parent. Practically, this often showed itself in disputes where fathers sought overnight time with their infant children who lived primarily with mothers. In light of the "psychological parent" notion as well as early theorizing about infant attachments, professionals in the family court system—judges, therapists, child custody evaluators, and lawyers—strongly discouraged overnights or extended stays of the infant with the noncustodial parent, usually the father.[16]

But the "common sense" overnight proscriptions were not based on child development research.[17] And those categorical judgments did not account for the quality of the child's interactions with each parent, the nature of both parents' involvements with the child, or the child's need to maintain and strengthen relationships with both parents after the marital separation.[18] In fact, research has found that infants and toddlers readily adapt to transitions from one stable caretaking arrangement to another.[19] And developmental psychologists have found that emotional attachments between children and their parents deepen when children are able to interact with parents in a variety of contexts.[20] Overnights provide opportunities for a wide range of involvements between children and their nonresidential parents.[21] There are no research findings that maintain that infants and toddlers are emotionally harmed when they spend overnight time with their nonresidential parent,[22] although some MHPs maintain that the research is not clear enough for social policy to promote infant overnight periods with the nonresidential parent.[23] The research, fairly considered, indicates that overnights for infants and toddlers should neither be made mandatory nor be routinely excluded but rather should be among the options considered when fashioning parenting arrangements.[24]

Finally, "common sense" arguments cut both ways on the infant overnight issue. For example, infants and toddlers often tolerate sleeping apart from their mothers and away from their beds—at day care centers, in cars, in strollers, and at grandparents' homes, among other places. Or, parents may take a vacation within the first few years of the child's life and leave the child in the care of another adult—perhaps not even a family member.[25] But while these "common sense" notions to counter infant overnights apart from the residential parent seem self-evident, even these must be considered in light of the scientific–critical thinking mind-set before the court might deem such testimony reliable.

EXPOSING IPSE DIXIT ASSERTIONS

Expert witnesses may hide analytical gaps in their reasoning and testimony when they confidently base their conclusions and opinions on unproven assertions and expect the court to accept those assertions at face value. *Joiner* highlights the requirement that experts must support their opinions when it notes that while experts commonly extrapolate from their data, "nothing in either *Daubert* or the Federal Rules of Evidence requires a district court to admit opinion evidence which is connected to existing data only by the *ipse dixit*—a dogmatic and unproven statement[26]—of the expert."[27] Further, *Viterbo v. Dow Chemical* states, "When an expert brings to the court little more than his credentials and a subjective opinion, this is not evidence that will support a judgment."[28]

Often, when pressed with the "How do you know what you say you know?" challenge, experts who use their reputations instead of a scientific–critical thinking mind-set to buttress their subjective opinions will be quickly exposed. But qualifications-focused questions may also unmask many of these experts' attempts to overstate or mischaracterize their professed qualifications before the court. If lawyers discover such "puffing," they might then ask how the expert's opinion should be deemed reliable if the expert cannot even recount professional accomplishments and experiences reliably. As noted in Chapter 4, MHP experts may tout forensic psychology board certifications or diplomates; lawyers should focus on the nature of those diplomates and how the experts earned those diplomates (*see* Chapter 4). Because MHPs value diplomate status as evidence of expertise, a lawyer's inquiry often will quickly uncover qualifications "puffing."

Experts may also try to enhance themselves in court by mischaracterizing other aspects of their training. For instance, many prestigious universities offer one- or two-week workshops or training programs on a number of topics and then provide certificates for completing the programs. Some MHPs list those certificates on their vitae more prominently than their graduate degrees. Lawyers should not allow the name of a prestigious school in testimony or in a vita to go unchallenged—particularly in a deposition. Ask MHPs what kind of training earned the certificate, how long the training lasted, and how the training informs their overall practice.

In addition, experts may mischaracterize past work experiences as training in a particular area. For example, one MHP listed a job stint with a clinic serving minorities as a "residency," implying that she obtained special experiences and training serving that population group. While that job presumably provided some useful experiences, it was not part of a "residency" training program—the MHP "puffed" the experience into something it was not to enhance her credibility. As with experts' touting of board certifications or certificates from prestigious universities, lawyers should question the nature of residency programs that experts claim to have attended. Probe deeply, at least in trial preparation, to determine the true nature of experts' credentials.

Finally, experts may try to support ipse dixit opinions by basing those opinions on their clinical experiences. When backed into a corner by the "How do you know what you say you know?" line of inquiry, these experts will finally invoke experiences from their professional practices as sources of proof for their assertions—for example, to support claimed competence, an expert might report having treated sexually abused children for several years. Of course, those clinical experiences are rarely studied systematically, and the expert's methods may only faintly resemble methods recommended in the professional literature. And families who seek help from that therapist may not be representative of the family about which the expert is offering an opinion—the therapist may have treated children already determined to have been sexually abused but have little experience evaluating sexual abuse allegations in a family court dispute. As discussed earlier, experience, according to Federal Rule of Evidence 702, is a factor that may qualify a witness to provide expert testimony. But unsupported "experience" is not reliable. Recall that the Advisory Committee Notes for Rule 702 give some guidance about how to evaluate experts who rely solely or primarily on experience testimony, noting that "the witness must explain how that experience leads to the conclusion reached, why that experience is a sufficient basis for the opinion, and how that experience is reliably applied to the facts."[29]

EXPOSING ATTEMPTS TO INVOKE THE GENERAL ACCEPTANCE FACTOR ABSENT SUPPORT

Another way that MHP experts may hide analytical gaps in their conclusions and opinions is by resorting to a general acceptance argument to convince courts of their testimony's reliability absent other reliability indices.

As noted in the Chapter 3 discussion of the *Frye* test and case law, the general acceptance standard, by itself, may be problematic. Giannelli noted that the most important flaw in *Frye* might be that the test obscures critical problems in the use of a particular technique.[30] And case law has emphasized that "courts should consider the quality, as well as the quantity, of the scientific literature and opinion supporting or opposing the technique."[31]

Consider a child custody evaluation in which a key measure used to understand the child is a play technique known as *Family as Animals in the Sand*,[32] adapted from a drawing technique[33] and a variant of Sandplay Therapy methods.[34] In this technique, the child chooses miniature animals to represent each family member, places the animals in a sandtray—a 19.5 × 28.5 × 3.5 inch box filled with sand[35]—and then creates an "environment" in the sandtray.[36] This environment supposedly depicts "a 3-dimensional representation of the child's perception of the family."[37] Various features of this supposed family depiction are noted: the order in which family members are placed; family members' proximity to one another, especially the child animal; and the level of potential danger if some animals are highly aggressive and frightening while others are small and vulnerable.[38]

Unfortunately, the *Family as Animals in the Sand* technique is unable to provide reliable information about the child's perceptions of family members—the purpose for which the method is used. For instance, if a girl places the animal representing herself close to the animal representing her father, she could be representing either her perception of her actual relationship with her father or her wish for such a close relationship.[39] In addition, such animal placement could symbolically depict an impaired father-daughter relationship.[40] No empirical research supports relative placement of symbolic objects in a sand environment through use of this technique—or in drawings, for that matter—as a method by which to gain reliable, trustworthy information about the child's perception of family relationships. It would seem that attempts by the evaluator to use observations from such techniques to support conclusions and expert opinions of the girl should fail: the analytical gaps in the evaluator's links between the data and proffered opinion appear quite wide, and the evaluator's reasoning does not reflect a scientific–critical thinking mind-set.

Given this analysis, the expert might further hide the wide analytical gap by noting that sandplay therapy is a generally accepted technique among many MHPs. First, the expert might note that the *Family as Animals in the Sand* technique is included in literature that discusses its use in child custody cases.[41] Second, the expert might call the court's attention to training conducted for MHPs who might consider using the technique in child custody evaluations.[42] In addition, the expert might refer to professional credentials—an MHP license with an added credential such as *Registered Play Therapist*. Finally, the expert might call the court's attention to the professional organization Sandplay Therapists of America.[43] This organization publishes a professional journal, the *Journal of Sandplay Therapy*, and provides continuing education and five membership categories, four of which have training components.[44]

Despite these indices that might seem to weave a case for general acceptance of conclusions and opinions derived from use of the *Family as Animals in the Sand* technique, strong arguments may be marshaled against using a general acceptance assertion to support the technique. Those arguments would highlight the lack of research support for the technique and would emphasize the ipse dixit quality of expert testimony that relies on the technique—without the empirical evidence or a scientific–critical thinking rationale, the expert's opinion is reduced to dogmatic, unproven assertions.[45] While referencing Rule 702's requirement that expert testimony "assist the trier of fact to understand the evidence or to determine a fact in issue," Psychologist David Martindale notes the important distinction between perceived helpfulness and actual helpfulness.[46] Many procedures used by MHPs in their practices might be perceived as helpful by those MHPs and their patients. But expert testimony can only be helpful as evidence if it is reliable. More authoritatively, Justice Breyer in *Kumho Tire* noted that *Daubert*'s general acceptance factor does not "help show that an expert's testimony is reliable where the discipline itself lacks reliability, as, for example, do theories grounded in any so-called generally accepted principles of astrology or necromancy."[47]

Each of the four ways MHPs may hide the analytical gaps in their reasoning that were highlighted in this chapter compromise the quality and reliability of an expert's conclusions and opinions. Using a scientific-critical thinking mind-set, lawyers should prepare themselves to identify and challenge MHP experts who adopt these approaches in their testimony.

The analytical gap problems discussed in the next two chapters, the misapplication or misrepresentation of research and the adoption of confirmatory bias, are more difficult to identify and, arguably, have more pernicious effects in family law cases. In these instances, the lawyer's challenge to the MHP expert, "How do you know what you say you know?", is heightened. Let's explore these problems and address ways to handle them.

NOTES

1. S.I. Hayakawa & Alan R. Hayakawa, Language in Thought and Action 84–85 (5th ed. 1990) (S.I. Hayakawa noted that the "Abstraction Ladder" is based on the "Structural Differential," a diagram originated by Alfred Korzybski to explain the process of abstracting. S.I. Hayakawa—professor, college president, and U.S. Senator—died in 1992.).

2. *Id.*

3. *Id.* at 93.

4. *See id.* at 88.

5. *Id.*

6. *Id.* at 93.

7. *See* Kumho Tire Co., Ltd. v. Carmichael, 526 U.S. 137, 149 (1999) (the objective is for expert testimony to be reliable or trustworthy).

8. JOSEPH GOLDSTEIN, ANNA FREUD & ALBERT J. SOLNIT, BEYOND THE BEST INTERESTS OF THE CHILD 98 (1979) [hereinafter GFS BEYOND].

9. JOSEPH GOLDSTEIN, ANNA FREUD & ALBERT J. SOLNIT, BEFORE THE BEST INTERESTS OF THE CHILD 13 (1979) [hereinafter GFS BEFORE].

10. GFS BEYOND, *supra* note 8, at 99.

11. *Id.*

12. *Id.*

13. Marsha Garrison, *Child Welfare Decisionmaking,* 75 GEO. L.J. 1745, 1763 (1987).

14. Michael E. Lamb, *Placing Children's Interests First: Developmentally Appropriate Parenting Plans,* 10 VA. J. SOC. POL'Y & L. 98 (2002).

15. *See* Richard A. Warshak, *Blanket Restrictions: Overnight Contact Between Parents and Young Children,* 38 FAM. & CONCILIATION CTS. REV. 422, 423 (2000).

16. Joan B. Kelly & Michael E. Lamb, *Using Child Development Research to Make Appropriate Custody and Access Decisions for Young Children,* 38 FAM. & CONCILIATION CTS. REV. 297, 305 (2000).

17. *Id.;* Warshak, *supra* note 15, at 423.

18. *See* Michael E. Lamb, Kathleen J. Sternberg & Ross A. Thompson, *The Effects of Divorce and Custody Arrangements on Children's Behavior, Development, and Adjustment,* 35 FAM. & CONCILIATION CTS. REV. 393 (1997) (this document summarized the research at the time of publication and was written on behalf of eighteen prominent MHPs in the field).

19. Kelly & Lamb, *supra* note 16, at 305.

20. Warshak, *supra* note 15, at 435.

21. *Id.* at 436.

22. Kelly & Lamb, *supra* note 16, at 306; Warshak *supra* note 15, at 435.

23. Judith Solomon & Zeynep Biringen, *Another Look at the Developmental Research: Commentary on Kelly and Lamb's "Using Child Development Research to Make Appropriate Custody and Access Decisions for Young Children",* 39 FAM. & CONCILIATION CTS. REV. 355, 361 (2001).

24. Richard A. Warshak, *Who Will Be There When I Cry in the Night? Revisiting Overnights—A Rejoinder to Biringen et al.,* 40 FAM. & CONCILIATION CTS. REV. 208, 217 (2002).

25. Warshak, *supra* note 15, at 433.

26. NEW OXFORD AMERICAN DICTIONARY (2d ed. 2005); BLACK'S LAW DICTIONARY 833 (7th ed. 1999) (*Ipse dixit* is Latin for "he himself said it." It stands for the proposition that something is asserted but not proved.).

27. General Electric Co. v. Joiner, 522 U.S. 136, 146 (1997).

28. 826 F.2d 420, 421 (5th Cir. 1987).

29. FED. R. EVID. 702 advisory committee's notes.

30. Paul C. Giannelli, *The Admissibility of Novel Scientific Evidence: Frye v. United States, a Half Century Later,* 80 COLUM. L. REV. 1197, 1226 (1980).

31. People v. Leahy, 882 P.2d 321, 336 (Cal. 1994).

32. Anita Trubitt, *The Incorporation of Play Therapy Modalities in a Comprehensive Child Custody Evaluation,* 24 AFCC NEWS 6, 6 (Spring 2005).

33. *Id.*

34. *See* Anita Trubitt, *Anita Trubitt Description of Training Workshop,* http://www.anitatrubitt .com/TrainingDescription.html (last visited July 25, 2007).

35. *See* http://members.aol.com/sandplayetc/sandtrays.htm (last visited July 25, 2007).

36. Trubitt, *supra* note 32, at 6.

37. *Id.*

38. *Id.*

39. *See* Leonard Handler, *The Clinical Use of Drawings, in* MAJOR PSYCHOLOGICAL ASSESS- MENT INSTRUMENTS 206, 219 (C.S. Newmark ed., 1996); *see also* David A. Martindale, *Play Ther- apy Doesn't Play in Court,* 3 J. CHILD CUSTODY 77, 81 (2006) (critique of Trubitt's inclusion of "projective play therapy modalities" into child custody evaluations).

40. *Id.*

41. *See* ANITA TRUBITT, PLAY THERAPY GOES TO COURT: IMPLICATIONS AND APPLICATIONS IN CONTESTED CHILD CUSTODY (2d ed. 2004); Trubitt, *supra* note 32, at 6.

42. *See* Trubitt, *supra* note 34 (Trubitt conducts training for MHPs who might serve the court as a child custody evaluator. The training consists of: "(1) the specific play therapy modali- ties as powerful assessment tools that are used either by the custody evaluator or the therapist in high-impasse divorce or paternity court cases; (2) how to work in that system in ways that do not pose serious risk to the family or the therapist; and (3) ways of working collaboratively with other professionals (i.e., attorneys/custody evaluators) involved in family court cases.").

43. *See* Sandplay Therapists of America at http://www.sandplay.org (last visited July 25, 2007).

44. *Id.*

45. *See* Martindale, *supra* note 39, at 77.

46. *Id.* at 83.

47. *Kumho Tire Co.,* 526 U.S. at 151.

CHAPTER 7

Exposing Misapplied or Misrepresented Research: The Example of Domestic Violence

Experts who misapply or misrepresent research to support their reports and testimony present special challenges for lawyers, particularly when different literatures appear to support different sides of intense professional and social controversies. Nevertheless, lawyers who understand certain key elements of research studies will more easily expose the analytical gaps in the reasoning of such experts. One concern on which lawyers should focus is whether people studied in the research cited to support an opinion are similar to people to whom the expert applies the research findings. The less the comparison applies—for instance, generalizing solely from a study of unmarried college students to a couple going through a divorce—the greater the analytical gap in the expert's reasoning. Comparing apples to oranges does not support reliable testimony.

Domestic violence allegations in family courts reflect such issues and, thus, present unique emotional, conceptual, and legal challenges to lawyers trying to manage their cases effectively. Such allegations might be dramatic and compelling with supportive photographs and police reports, or they may devolve to "he said, she said" accusations with little, if any, corroboration. It is easy to see how these concerns may combine to muddy the case's legal analysis and management.

CONCEPTUAL CHALLENGES IN DOMESTIC VIOLENCE CASES

To address how experts in domestic violence cases use the professional literature to support their opinions, lawyers must first heed the field's conceptual differences.[1] Professionals—both MHPs and lawyers—differ in their approaches to domestic violence. For example, Dalton characterized the two main approaches as "colliding paradigms." She noted that partner abuse specialists, representing one paradigm, conceptually address domestic violence concerns differently than the majority of MHPs who work in the family court system.[2] Dalton said that where partner abuse specialists see abuse, other

131

MHPs tend to see conflict, and that while partner abuse specialists will always suspect that violence in a relationship indicates the presence of a power and control dynamic, MHPs more quickly associate violence with conflict between relatively evenly matched partners.[3] While calling for dialogue between these views, Dalton characterized the paradigm of partner abuse specialists as the "new paradigm" which the family court system should adopt.[4]

Straus also noted two camps: service providers-activists and academics-researchers.[5] He claimed that the first camp focused on domestic violence against women, while his work—represented by academics-researchers—sought to understand domestic violence regardless of the perpetrator's gender.[6] Straus acknowledged that while service providers must employ a broad definition of violence to meet the needs of women victimized by physical and emotional assaults—among other injuries—understanding partner assaults regardless of the gender of perpetrator or victim also was important.[7]

Although Dalton and Straus wished for greater dialogue between the two approaches, each realized their marked differences. And while Dalton hoped for an integrated acceptance of the "new paradigm" she advocated,[8] Straus doubted that would happen.[9] Yet, Straus emphasized that society benefits from the agendas and professional contributions of both sides.[10]

Unfortunately, some adherents to the different approaches in the domestic violence field have not carried out the debate in the civil manner of Dalton and Straus. The high stakes in family court that attend abuse and domestic violence allegations understandably roil emotions. As a result, these conflicting camps have traded harsh charges to the point of accusing each other of misrepresenting and distorting scientific findings to serve political agendas.[11]

To further complicate matters, proponents endorsing one or the other of the "colliding paradigms" in domestic violence cases often invoke different literatures or different interpretations of the same literature to support their positions, raising questions about how one should gauge the reliability of either body of literature. That is, when an MHP expert invokes one literature set to support an opinion while dismissing the other, *Frye-Daubert* concerns may be invoked. Unfortunately, oversimplification is responsible for many of the failures of family courts in domestic violence cases.[12] No one paradigm adequately addresses the diversity of the individuals and families who bring the overlapping issues of child custody and domestic violence into family court.[13]

DEFINITIONS AND LEGAL IMPLICATIONS

Difficulties with domestic violence allegations begin with definition. The field has not reached consensus about how to define domestic violence.[14] Definitions vary—based on the nature of the act, the physical or psychological impact on the victim, the intent of the perpetrator, mitigating situation influences, and community standards concerning appropriate conduct.[15] Narrowly focusing on only one or two of these factors—for instance, defining domestic violence as a physical assault that results in injuries requiring medical attention—results in clearer definitions at the expense of ignoring other important variables. Definitions that are too broad or inclusive—for example, any negatively interpreted physical contact in a relationship—sacrifice clarity, particularly when intent and community standards are considered.[16] While these varied definitions create problems in understanding the meanings and implications of results in the MHP literature, the concern is paralleled on the legal side: states define domestic violence differently, if at all, leading to a lack of clarity about how physical altercations in the family might be treated by courts.[17]

Nevertheless, domestic violence becomes an important legal concern in child custody disputes because virtually all states, by statute, require courts to consider domestic violence in child custody determinations. Statutes vary from making domestic violence one of several factors to consider in custody determinations to imposing presumptions against batterers or imposing special procedural considerations in cases involving domestic violence.[18] For example, in Utah, "any history of, or potential for, child abuse, spouse abuse, or kidnapping" is one of ten best interest factors for the court to consider when determining joint legal or physical custody of the child.[19] The more detailed Texas law states, "[I]n determining whether to appoint a party as a sole or joint managing conservator, the court shall consider evidence of the intentional use of abusive physical force by a party against the party's spouse . . . committed within a two-year period preceding the filing of the suit or during the pendency of the suit."[20] And "the court may not appoint joint managing conservators if credible evidence is presented of a history or pattern of past or present . . . physical or sexual abuse by one parent directed against the other parent. . . ."[21] To tie this provision to another child custody issue, Texas notes that in court-ordered joint custody, the court has the option to restrict the child's primary residence to a geographic area[22]—if no joint custody exists, the parent with primary custody may move with the child to a location far from the other parent. Clearly, domestic violence allegations raise the legal stakes and emotional temperature for several reasons and put courts on notice that the physical and emotional well-being of family members, beyond just the expected stress of a contested divorce, are being made issues in the case.

As a result, lawyers involved in these cases must be aware of spurious claims of proponents in the literature and experts on the stand who seek to promote their agendas rather than enlighten the court about the case at hand. "How do you know what you say you know?" will be the constant inquiry of discerning lawyers as they navigate this difficult area.

LOOKING AT THE LITERATURES

The two domestic violence approaches invoke different literatures to support their seeming contradictory views—much, though not all, of the literature from each camp might be deemed generally accepted. One camp's literature is primarily based on crime and police reports as well as on women who have sought services of women's shelters and other treatment programs to escape and address the serious violence they and their children have experienced. This literature concludes overwhelmingly that male violence is more a problem than female violence.[23] The other camp's literature focuses on research subjects from the community and family physical altercations found to exist in a number of intimate relationships—couples married, cohabiting, or dating. This literature concludes that women and men are equally violent in their relationships and that women may initiate physical altercations with men.[24] Given these stark differences, how should lawyers gauge the reliability of this literature, particularly when experts—retained or court-appointed—may offer contrasting testimony citing literature upheld by either camp that might be deemed generally accepted?

The problem of matching subjects in domestic violence research with family members in a particular case is a critical expert testimony concern. For instance, using findings based on crime cases or victims in women's shelters to characterize the usually more minor and different quality of violence among couples in the general population is unwarranted.[25] Likewise, research findings are misapplied when family conflict studies of the general population are used to characterize relationships in which one partner uses violence to control, intimidate, or injure the other partner.[26] Expert opinions based on these misapplications of the research represent unreliable testimony. To further understand these issues, let us take a closer look at some key domestic violence literature. Then we will illustrate how experts may misapply and misuse this literature.

The Different Faces of Domestic Violence

No standard psychological profile fits domestic violence perpetrators,[27] and no psychological or medical test can determine whether certain people are abusers. Many abusers do not fall under any formal diagnostic category for mental disorders.[28] In addition, empirical evidence demonstrates that not all domestic violence perpetrators are alike, and not all domestic violence is alike.[29] Yet, some writers have described "typical characteristics of batterers as parents."[30] Such general, unreliable lists do not accurately reflect the literature, and they overlook the complexity of relationships in families in which domestic violence occurs. In addition, the false positives concerns—some batterers may be described by some of those listed characteristics, but so may many other people who are not batterers—are glossed over when those lists are used. Lawyers should keep these findings in mind when experts support an opinion about whether domestic violence occurred by referencing the alleged perpetrator's psychological characteristics.

Domestic violence arises from multiple sources that may follow different patterns in different families.[31] Nevertheless, the literature reveals a convergence among researchers of classifications or typologies in domestic violence.[32] Such typologies improve our ability to understand family and relationship dynamics in domestic violence situations.[33] But as with symptom or behavior lists, typologies may be misapplied if characteristics of a particular type, by themselves, are used to prove that a person is a spouse abuser—such misapplications are not supported in the literature.

Michael Johnson's typology model provides a useful way to understand domestic violence issues and integrate the different literatures.[34] He reviewed the literature from large-sample survey research and shelter populations and noted three qualitatively different types of intimate partner violence: intimate terrorism; violent resistance; and common couple, or situational couple, violence.[35] Johnson distinguished the types by the nature of control inherent in each.

Intimate terrorism, Johnson's first type, "is defined by the attempt to dominate one's partner and to exert general control over the relationship," demonstrated by the use of power and control tactics, including violence.[36] Intimate terrorism generally is frequent and brutal; it is associated with the common understanding of domestic violence or spousal abuse. Male batterer typology research further divides this class into two profiles who engage in moderate to severe partner violence: violent-antisocial batterers who are more likely to also engage in violence outside the home, and batterers who are more psychologically distressed, emotionally insecure, and emotionally volatile and who generally confine their violence within the home.[37] Other researchers also note that for a small number of batterers, the violence arises from disordered thinking and serious distortions of reality that involve paranoid ideation.[38] Johnson's second type, *violent resistance*, is violence in response to intimate terrorism, although not specifically identified with self-defense.[39]

Situational couple violence, Johnson's third intimate partner violence type, is unlike intimate terrorism because there is no relationship-wide pattern of controlling behaviors in these altercations; situational couple violence is qualitatively different from intimate terrorism.[40] Situational couple violence characteristically occurs when a couple's specific conflicts escalate to physical altercations—matters understood primarily through family conflict theory.[41] In general, this violence type "is an intermittent response to the occasional conflicts of everyday life, motivated by a need to control in the specific situation, but not a more general need to be in charge of the relationship."[42] Johnson noted that situational couple violence is less severe than intimate terrorism, generally does not escalate, and is more likely to be mutually violent.[43] Nevertheless, Johnson also noted that violent acts in either intimate terrorism or situational couple violence may range from minor pushing and shoving to life-threatening behaviors, and from isolated to more frequent occurrences.[44]

As with the intimate terrorism type, a large body of domestic violence literature supports the validity of categorizing situational couple violence in this manner. Also, as noted earlier, this literature arises primarily from general population community samples, not from police crime reports or battered women's shelters where most of the samples that primarily inform intimate violence literature are based—a critical point for family lawyers involved in cases with domestic violence allegations. As Johnson implores, don't mix apples and oranges.[45] Don't let the other side do so either.

Researchers other than Johnson also have distinguished situational couple violence from the intimate terrorism that is more commonly understood as domestic violence.[46] Two issues stand out in the situational couple violence literature: the surprising prevalence of violence and physical altercations in relationships in the general population, and findings that men and women do not differ in the rates at which they initiate physical altercations in their relationships.

The notion of situational couple relationship violence is controversial. Predictably, proponents of the different approaches to domestic violence clash in family law courts and in everyday life over this notion; argued positions may take on a "gender-wars edge." In one community example, efforts in several cities to enforce spouse abuse laws enacted to protect women resulted in unexpected results: the numbers of women arrested for domestic assault significantly increased.[47] Some people puzzled over the increase, others felt that the law finally was catching up to the reality that men can be domestic violence victims, and still others suggested that police needed better training in using their discretion when responding to domestic violence calls.[48] One startling issue raised was whether, given the high arrest rate of women, the bar for arresting people for domestic violence was too low.[49] Each of these issues invokes significant concerns. And each of these issues represents perspectives in family law cases that could be flashpoints when domestic abuse allegations are raised.

The domestic violence literature from community samples shows consistent findings about situational couple violence. Rates for men and women are comparable,[50] the violence is usually minor, and outcomes generally do not result in injury—but note that injuries, occasionally serious ones, may occur during these altercations.[51] In addition, escalation of the violence in this group from emotional and verbal abuse to severe, physically violent abusive behavior is not inevitable;[52] that trend is more characteristic of intimate terrorism.[53] Most common situational couple altercations maintain only minor levels of violence—for instance, arguments that "get out of hand" and result in pushing or shoving. These couples may also desist from violence over time.[54] A growing consensus in the domestic violence field views situational couple violence as relationship-based with both partners contributing to the problems, while the more severe and frequent violence represented by intimate terrorism is increasingly viewed as caused by individual characteristics of the perpetrator.[55] An implication in child custody litigation is that experts who testify that a single act of violence is the "tip of an iceberg" and that, based on a single act of violence, the court can expect the parent to be violent in the future may stand on weak ground.

Unfortunately, situational couple violence is more prevalent in the general population than one might think. A large U.S. representative sample found that over a one-year period, approximately 12 percent of men and 12 percent of women committed violent acts—defined as "an act carried out with the intention or perceived intention of causing physical pain or injury"[56]—against each other in their marital or cohabiting relationships;[57] about 8 percent of the acts for both sexes were characterized as minor violence acts (that is, threw something, pushed/grabbed/shoved, or slapped).[58] A smaller Canadian study yielded similar results.[59]

Other findings independently confirmed the unexceptional nature of situational couple violence. For example, Jacobson and Gottman, in their well-known study of severe abusive relationships, decided to include a "low-level violent" group of couples to see if those couples might, over time, become more violent.[60] To their admitted surprise, the authors discovered that husbands in this group did not escalate to become "batterers." Rather, those couples comprised a stable group who periodically had arguments that escalated into pushing and shoving, but not beyond those behaviors.[61]

Further, research review indicates that the prevalence of partner aggression changes by age: physical aggression against a partner increases to a marked frequency—estimated as high as 35 to 40 percent—during adolescence through the midtwenties but then decreases steadily.[62] That is, in dating relationships and early in marriages, physical aggression—pushing, grabbing, slapping—is much more prevalent than in marriages of middle-aged partners.[63] Despite the decrease of these behaviors over time, if such physical aggression occurs in these relationships on different occasions, this problem relational pattern may become quite stable.[64]

Another variant of partner violence that occasionally inflames family law cases but may not rise to the level of "battering" is that which occurs around the marital separation or divorce. Minor incidents of violence—hitting, throwing objects—are common around the separation period; husbands and wives are almost equally likely to engage in these behaviors. Johnston and Campbell classified separation and post-divorce violence as a special type of interparental violence "that can and should be clearly distinguished from other forms of abuse."[65] This group was marked by uncharacteristic acts of violence that were precipitated by the separation or were reactions to stressful or traumatic post-divorce events. Often, the violence was perpetrated by the partner who felt abandoned. In these cases, violence had not occurred during the marriage.[66] Lawyers will want to ensure that experts considered evidence relevant to this important distinction.

While the prevalence of situational couple violence and other partner violence variants may be relatively high,[67] this does not mean that partners who engage in these behaviors and their children escape the negative consequences of such family interactions. This problem merits serious concern.[68] Apart from the moral wrong of assaults in relationships,[69] a pattern of repeated physical aggression is associated with serious marital discord.[70] Also, minor levels of aggression between spouses can result in injury and emotional damage, and such effects are greater when they result from men's physical aggression than from women's.[71] In addition, even minor assaults by women put women in danger of much more severe retaliation by men.[72] Finally, children exposed to physical altercations between their parents, whether minor or severe, are at risk for the development of emotional and behavioral problems.[73]

Despite these concerns, a surprising number of couples do not view the situational couple violence aspect of their relationship as a problem. Jacobson and Gottman noted that couples in their "low-level violent" group did not consider physical altercations as significant relationship problems.[74] One study found that more than a third of women who reported being victims of one or more physical assaults—defined broadly and inclusively—in their current or most recent relationship did not regard themselves as having experienced "physical abuse," as a "victim of violence," or as a "battered woman."[75] Results suggested that the relationship context influenced labeling of the assault: women experiencing more frequent and more severe assaults were more likely to apply labels; lower relationship commitment and having ended the relationship also were associated with increased self-labeling.[76] Other research revealed that over 60 percent of couples seeking marital therapy experienced physical violence in their relationships but less than 10 percent of those couples spontaneously reported or identified the violence as a presenting problem.[77] These couples—both men and women—did not report partner aggression as a presenting problem because the experiences, like slapping or hitting, were infrequent; were deemed mild rather than severe, and, therefore, not a problem; and were secondary to or caused by other marital problems.[78]

Although many of these couples do not view their physical altercations as problems during the marriage, those same altercations may become characterized differently—by spouses, their advocates, and their lawyers—during the divorce process. Johnston and Campbell noted that post-separation altercations, even if uncharacteristic of behaviors during the marriage, may cause the abandoned or aggrieved spouse to crystallize a new, "negative identity" of the other spouse and use that new identity to explain why the other spouse cannot be trusted or why the other spouse may present a possible danger to the children.[79] Such a recasting of the other spouse or of the past marital dynamics may lead to an impasse in the divorce negotiations—discussed in Chapter 2—that could complicate opportunities to resolve key divorce issues and significantly aggravate the emotional tenor of the divorce process.

The Issue of Female-Initiated Violence

The most long-standing and acrimonious debate in the domestic violence literature has involved the issue of whether women initiate violence in their relationships at the same rate as men.[80] In the mid-1980s, it was deemed politically incorrect for researchers to consider studying female aggression.[81] Even more recently, presenting data on gender differences in aggression was characterized as "socially sensitive,"[82] and many advocates for battered women still fear the possible negative repercussions of research on female aggression.[83] Their concern is that such research may be misused or misrepresented, and that, as a result, abused women will suffer further from resulting unfavorable laws or unfair court decisions.

As noted earlier, a significant body of research clearly indicates that men and women engage at about an equal frequency in physically aggressive acts in their intimate relationships, particularly in community research samples that more likely tap situational couple violence, not the crime studies or shelter surveys whose samples reflect intimate terrorism experiences.[84] And, counter to the rationales of some that women's physical aggression is primarily self-defensive, some research indicates that when asked, more women than men report initiating an attack[85]—among the reasons were to engage their partner's attention, particularly emotionally.[86] Other research noted that women were more likely to express aggression physically in their partner relationships,[87] significantly more when they were in their twenties than when they were over thirty years old[88]— recall research noted earlier regarding the high frequency of physical aggression in partner relationships of adolescence through the twenties.

Although the community sample research shows a general equivalence in the frequency of male and female physically aggressive acts in their relationships, another key finding is evident: women are more likely than men to be physically injured and to suffer psychological consequences of partner aggression.[89] Research indicating that many men and women are involved in relationships with low-level, often mutual, violence does not negate the problem of severe relationship violence in which men are likely the primary perpetrators and women the primary victims.[90] And women are more vulnerable to physical, financial, and emotional injuries, especially if situational couple violence incidents escalate unexpectedly.[91] Nevertheless, research also indicates that a substantial minority of men are injured when injuries are sustained in physical altercations.[92]

The implications of this research? Experts should attend to all physical violence allegations in child custody cases—from women and from men—and to the nature and sources of those allegations.

Looking Inside the Literature

After focusing on what body of literature experts use to support their opinions in a particular domestic violence case, understanding how experts use the literature they invoke is the lawyer's next task—at times, no small feat. Research from reputable journals and books and, particularly, statistics appearing to support that research may seem authoritative when pronounced confidently from the stand. But while good research may support reliable testimony, mischaracterized research will expose experts' biases and highlight analytical gaps in their reasoning.

The authors of a chapter titled *Child Witnesses of Domestic Violence*[93] illustrate how experts' biases may be reflected in the interpretation and reporting of research. For example, at the outset of their piece, the authors make a point of replacing the term *marital violence* with *wife assault*[94] (emphases in original), justifying this by reference to *police and court reports* (emphasis added) indicating that 95 percent of instances of marital violence involve women as victims and men as perpetrators.[95] But the authors do not distinguish wife assault from situational couple violence even though community survey research, as opposed to police and court reports, indicates that situational couple violence is the more prevalent type of physical altercations in marriages and that men and women perpetrate these altercations at about equal frequencies.

The authors then underline their approach to domestic violence in their assertion about a significant research study. After noting "the pressing social and legal problem of family violence and wife assault," they write that "Straus and Gelles (1986), in a well-conducted, large-scale survey, found that severe husband-to-wife violence occurred in 11.3 percent of American homes."[96] However, the study found that the *overall* rate of violence from husband to wife was 11.3 percent, not the rate of severe violence;[97] overall violence in the study included "minor violence acts" more associated with Johnson's situational couples violence category. "Severe" husband-to-wife violence occurred in 3 percent of the couples surveyed.[98]

In addition to misstating Straus and Gelles's study results, the authors omit reporting that Straus and Gelles also found that the overall rate of wife-to-husband violence was 12.1 percent,[99] essentially equal to husband-to-wife rates, and that "severe" wife-to-husband violence occurred in 4.4 percent of couples surveyed.[100] These findings counter the authors' earlier stated premise that men perpetrate physical altercations in marriages the vast majority of the time.[101]

Finally, this example highlights a problem with the domestic violence literature in that professionals from different perspectives too readily dismiss data that do not support their position.[102] The research shows different kinds of domestic violence by both men and women. Johnson, as a result, emphasizes that it is scientifically unacceptable to make assertions about domestic violence without specifying the type of violence to which one is referring.[103]

In a recent writing, one of the authors of the above-cited chapter has acknowledged "common couple aggression" as distinct from other spousal violence types. In addition, he has presented useful considerations for child custody arrangements that depend on the spousal violence type and the nature of the spousal relationship. He notes that given the wide range of family violence, "understanding the context and pattern of the violence is more informative than merely focusing on the most serious or most recent incident of aggression."[104] Lawyers should take heed that MHP experts reflect this understanding of the domestic violence literature in their conclusions and opinions.

EXPOSING THE GAPS IN DOMESTIC VIOLENCE TESTIMONY

Because MHP experts may cite one camp's domestic violence literature to support their position, lawyers may encounter difficulties when they try to expose analytical gaps in experts' testimony when experts tie their data to their conclusions and opinions. But the lawyers' general approach still applies: use the "How do you know what you say you know?" lever to make experts "show their work"; don't accept their conclusions unchallenged. In addition, use the scientific–critical thinking mind-set that judges essentially are charged to employ when they consider the reliability and admissibility of expert testimony.

Three questions that will help lawyers meet this task:

- Is the expert familiar with the domestic violence literature?
- Does the expert acknowledge that the domestic violence literature reflects different types of violence that may have different causes?
- What methods does the expert use to generate data that inform the evaluation conclusions and expert opinions?

Is the Expert Familiar with the Domestic Violence Literature?

To start, MHPs should be familiar with the domestic violence literature and how various professionals—psychologists, counselors, social workers, and lawyers—in the field use the literature to support their positions. They should be able to describe and contrast the approaches to domestic violence. As emphasized in this chapter, this requirement is essential because some professionals who identify themselves with one or the other approach in the domestic violence field base their positions on specific literature while they at times dismiss data that do not support their positions.[105] Those professionals, then, may inappropriately generalize research results to people not represented in the samples on which the research findings are based. Disregard of or selective attention to the domestic violence literature should beg the question about whether the MHP expert is biased. Biased testimony is unreliable testimony.

Does the Expert Acknowledge That the Domestic Violence Literature Reflects Different Types of Violence That May Have Different Causes?

This issue is key in child custody evaluations in which partner violence is alleged by one or both partners. As noted earlier, the prevalence of situational couple violence in young marriages is high.[106] But intimate terrorism violence also occurs in all-age marriages, albeit at a lower rate than situational couple violence.[107] Partner violence allegations in child custody disputes may cause one spouse to minimize or deny intimate terrorism violence or may cause another spouse to exaggerate situational couple violence. Or, one or the other spouse may be realistically describing the nature of the partner violence in their relationship. If the expert is unable to acknowledge different types of partner violence, either the expert may be unfamiliar with the domestic violence literature, or the expert may be revealing an allegiance for one or the other domestic violence camps and may be misapplying research or disregarding important findings that could be useful to the court.

What Methods Does the Expert Use to Generate Data That Inform the Evaluation Conclusions and Expert Opinions?

Conducting an evaluation using reliable, accepted methods that will produce reliable data on which to base expert opinions is a challenge when addressing domestic violence concerns. The expert evaluator's task is to unravel the past scenarios of aggression and violence and to assess implications for the children as the family structure changes as a result of the divorce.[108] Many instruments and inventories purport to measure issues related to partner violence,[109] but most are not psychometrically strong. This leads to reliability and validity questions and concerns about examinees' attempts to misrepresent themselves through their responses to inventory questions. Also, several partner violence–oriented structured interviews have been developed to help researchers and clinicians obtain information about dimensions of partner violence.[110] But researchers note that the field's heavy reliance on research participants' self-reports in interviews and inventories presents problems.[111] The primary reliance on client self-reports about alleged abuse absent corroborating evidence is also an evaluation concern that may compromise the legal reliability of the expert opinions that flow from these procedures—recall that no standard psychological profile fits domestic violence perpetrators,[112] and no psychological tests can identify whether abuse has occurred. Thus, experts who testify that a litigant fits a battering spouse profile will be unable to provide a reliable scientific basis for this opinion.

Given these apparent limitations, how, then, should MHPs investigate partner violence allegations? In sum, the most important methodology for approaching domestic violence cases is likely to be a thorough and informed evaluation.[113] Lawyers should expect MHPs to address these concerns from a scientific–critical thinking mind-set, appropriately weighing data and considering plausible alternative explanations of the allegations raised. Certainly, inventories and structured interviews—properly employed and appropriately considered as data—may provide useful information. But MHP evaluators should also draw on additional information to determine the type of violence that occurred in the relationship, the context of that violence, and the likelihood of the violence recurring. Austin notes six sources of information to consider:[114]

- Objective verification from records (medical and police)
- Pattern of abuse complaints—did allegations surface only in the context of a child custody case?
- Corroboration by credible others
- Absence of disconfirming verbal reports by credible third parties
- Psychological profile and history of abusive behavior by the alleged perpetrator of marital violence
- Psychological status of the alleged victimized partner

Even using these guidelines, experts may be unable to offer reliable opinions about the quality or extent of domestic violence allegations in a particular case. In such an event, the expert, guided by a scientific–critical thinking mind-set, will not hesitate to say "I don't know" when asked for an opinion and will express a need for further reliable data with which to inform an opinion.

Domestic violence presents serious challenges to courts, lawyers, MHPs, and, most of all, the families in which it occurs. The complexity of these issues—not all of which were discussed in this chapter—and the attendant sharp emotions highlight the importance of reliable expert testimony.

In this chapter, domestic violence was used to illustrate how MHPs might try to hide the analytical gaps in their opinions by misapplying and misrepresenting social science research to support their opinions. Lawyers should ensure that experts appropriately apply and represent the research on which they rely. *Frye-Daubert* concerns should be invoked when lawyers expose experts who fall short of this obligation. Again, an approach that demands of experts "How do you know what you say you know?" will provide lawyers the lever to evaluate effectively the quality of MHPs' materials and expert testimony.

NOTES

1. *See* Amy Holtzworth-Munroe, *Male Versus Female Intimate Partner Violence: Putting Controversial Findings into Context,* J. Marriage & Fam. 1120, 1120 (2005).

2. *See* Clare Dalton, *When Paradigms Collide: Protecting Battered Parents and Their Children in the Family Court System,* 37 Fam. & Conciliation Cts. Rev. 275 (1999).

3. *Id.*

4. *Id.* at 290.

5. Murray A. Straus, *The Controversy over Domestic Violence by Women: A Methodological, Theoretical, and Sociology of Science Analysis, in* Violence in Intimate Relationships 17, 37 (X.B. Arriaga & S. Oskamp eds., 1999).

6. *Id.*

7. *Id.* at 38.

8. Dalton, *supra* note 2, at 290.

9. Straus, *supra* note 5, at 40.

10. *Id.*

11. Holtzworth-Munroe, *supra* note 1, at 1124.

12. Leslie Ellen Shear, *Child Custody and Domestic Violence: The Tangled Roles of Inquiry and Advocacy in Improving the Family Justice System's Response to Complex Challenges,* 1(3) J. Child Custody 107, 108 (2004).

13. *Id.* at 112.

14. Robert E. Emery, *Family Violence,* 44 Am. Psychol. 321, 321 (1989).

15. *Id.*

16. *Id.*

17. *See* Annette M. Gonzalez & Linda M. Rio Reichmann, *Representing Children in Civil Cases Involving Domestic Violence,* 39 Fam. L.Q. 197, 213 (2005).

18. Chart 2—Custody Criteria, 39 Fam. L.Q. 917 (2006).

19. Utah Code Ann. § 30-3-10.2 (2)(i) (2005).

20. Tex. Fam. Code Ann. § 153.004 (a).

21. Tex. Fam. Code Ann. § 153.004 (b) (Texas statutes use the term "conservatorship" to refer to custody).

22. Tex. Fam. Code Ann. § 153.134 (b)(1)(A).

23. *See* John Archer, *Sex Differences in Aggression Between Heterosexual Partners: A Meta-Analytic Review,* 126 Psychol. Bull. 651, 651 (2000); *see also* Holtzworth-Munroe, *supra* note 1, at 1120.

24. *Id.*

25. Straus, *supra* note 5, at 29.

26. *Id.*

27. *See* Amy Holtzworth-Munroe & Gregory L. Stuart, *Typologies of Male Batterers: Three Subtypes and the Differences Among Them,* 116 Psychol. Bull. 476, 494 (1994); *see also* Daniel G. Saunders, *Woman Battering, in* Assessment of Family Violence 243, 244 (Robert T. Ammerman & Michel Hersen eds., 1999).

28. *See* L. Kevin Hamberger, Jeffrey M. Lohr, Dennis Bonge & David F. Tolin, *A Large Sample Empirical Typology of Male Spouse Abusers and Its Relationship to Dimensions of Abuse,* 11 Violence & Victims 277 (1996).

29. *See* Holtzworth-Munroe & Stuart, *supra* note 27, at 494; Amy Holtzworth-Munroe, Jeffrey C. Meehan, Katherine Herron, Uzma Rehman & Gregory L. Stuart, *Testing the Holtzworth-Munroe and Stuart (1994) Batterer Typology,* 68 J. Consulting & Clinical Psychol. 1000, 1000 (2000).

30. Allen M. Bailey, *A Review of* The Batterer as Parent *by Lundy Bancroft & Jay G. Silverman,* 39 Fam. L.Q. 221, 226 (2005) (citing Lundy Bancroft & Jay G. Silverman, The Batterer as Parent: Addressing the Impact of Domestic Violence on Family Dynamics (2002)).

31. Janet R. Johnston & Linda E.G. Campbell, *A Clinical Typology of Interparental Violence in Disputed-Custody Divorces,* 63 Amer. J. Orthopsychiatry 190, 191 (1993).

32. Mary M. Cavanaugh & Richard J. Gelles, *The Utility of Male Domestic Violence Offender Typologies,* 20 J. Interpersonal Violence 155, 158 (2005).

33. Holtzworth-Munroe et al., *supra* note 29, at 1000.

34. *See* Michael P. Johnson, *Apples and Oranges in Child Custody Disputes: Intimate Terrorism vs. Situational Couple Violence,* 2(4) J. Child Custody 43 (2005).

35. *Id.* at 45; *see* Michael P. Johnson, *Patriarchal Terrorism and Common Couple Violence: Two Forms of Violence Against Women,* 57 J. Marriage & Fam. 283, 284 (1995).

36. Michael P. Johnson & Janel M. Leone, *The Differential Effects of Intimate Terrorism and Situational Couple Violence,* 26 J. Fam. Issues 322, 323 (2005).

37. *See generally* Hamberger et al., *supra* note 28 (two of three clusters noted in their research are the antisocial and passive aggressive–dependent batterers); Holtzworth-Munroe & Stuart, *supra* note 27, at 482 (two of three clusters noted in their research are the generally violent–antisocial and dysphoric-borderline batterers); Neil Jacobson & John Gottman, When Men Batter Women: New Insights into Ending Abusive Relationships 28–29 (two clusters are "cobras," who are severely violent and "systematically cold," and "pit bulls," whose violence arises from their emotional dependency, their emotional insecurity, and their fear of feeling abandoned).

38. *See* Johnston & Campbell, *supra* note 31, at 197.

39. Johnson, *supra* note 34, at 45.

40. Johnson & Leone, *supra* note 36, at 325 (in Johnson's 1995 article, Johnson refers to this category as "common couple violence." More recently, he has relabeled this category as "situational couple violence." The latter term will be used in this chapter.).

41. *Id.* at 324.

42. Johnson, *supra* note 35, at 286 (citing R.M. Milardo & R. Klein, *Dominance Norms and Domestic Violence: The Justification of Aggression in Close Relationships.* (1992) (Paper presented at the Pre-Conference Theory Construction and Research Methodology Workshop, National Council on Family Relations annual meeting, Orlando, FL)).

43. Johnson & Leone, *supra* note 36, at 325.

44. *Id.* at 324.

45. Johnson, *supra* note 34, at 43.

46. *See* Straus, *supra* note 5, at 19.

47. Carey Goldberg, *Spouse Abuse Crackdown, Surprisingly, Nets Many Women,* N.Y. Times, Nov. 23, 1999, at A16.

48. *Id.*

49. *Id.*

50. *See* Archer, *supra* note 23, at 664.

51. Jacobson & Gottman, *supra* note 37, at 227; *see also* Johnson, *supra* note 35, at 285.

52. Richard J. Gelles, *The Politics of Research: The Use, Abuse, and Misuse of Social Science Data—The Cases of Intimate Partner Violence,* 45 Fam. Ct. Rev. 42, 46 (2007).

53. Johnson, *supra* note 35, at 286; *see* Holtzworth-Munroe, *supra* note 1, at 1121.

54. Holtzworth-Munroe, *supra* note 1, at 1121; *see also* JACOBSON & GOTTMAN, *supra* note 37, at 25.

55. Holtzworth-Munroe, *supra* note 1, at 1123.

56. Murray A. Straus & Richard J. Gelles, *Society Change and Change in Family Violence from 1975 to 1985 as Revealed by Two National Surveys,* 48 J. MARRIAGE & FAM. 465, 470 (1986).

57. *Id.*

58. *Id.* at 470–71.

59. *See* Marilyn Kwong, Kim Bartholomew & Donald G. Dutton, *Gender Differences in Patterns of Relationship Violence in Alberta,* 31 CANADIAN J. BEH. SCI. 150, 156 (1999).

60. JACOBSON & GOTTMAN, *supra* note 37, at 25.

61. *Id.*

62. K. Daniel O'Leary, *Developmental and Affective Issues in Assessing and Treating Partner Aggression,* 6 CLINICAL PSYCHOL.: SCI. & PRAC. 400, 400–402 (1999) (because there are no longitudinal studies that contain data from broad age spans, O'Leary relies on data from various cross-sectional studies to estimate developmental trends).

63. *Id.* at 402.

64. *Id.* at 400.

65. Johnston & Campbell, *supra* note 31, at 196; Janet R. Johnston, *Response to Clare Dalton's "When Paradigms Collide: Protecting Battered Parents and Their Children in the Family Court System,"* 37 FAM. & CONCILIATION CTS. REV. 422, 425 (1999).

66. Johnston & Campbell, *supra* note 31, at 196.

67. K. Daniel O'Leary, Julian Barling, Ileana Arias & Alan Rosenbaum, *Prevalence and Stability of Physical Aggression Between Spouses: A Longitudinal Analysis,* 57 J. CLINICAL & CONSULTING PSYCHOL. 263, 267 (1989).

68. *Id.*

69. Straus, *supra* note 5, at 21.

70. O'Leary, *supra* note 62, at 403; *see also* O'Leary et al., *supra* note 67, at 267.

71. *See* Michelle Cascardi, Jennifer Langhinrichsen & Dina Vivian, *Marital Aggression: Impact, Injury, and Health Correlates for Husbands and Wives,* 152 ARCHIVES INTERNAL MED. 1178 (1992).

72. Straus, *supra* note 5, at 21.

73. *See, e.g.,* E. Mark Cummings, *Children Exposed to Marital Conflict and Violence: Conceptual and Theoretical Directions, in* CHILDREN EXPOSED TO MARITAL VIOLENCE 55, 56 (George W. Holden et al. eds., 1998); E. Mark Cummings et al., *Marital Aggression and Children's Responses to Everyday Interparental Conflict,* 12 EUR. PSYCHOL. 17 (2007); Kathleen Sternberg et al., *Effects of Domestic Violence on Children's Behavior Problems and Depression,* 29 DEV. PSYCHOL. 44 (1993).

74. JACOBSON & GOTTMAN, *supra* note 37, at 25.

75. *See* Hemby & Gray-Little, *Labeling Partner Violence: When Do Victims Differentiate Among Acts?,* 15 VICTIMS & VIOLENCE 173 (2000).

76. *Id.*

77. Miriam K. Ehrensaft & Dina Vivian, *Spouses' Reasons for Not Reporting Existing Marital Aggression as a Marital Problem,* 10 J. FAM. PSYCHOL. 443, 450 (1996).

78. *Id.*

79. Johnston & Campbell, *supra* note 31, at 197.

80. *See* Amy Holtzworth-Munroe, *Female Perpetration of Physical Aggression Against an Intimate Partner: A Controversial New Topic of Study,* 20 VIOLENCE & VICTIMS 251, 252 (2005).

81. *Id.* at 251.

82. K. Daniel O'Leary, *Are Women Really More Aggressive Than Men in Intimate Relationships? Comment on Archer (2000),* 126 PSYCHOL. BULL. 685, 685 (2000).

83. Holtzworth-Munroe, *supra* note 80, at 257.

84. Archer, *supra* note 23, at 664.

85. *Id.; see also* Kwong et al., *supra* note 59, at 158 (in a Canadian sample, both genders reported that women initiate violence and are sometimes the sole perpetrators of aggression in relationships).

86. *See* Martin S. Fiebert & Denise M. Gonzalez, *College Women Who Initiate Assaults on Their Male Partners and the Reasons Offered for Such Behavior,* 80 PSYCHOL. REP. 583 (1997).

87. *See* Archer, *supra* note 23, at 664.

88. *See* Fiebert & Gonzalez, *supra* note 86, at 583.

89. Holtzworth-Munroe, *supra* note 80, at 253; *see also* Michael P. Johnson, *Domestic Violence: It's Not About Gender—Or Is It?,* J. MARRIAGE & FAM. 1126, 1129 (2005); Straus, *supra* note 5, at 22.

90. Kwong et al., *supra* note 59, at 159.

91. Murray A. Straus, *Physical Assaults by Women Partners: A Major Social Problem, in* WOMEN, MEN, AND GENDER: ONGOING DEBATES 210, 219 (M.R. Walsh ed., 1997).

92. Archer, *supra* note 23, at 665.

93. Marlies Sudermann & Peter G. Jaffe, *Child Witnesses of Domestic Violence, in* ASSESSMENT OF FAMILY VIOLENCE 343 (Robert T. Ammerman & Michel Hersen eds., 2d ed. 1999).

94. *Id.* at 343.

95. *Id.* (citing DONALD G. DUTTON, THE DOMESTIC ASSAULT OF WOMEN (1988); *but see* Donald G. Dutton, *Domestic Abuse Assessment in Child Custody Disputes: Beware the Domestic Violence Research Paradigm,* 2(4) J. CHILD CUSTODY 23, 32 (2005) (Dutton now disputes the validity of this statistic).

96 *Id.* at 344.

97. Straus & Gelles, *supra* note 56, at 470.

98. *Id.*

99. *Id.*

100. *Id.*

101. Sudermann & Jaffe, *supra* note 93, at 343.

102. Johnson, *supra* note 34, at 48.

103. Johnson, *supra* note 89, at 1126.

104. Peter G. Jaffe, Claire V. Crooks & Nick Bala, *Making Appropriate Parenting Arrangements in Family Violence Cases: Applying the Literature to Identify Promising Practices* 40. Report to the Department of Justice, Canada (2006).

105. Johnson, *supra* note 34, at 48.

106. O'Leary, *supra* note 62, at 400.

107. *See* Straus & Gelles, *supra* note 56, at 470.

108. William G. Austin, *Partner Violence and Risk Assessment in Child Custody Evaluations,* 39 FAM. CT. REV. 483, 491 (2001).

109. *See* JILL H. RATHUS & EVA L. FEINDLER, ASSESSMENT OF PARTNER VIOLENCE (2004).

110. *Id.*

111. Holtzworth-Munroe, *supra* note 80, at 257.

112. Holtzworth-Munroe & Stuart, *supra* note 27, at 494; Saunders, *supra* note 27, at 244.

113. Diane R. Follingstad, *Battered Woman Syndrome in the Courts, in* 11 HANDBOOK OF PSYCHOLOGY, FORENSIC PSYCHOLOGY 484, 501 (Alan M. Goldstein ed., 2003).

114. Austin, *supra* note 108, at 492.

CHAPTER 8

Exposing Confirmatory Bias: The Example of Sexual Abuse Allegations

Cognitive biases may infect many professions—stockbrokers, physicians, even football coaches—in which judgments affect outcomes. As noted earlier, social science judgments are not immune from such effects. Usually, biases are applied unintentionally, leading to systemic judgment errors and inaccurate results.[1] But sometimes, people apply their biases purposely when they distort research findings or conventional wisdom to advocate their positions.[2] Regardless, biases hinder critical thinking because they keep people from considering relevant information required for informed judgments.[3]

Confirmatory bias harms expert testimony because it compromises, sometimes dramatically, the quality and reliability of that testimony. Confirmatory bias orients experts to seek certain data or evidence that supports favored positions and to discount or ignore evidence inconsistent with those favored positions. As a result, confirmatory bias funnels experts' considerations and interpretations of data toward unexamined values or already preconceived opinions.

Expert MHPs are particularly vulnerable to confirmatory bias in cases involving sexual abuse allegations. Lawyers also face unique challenges when they attempt to find that bias and expose the resulting analytical gaps in experts' empirical and reasoning threads. The stakes are high. While emotional, access, or property issues may complicate child custody disputes, sexual abuse allegations may be the most inflammatory and difficult issue for lawyers to manage. Parents'—and lawyers'—emotional reactions to the allegations may quickly overwhelm the careful, rational search for facts. Impasses, discussed in Chapter 2, that prevent a case's resolution will harden further. And supporters of those impasses—therapists, stepparents, and even lawyers—may steel the parents' resistances to information that might offer different views on the allegations. The consequences for each family member are significant. If the allegations are proven true, the child's emotional development may be impaired; if false, the child's well-being and trust in close relationships may still be compromised. For parents, any motivation they might have to resolve their custody dispute and co-parent their child constructively may be destroyed—whether the allegations are true or false.

Often, courts will appoint an MHP to conduct an evaluation for neutral, professional feedback about the sexual abuse allegations. While the product of a competent evaluation may still not tamp down the parents' enmity toward each other, the consequences of a poor evaluation may aggravate the emotional damage to the child and to the child's relationships with his or her parents and, thus, spin the case out of control.[4]

Given the serious, emotional nature of sexual abuse allegations, family lawyers must manage their clients sensitively and attempt to understand the issues and materials that comprise sexual abuse investigations. But, like other evidence in court, the building blocks of opinions involving sexual abuse claims must "have a reliable basis in the knowledge and experience of the discipline" from which the evidence is proffered.[5] And the expert, while offering the opinion, must "employ in the courtroom the same level of intellectual rigor that characterizes the practice of an expert in the relevant field"—the applicable professional standards test.[6] Finally, the analytical gap test: The greater the gaps between the expert's data and conclusions, the less legally reliable or trustworthy those conclusions will be.[7] Our four-step *Frye-Daubert* Analysis Model from Chapter 3 should guide you through these issues.

In this chapter, lawyers will understand how confirmatory bias may affect the investigation of sexual abuse allegations in child custody cases. First, we will look at the broad range of sexual abuse behaviors and highlight the professional literature that addresses whether certain behaviors or psychological symptoms reliably distinguish children who have been sexually abused from those who have not. Then, we will explore key principles when considering sexual abuse allegations. Last, we will examine forensic interview techniques that heighten the probability of accurate responses from young children as well as techniques that are more likely to elicit inaccurate responses. Understanding this chapter's material will help lawyers expose the analytical thinking gaps in experts'— their own and their opponents'—reasoning that may be created by confirmatory bias in these difficult cases. In this task, lawyers should keep in mind the question to MHPs that is this book's theme—"How do you know what you say you know?"—to navigate this emotional and contentious subject.

BEHAVIORS AND SYMPTOMS: PROBLEMS IN SEXUAL ABUSE VALIDATION

Definitions

Assessing child sexual abuse and gauging its effects on abused children must account for several factors. First, the mental health literature has not settled on a specific definition of *child sexual abuse*—each word in the term has been defined differently by researchers and clinicians.[8] Legal concepts of child sexual abuse, while more defined, include a broad range of behaviors—including exhibitionism, kissing, fondling, digital penetration, intercourse, oral or anal sex, and insertion of objects into the sex organs.[9] Further, any number of persons—family members, familiar adults, or strangers—may perpetrate these acts. Also, children may be victimized once or over short or long periods of time—frequently or irregularly.[10]

In addition, sexually abused children and adolescents vary greatly in their emotional and behavioral reactions to the abuse. There is no single profile of a sexually abused child at a particular age,[11] and the variability of children's reactions to abuse increases even more with development. A four-year-old abused child may react and look clinically differently than a fourteen-year-old abused adolescent.[12] Or, neither may show any discernable effect.[13]

Nevertheless, some MHPs have presumed to identify child sexual abuse victims with checklists comprised of symptoms or "behavioral indicators" purporting to distinguish behaviors of children who have been abused.[14] But research has consistently found that no single symptom or symptom pattern identifies the majority of sexually abused children.[15] An often-cited extensive literature review noted that sexually abused children manifested more symptoms than non-sexually abused children, but the number of symptoms is broad and symptoms do not fall into a clear pattern. In addition, approximately one-third of sexually abused children showed no apparent adverse symptoms.[16] And although sexualized behavior may be the most common symptom manifested by sexually abused children, as many as half of these children did not show such behaviors—note also that non-sexually abused children may manifest sexualized behaviors.[17]

Likewise, while sexually abused children may manifest PTSD-type symptoms—such as fears, nightmares, somatic complaints, and autonomic arousal—it often is unclear if those PTSD-type symptoms are abuse-related or could have arisen from other causes. For example, many children from four to seven years old in the general population argue a lot, experience fears and worries, show mood changes, become excessively dependent, cry a lot, and have difficulties concentrating.[18] And children in psychological treatment show higher percentages of these symptoms than children not in treatment.[19]

Finally, the reviewed literature indicated that "molestations that included a close (in relation) perpetrator; a high frequency of sexual contact; a long duration; the use of force; and sexual acts that included oral, anal, or vaginal penetration lead to a greater number of symptoms for victims."[20] Consequently, different variables in children's abuse experiences and children's coping styles may lead to different symptoms, if any.[21]

What About Sexualized Behaviors?

As noted earlier, a critical issue when evaluating child sexual abuse allegations is that children may manifest sexualized behaviors for reasons other than reflecting sexual abuse experiences. For example, psychologist William Friedrich detailed in an extensive study[22] that children who reportedly had no sexual abuse history exhibited a broad range of sexualized behaviors.[23] Because sexual behavior in children varied by age, analyses were conducted for three age groups: two- to five-year-olds; six- to nine-year-olds; and ten- to twelve-year-olds. Friedrich asked mothers to rate their children's behaviors over the previous six months from a questionnaire that included the Child Sexual Behavior Inventory, a parental report measure he developed[24]—Friedrich noted that he used mothers to rate the children's behaviors because mothers tend to underreport child behaviors less than fathers.[25] Friedrich's results showed that the overall frequency of sexualized behaviors peaked at five years old for both boys and girls and then dropped off over the next seven years[26]—interestingly, this is the preschool to early-elementary school developmental period when sexual abuse allegations seem to be most hotly contested and with which much of the research on children's suggestibility and interviewing techniques has dealt.

The items most frequently endorsed by mothers in the study of their two- to five-year-old boys were: stands too close to people (29.3 percent); touches sex (private) parts when in public places (26.5 percent); touches or tries to touch their mother's or other women's breasts (42.4 percent); touches sex (private) parts when at home (60.2 percent); and tries to look at people when they are nude or undressing (26.8 percent).[27] Of six- to nine-year-old boys, mothers noted that 39.8 percent touch their sex (private) parts when at home, and 20.2 percent try to look at people when they are nude or undressing.[28]

The items most frequently endorsed by mothers in the study of their two- to five-year-old girls were: stands too close to people (25.8 percent); touches or tries to touch their mother's or other women's breasts (43.7 percent); touches sex (private) parts when at home (43.8 percent); and tries to look at people when they are nude or undressing (26.9 percent).[29] Of six- to nine-year-old girls, 20.7 percent touch their sex (private) parts when at home, and 20.5 percent try to look at people when they are nude or undressing.[30]

Besides reporting tallies of mothers' ratings of children's behaviors, Friedrich emphasized that children's sexual behaviors, as well as other children's behaviors, must be interpreted in light of individual and family variables[31]—he agreed with the observation that his findings underestimated the true frequency of childhood sexual behavior in a normative population.[32] For example, he noted that mothers will vary in their willingness to endorse sexual behavior in their children. That is, more highly educated mothers and mothers who reported their beliefs that sexual feelings and behaviors in children were normal reported more sexual behaviors in their children—an observation noted in previous literature.[33] And, of course, as children grow older, they begin to hide their knowledge about sexual matters from adults.[34]

As might be expected, young children also manifest sexualized behaviors outside the home. Among staff observations in preschool settings, children's curiosity about genitalia looking and limited touching were more commonly observed, and drawing or modeling of genitalia and simulating sexual intercourse were also reported.[35] And a study examining children referred and evaluated for sexual abuse at a forensic child abuse evaluation clinic found no significant relationship between a sexual abuse determination and the presence or absence of sexual behavior problems.[36]

Besides the commonality of some sexualized behaviors among young children—in psychological treatment and not in treatment—who have not been sexually abused, children also may manifest such behaviors for reasons other than sexual abuse. For example, life stress as well as physical abuse and domestic violence may unsettle some children to the point that they exhibit acting-out problems and difficulties inhibiting their behaviors—including sexual-type behaviors.[37]

In addition, family boundary violations may contribute to problem sexual-type behaviors in young children.[38] Dr. Toni C. Johnson notes several boundary problems that may contribute to problem sexual behaviors in children.[39] Among those are the following:

- Children become confused based on sexual content they view on television, on videos, or in magazines.
- Children do not receive adequate supervision.

- Children live in homes with a sexualized environment.
- Children live in homes with little or no physical, sexual, or emotional privacy.
- Children are used to fulfill a parent's emotional needs that may be sexualized.
- Children have observed physical violence, particularly between their parents or caregivers, due to sexual jealousy and sexual mistrust.
- Children have been sexually abused.

Johnson noted that when sexual abuse allegations due to concerns about the child's sexual behaviors cannot be substantiated, it is important to assess with each parent the child's sexual behaviors and the boundaries in the child's home with each parent.[40]

In sum, the research or professional literature does not support expert opinions about sexual abuse based solely on behaviors or other symptoms of alleged victims. Lawyers should expect MHPs to rely on a number of information sources and to keep their minds open to alternative explanations for behaviors and statements interpreted or labeled as sexual abuse outcries or disclosures.[41] Recall that MHPs best guard against confirmatory biases when they actively consider alternative hypotheses. Such methodology is a hallmark of competent forensic evaluations and reflects a scientific–critical thinking approach to allegations of sexual abuse.

KEY PRINCIPLES WHEN CONSIDERING SEXUAL ABUSE ALLEGATIONS

Allegations—True or False?

Because there is no generally accepted sexual abuse victim profile and no psychological, behavioral, or medical markers of most sexual abuse, children's statements that give rise to sexual abuse allegations become the focus of MHP therapists or evaluators and courts. Consequently, the context—how and to whom a child disclosed the alleged abuse—and the contents of children's statements often become critical pieces of evidence when determining the allegations' validity. Thus, lawyers should understand several key principles from the research that address concerns about children's disclosures and statements used to support sexual abuse allegations.

The research should not be read to nitpick reliable statements by young children who have been sexually abused. Sexual abuse is a serious concern that may compromise a child's emotional and social development. Protecting children from abuse serves their best interests. But flawed interviews that muddy sexual abuse allegations or false allegations may also compromise children's emotional and social development, create anxieties in the children's relationships with their parents, and place those children in the midst of untenable loyalty concerns over their parents that could affect their perceptions of relationships and family as they grow older.

To further highlight the complexity, psychologist Kathryn Kuehnle notes several alternatives that professionals should consider when evaluating allegations:[42]

- The child is not a victim of sexual abuse, but a sincere, overly vigilant parent inaccurately believes the child has been abused.
- The child is not a victim of sexual abuse, but a parent is using the abuse allegation to manipulate the child and the court system during litigation.

- The child is not a victim of sexual abuse and is credible, but the child is estranged from the parent accused of the abuse and has misperceived an innocent or ambiguous interaction.
- The child is a victim of abuse but will not disclose the abuse because the child fears the consequences of such disclosure.
- The child is a victim of sexual abuse but will not disclose the abuse due to misguided loyalty to the parent accused of the abuse.
- The child is a victim of sexual abuse but does not have the verbal skills to provide a credible description of the abuse.
- The child is a victim of sexual abuse and is a credible reporter of the incidents.

In sum, the evaluation of sexual abuse allegations is complex; the need for competent, comprehensive examinations that address alleged child statements and the statements' contexts are essential. But MHPs will not always be able to proffer an opinion about the allegations in a given case—an aspect of the scientific–critical thinking mindset is the willingness to express uncertainty if the data do not lead to a defensible, reliable opinion. Lawyers must recognize that an MHP's uncertainty in difficult cases is not bad—evaluations are not lie detectors or crystal balls. In fact, an opinion of uncertainty may highlight the objectivity and credibility of the expert's overall testimony and keep tight the analytical reasoning threads through that testimony.

Children's Disclosure Statements

Over the past twenty-five years, MHPs have developed and used various syndromes as models to determine the validity of children's "outcries" of alleged sexual abuse and to explain inconsistent behaviors and statements by sexual abuse victims. An example of a model frequently referenced in the mental health literature and in case law is the Child Sexual Abuse Accommodation Syndrome (CSAAS); MHPs have also used other terms—Sexually Abused Child Syndrome and Child Sexual Abuse Syndrome—to describe supposed characteristic behaviors of child sexual abuse victims.[43] CSAAS, first defined by Roland Summit in 1983, posits that sexually abused children show five characteristics: secrecy with the perpetrator about the abuse;[44] helplessness and dependence on the abuser;[45] entrapment and accommodation where the child's only healthy survival option is to accept the situation;[46] delayed, conflicted, and unconvincing disclosure;[47] and retraction of the disclosure when the child recognizes the resulting recriminations and family discord and attempts to restore family peace.[48] Summit claimed that because abused children are powerless, they find various means to accommodate—emotionally and otherwise—abusers' demands without complaint: by keeping the abuse secret, by exhibiting behavior problems, by turning to imaginary companions, or by experiencing altered states of consciousness.[49] Summit viewed his CSAAS model as providing a "common language" and a "recognizable map" for understanding child sexual abuse.[50]

Summit's model has significantly influenced MHPs' and law enforcement's notions of sexually abused children.[51] But after Summit introduced his model, MHP experts began to misuse CSAAS or its elements as a diagnostic tool to validate children's sexual abuse allegations,[52] and prosecutors misused CSAAS or similar syndromes to prove the reliability of children's allegations.[53] Consequently, since the early to mid-1990s, courts have largely rejected CSAAS when it has been invoked to persuade the jury that children's statements about sexual abuse are truthful or diagnostic of abuse.[54] Further, in 1992, Summit qualified his earlier writing by emphasizing that "[i]t should be understood without apology that the CSAAS is a clinical opinion, not a scientific instrument,"[55] and that CSAAS "is used appropriately in court testimony not to prove a child was molested but to rebut the myths which prejudice endorsement of delayed or inconsistent disclosure" of the child's abuse statements.[56]

While most courts will not accept offering CSAAS as evidence to establish that a child has been sexually abused,[57] many have followed Summit's characterization of his model by allowing CSAAS-based testimony to be offered on rebuttal for rehabilitative purposes to explain children's inconsistent reports when those abuse disclosures are delayed or recanted.[58] Of course, this distinction begs the question: Why is CSAAS-based testimony reliable on rebuttal to explain children's reporting inconsistencies if that testimony is not deemed sufficiently reliable to offer the jury that the CSAAS model proves that the abuse occurred?[59] A critical concern is that use of CSAAS elements on rebuttal provides opportunities for testimony not allowed previously in trial to enter into jurors' considerations by the back door.[60] In fact, several jurisdictions have wrestled with the problem of admitting CSAAS testimony for any purpose—including for rebuttal.[61]

Despite these legal concerns and Summit's cautions, many professionals still use the CSAAS model to determine the validity of sexual abuse allegations,[62] and other professionals assert that the elements of CSAAS characterize an abused child's behaviors and reactions.[63] However, CSAAS's reliability is compromised on two counts: conceptually and empirically. Conceptually, CSAAS elements are contradictory:[64] If a child says that sexual abuse occurred, the CSAAS model explains how the child's behaviors are consistent with abuse; if the child qualifies or recants the sexual abuse statements, those actions also are victim characteristics. In addition, because CSAAS describes behaviors that are not unique to sexually abused children, it would be classified as "less certain" in Myers's "continuum of certainty" syndrome model—discussed in Chapter 4—and, therefore, should have lower probative value in court.[65]

CSAAS is also compromised empirically. One way to test the reliability of syndromes is to examine their elements. If the elements of proposed syndromes can be supported sufficiently by research, the syndromes, or, at least, their supporting elements, should pass muster under a *Frye-Daubert* analysis.[66] As a whole, empirical research does not support the elements of CSAAS. A recent comprehensive review of CSAAS elements analyzed two data sets: retrospective studies in which adults with intrafamilial child sexual abuse histories were asked to recall their disclosures in childhood, and studies of disclosure patterns of children treated or evaluated for sexual abuse.[67] The review's findings indicated that a large proportion of sexually abused children delay disclosing their abuse for long periods of time or fail to report the child sexual abuse incidents they experienced—two-thirds of adults who claimed to have been abused as children reported that they did not tell anyone about the abuse in their childhoods.[68] In sum, these retrospective studies support CSAAS's first element that asserts that many child sexual abuse incidents go unreported and stay secret with child victims.[69] Interestingly, a recent study found that in sexual abuse cases involving alleged perpetrators who were not family members, children's willingness to disclose abuse to their parents promptly and spontaneously decreased when they expected negative reactions from their parents, especially when the abuse was more serious.[70]

However, review of studies of disclosure patterns of children treated or evaluated for sexual abuse found that "there is little evidence to suggest that denials, recantations, and re-disclosures are typical when abused children are directly asked about abuse."[71] The research showed that when directly questioned in a formal setting, only a small percentage of abused children denied or recanted their abuse disclosures.[72] Interestingly, children were most likely to recant in cases where the findings of sexual abuse were least certain; children were least likely to recant in cases where the findings of sexual abuse were most certain.[73] Finally, supporters of the notions that abused children normally deny and recant their abuse statements and that disclosure of sexual abuse is a drawn-out process relied on studies that showed significant scientific shortcomings[74] and were deemed the weakest methodologically.[75]

In sum, retrospective research show that most adults who claim histories of child sexual abuse recall that they never told anyone about the abuse during childhood.[76] But most children interviewed about sexual abuse who make abuse disclosures do not later recant.[77] In all, only a minority of young children reflect the CSAAS model's disclosure pattern.[78]

Consequently, lawyers should challenge experts who use CSAAS elements as assumptions to support their conclusions and opinions of sexual abuse allegations. Experts' attempts to connect children's statements and behaviors with those elements may reflect a wide analytical gap highlighted by confirmatory bias—that is, funneling of data into a largely unsupported syndrome while neglecting other plausible explanations for the statements.

Suggestibility and Its Concerns

Approaches

Once a child makes statements that an adult interprets as a sexual abuse disclosure, what factors may affect the quality of the disclosure? Are those statements always reliable—factually and legally? If not, is the investigative task then only a matter of deciding that those children are either telling the truth or lying? The answers are not simple. But while children, even preschoolers, can provide reliable information in well-conducted interviews about their experiences,[79] MHPs differ in their approaches to their investigations.

Some MHPs begin their investigations with a presumption that children almost never make up stories about being sexually abused,[80] and that evaluators must "approach an allegation of sexual abuse with a clear understanding of who has a vested interest in lying and who in telling the truth."[81] Accordingly, in a father-daughter incest example, the evaluator is to recognize that the child victim makes herself very vulnerable by telling the truth, while the perpetrator has everything to lose—his child, his marriage, even his freedom—if the child's story is believed.[82] And mothers may also have much to lose if the child's allegations are believed.[83] In sum, these MHPs hold that it is not in children's interests to make up sexual abuse allegations.[84] These MHPs also use notions derived from Summit's CSAAS model to support apparent inconsistencies in the children's reports.[85]

Other MHPs—before presuming the reliability of children's reports—examine the various possibilities that children's statements interpreted as sexual abuse may represent before concluding what those statements mean.[86] This approach invokes the forensic examiner's task to consider plausible, reasonable hypotheses in the evaluation process and guard against confirmatory bias that could prejudge the investigation or compromise the evaluation's conclusion.

Thinking About Memory

Psychologists have conducted a significant amount of empirical research since the mid-1980s that has addressed the reliability of children's reports of their experiences and has broadened the inquiry about the nature and context of children's disclosures.[87] Much of the research has focused on how the reliability of children's reports of their experiences may be influenced by characteristics and mind-sets of people to whom children make their reports and the relationships of those individuals to the children.[88] In addition, children's cognitive and emotional maturity levels and the contexts—including the effects of social demands and incentives, positive or negative—in which children make their reports may influence the reliability of children's reports.[89]

Understanding how memory works provides an important backdrop for this research. Current knowledge notes that memory develops through constructions and reconstructions of one's experiences; this process forms the mental experiences people use to create meanings about reality.[90] Memory does not act like a tape recorder, passively recording one's experiences and offering perfect recollections when prompted. Rather, memory of an event may be influenced by several factors at each stage—encoding the event, storing the event, and retrieving the event—that comprises the memory's development and expression. *Encoding*, or recording, an event may depend on particular elements of the event to which a person attends and a person's outlook or biases about the event; as a result, people viewing the same event may have different recollections of that event. Memories that are encoded and then *stored* may increase or decrease in strength as functions of time or of how often they are recalled. They may even change in part or in whole by subtle or overt suggestions or misapprehensions. Finally, in *retrieval*, people may not recall everything about parts of events they encoded or stored and may "fill in the blanks" with what typically happens—or should happen—when they relate the memory of their experiences.[91] In general, young children tend to provide briefer—albeit accurate—accounts of their experiences than do older children and adults.[92]

Two distinctions are important in memory retrieval: *script versus episodic memory*, and *recall versus recognition memory*.[93] When events occur regularly, children and adults develop script memories—like stereotypes, representative or typical memories.[94] Scripts enable people to remember important features of repetitive events while ignoring less central elements.[95] But in forensic investigations, recollections about specific events—episodic memory—rather than blended accounts of several incidents are important.[96] Forensic interviews with children must tap episodic rather than script memories, which are more vulnerable to suggestive "filling in" of details.[97]

The second important memory retrieval distinction is that between recall and recognition memory.[98] Adults and children asked to describe events from free recall ("Tell me what you remember about the concert.") generally produce brief but accurate accounts.[99] But when people are asked for more details ("Were the speakers on the stage?"), recognition memory rather than recall is invoked; in these instances, more details will be produced, but the probability of errors also increases.[100] The lesson? Competent interviews of children intended to produce reliable reports emphasize free recall questions over recognition memory questions—understandably, anxious parents rarely settle for free recall questions over the more specific feedback of recognition memory questions. When resorting to recognition questions, interviewers must take special care to minimize chances for errors in children's reports.[101] We will return to competent interview methods that are more likely to produce reliable reports by children later in this chapter.

The Different Facets of Suggestibility

The Scope of Suggestibility The suggestibility of children has a long research history and an evolving definition.[102] Earlier research viewed suggestibility as an unconscious process caused by exposure to information after the event and as primarily memory-based instead of involving social components.[103] Current views of suggestibility are broader and examine how children's memories and reports can be affected by factors both internal and external to the child.[104] For example, children can give reports about events while aware of how those reports differ from what happened—children may seek to please significant others, yield to social demands, or even lie.[105] And information children incorporate prior to the event may also influence their reports as when they have preexisting expectations about people or behaviors and use those expectations to interpret events.[106] In addition, children's memories or reports may be influenced by several other social factors: subtle or overt suggestions, stereotypes, and leading questions, as well as more blatant bribes and threats. The first three factors may alter memories of the events at issue in ways of which the child is unaware, whereas bribes and threats may alter the child's report while not altering underlying memories.[107] In sum, simplistic understandings of influencing children point only to whether children are telling the truth or to notions about whether the children have been "coached" to make certain statements. In contrast, suggestibility, as currently viewed, may take many forms—from overt and blatant to unintentional—and may or may not change children's underlying memories of the events they experience.[108]

The Breadth of Suggestibility Research has consistently indicated that preschoolers—age three to six years—are more vulnerable than older children to several types of suggestibility and, therefore, more likely to produce unreliable reports of their experiences, particularly in response to improper forensic interview or pre-interview interactions.[109] But vulnerability to suggestible influences is not just a quality of younger children. Recent research also demonstrates that older children are susceptible to suggestible influences.[110] Further, extensive research shows that adults' reports of their experiences also may be influenced by others' descriptions of those events,[111] that adults are subject to coercive, suggestible interviewing by perceived authorities,[112] and that adults can accept misinformation and incorporate it as their own—modifying memories or creating new, false ones.[113]

This is not to say that children cannot produce reliable reports of their experiences. They can—prior to and during a forensic interview—under conditions that minimize suggestibility and maximize opportunities to gain accurate, reliable information. But the quality of children's memories and reports depends on individual differences among children; on information to which children are exposed prior to a formal forensic interview; on the forensic interview's context, including the interviewer's skills; on the time elapsed since the event; and on the strength of certain memories.[114]

Lawyers, parents, and child protective agencies often turn to formal forensic interviews as primary tools to investigate sexual abuse allegations that first arise with children's statements—the forensic interview may be the most important component of an investigation or a trial involving a child witness.[115] Yet such interviews may not occur for several days, even weeks, afterward. No matter how much time elapses, much can occur—ranging from overheard conversations to deliberate coaching—that may compromise the reliability of a child's memories of the event(s) or report and, thereby, affect later statements made in even careful, well-conducted forensic interviews.[116] And prior to the forensic interview or interviews, children often undergo much questioning from family members, therapists, social workers, and other interested parties.[117] Out of concern for the children, many adults who conduct these "informal interviews" may understandably attempt to comfort the children rather than focus on gathering reliable information from them.

Parents or other trusted caretakers usually are the first recipients of children's statements that may be interpreted as reporting sexual abuse. No one expects parents to be neutral, unemotional responders: parents may interpret their children's behavior through filters comprised of their own experiences, their current attitudes, and their emotions toward their divorcing or ex-spouse. Where one parent sees a child innocently exploring the body, another parent sees an alarming indication of sexual abuse. Some divorcing parents may put a negative spin on any behavior that could loosely be interpreted to suggest sexual abuse. On the other hand, legitimate concerns about sexual molestation may have contributed to a parent's decision to seek a divorce. Parents' responses vary. The reactions of adults to children's disclosures set the stage for how those children may report those disclosures later.

> Tracking the child's memory "chain of custody" from the statement's first utterance is critical if the investigation is to yield reliable information and conclusions.[118]

In addition, lawyers in this process should ensure that MHPs have weighed other concerns that suggestibility encompasses that might compromise the reliability of children's reports: negative stereotyping by one parent of the other, children's errors in identifying the sources of information they report, incentives or social influences affecting children's reports, and misinformation transmitted—intentionally or unwittingly—to children.

Negative Stereotyping Research has demonstrated that the effects of negative stereotyping of another person may have powerful effects on young children's views and reports about that person.[119] People use stereotypes as simple, shortcut representations to organize their expectations of others and to interpret others' behaviors.[120] But if children are told repeatedly that a person "does bad things," they may incorporate that belief into their own reports and interpret incidents involving that person in light of that stereotype.[121]

A significant study pointed to the ease with which young children developed negative stereotypes of people presented to them prior to their interactions with those people, particularly when later questions about those stereotypes were paired with repeated erroneous and leading suggestions.[122] The harmful effects of negative stereotyping combined with erroneous leading suggestions were most evident in the youngest children.[123] Unfortunately, some children may also become subject to strong, unrealistic negative beliefs or stereotyping by one parent of the other in highly contentious custody battles. If the negative beliefs or stereotyping take hold, the children may develop severe, difficult-to-change distortions of the other parent that are not commensurate with their previous relationships with that parent.[124]

Source Attribution Concerns Notably, many of the false reports given by the children in the study just described were richly detailed.[125] This observation was similar to that in another study when preschool children were asked to think about events that did and did not happen to them.[126] When told to "think real hard and tell me if this ever happened to you . . ." about a particular event—for example, going to the hospital after getting a finger caught in a mousetrap—more than half the children produced false narratives for at least one fictitious event, and a quarter of the children gave false accounts for the majority of fictitious events. Besides their accounts being richly detailed, 27 percent of the children later refused to acknowledge that the events had not happened.

In a later study, preschool children were told that certain events happened and then asked to "make a picture of it in your head, and think real hard about each thing for a minute." The percentage of these make-believe happenings the children reported remembering increased over interview sessions to 43 percent by the twelfth session;[127] most of the children continued to believe that their false reports actually happened even when told otherwise.[128] In addition, these children's narratives were elaborate and quite descriptive of events that never occurred.[129]

These errors are referred to as problems in *source-monitoring* or as *source-attribution* errors. Source-attribution errors occur with the inability to remember and distinguish whether one actually engaged in the activity, heard about it, saw it, or thought about it.[130] The person is confused over the origin of a particular activity or thought. Young children are particularly vulnerable to these errors and are more likely than older children to have difficulty determining whether the information they "know" came from their own experiences or from other sources.[131] But even adults may have occasional difficulty distinguishing between events that happened and those they only thought about or heard related[132]—for example, when people recall a touchdown in a big game but confuse plays leading to the touchdown with plays from other games they may have watched, heard about, or read in the newspaper in previous weeks.

Other source-attribution concerns may affect reports children give of the memories of their experiences. For example, research has demonstrated that misinformation from parents may affect children's reports of their experiences, and that children who have heard their parents describe nonexperienced events sometimes reported having experienced those events when asked directly.[133] Parents in the studies did not overtly seek to change the children's thinking about nonexperienced events. Rather, after the children participated in certain events outside the home, researchers had parents read stories to the children about those experienced events and about other made-up events the children had not experienced. Many children in subsequent questioning reported that they had experienced the made-up events and even described those so-called experiences.[134]

This latter finding is contrary to the notion that information gained when children are asked to report in a free recall format is always highly accurate. Apparently, if children are exposed to inaccurate pre-interview information, their reports, even if detailed, may not reflect true happenings. Contrary to popular notions, the fact that children may provide detailed reports cannot solely be taken as validating the reality of those reports.[135] Finally, eight-year-old children were as likely to mention that they experienced the fictitious events as the youngest children, although the older children were more likely to realize they were describing events that did not occur when reminded.[136]

Effects of Incentives and Social Pressures   In addition to the harmful effects of negative stereotyping on children's perceptions and reports and the possibility that misinformation from parents outside of formal interviews may color or alter children's memories of events they experienced, research indicates, not surprisingly, that incentives and social pressures may affect children's reports. Reinforcing children, positively or negatively, as they report their experiences may affect the reliability of those reports—even within a few minutes.[137] Praising or rewarding children for their reports, particularly when given by warm, personable adults; indicating that children might be helpful or smart; or implying that children's reports or responses to questions were inadequate may compromise the reliability of those children's reports.[138]

Bribery and *threats* are the negative sides of incentives and social pressures that may compromise the reliability of children's statements. Bribery means trying to make people do things by giving them something that they want. When questioning a child, the interviewer—"informal" or formal—may, for example, promise the interviewed child that the interview will end "when you tell the truth." Or, the interviewer might tell the child expressing hunger that she or he can have lunch after the interview.[139] Of course, in some cases, the bribery may be even more obvious.

Threats may occur through spoken words, voice tone, and body language.[140] In one example, when a child gave answers that did not fit with the interviewer's belief in the alleged allegation, the interviewer said to the child, "Did your mom tell me a story? Maybe I need to get her to come in here."[141] In addition, the interviewer's voice tone was accusatory, and the child appeared threatened. On the other hand, the interviewer positively reinforced the child's statements that fit the interviewer's beliefs about the allegations while simultaneously pushing the child; the interviewer responded to an ambiguous statement by the child by saying, "Honey, you need to tell me the truth," and asking, "Why are you afraid to talk to me about this, sweetheart?"[142]

The effects of incentives and social pressures—particularly those that are positive—may be difficult to recognize. But parents, therapists, and forensic interviewers may cross the line, albeit, at times, unwittingly, when they respond positively or negatively—sometimes understandably—to particular statements of the child. Nevertheless, the reliability of children's statements in cases with sexual abuse allegations depends on children responding to properly framed interviewer questions and not to the social demands heightened by reinforced responses to the child.

The Legal Effects of Suggestibility Research

While the findings in this chapter have been widely accepted and incorporated into training for MHPs who conduct forensic interviews, some professionals in the field have expressed concerns about the implications of this research in court. For example, investigations into sexual abuse allegations usually result in judgments that may be deemed more or less probable depending on the data and interpretations of those data. As a result, Myers alleged that research studying the effects of suggestive interviewing techniques on children's recollections casts "doubt and skepticism" on children's abilities to report their experiences credibly.[143] In addition, Thomas Lyon cautioned that the suggestibility research reflects values trade-offs between two types of decision error: false positives and false negatives.[144] Lyon notes that interviewers must avoid either eliciting a false report of abuse or failing to elicit a report of abuse when abuse actually occurred.[145] But Lyon asserts that proponents of the more recent suggestibility research overemphasize false allegations of abuse and underestimate possibilities that abused children will not reveal abuse.[146] Lyon's cautions raise concerns that confirmatory bias may inappropriately orient MHPs and lawyers who might be biased against determining that abuse has occurred as well as those biased toward determining that abuse has occurred and that the research might be used by proponents of either bias to justify their expert opinions.

In response, Ceci et al. counter Lyon's concern by insisting that they persistently attend to the error trade-offs in their work,[147] but that when considering sexual abuse allegations, "the entire motivational, cognitive, and physical environment needs to be taken into consideration before making blanket claims about disclosure trade-offs."[148] The concern is not simply whether the child is telling the truth or a lie.[149]

In sum, the research of the past twenty years is compelling and has alerted MHPs and the legal system to factors that may compromise abuse investigations and the reliability of expert testimony in cases with sexual abuse allegations. These issues, however, still generate strong emotions and strongly held positions—fertile ground for confirmatory bias to take root and compromise the reliability of an expert's evaluation methodology and subsequent opinion testimony.

FORENSIC INTERVIEWS

As noted earlier, the forensic interview often is viewed as a key evidence piece in cases with child sexual abuse allegations. In most family court cases, physical or medical evidence, if any, to corroborate abuse allegations is equivocal at best, and the only possible witnesses will be the child and the alleged perpetrator of the abuse.[150] Assuming that the accused adult will deny involvement in any abuse of the child, investigators—and ultimately the court—will be left with the child's statement as the case's primary evidence. As with any other evidence, expert testimony and opinions about the meaning of the child's statement must be reliable to be admitted by the court. The methods and rationales experts use to support their conclusions about the statements must be based in research and professional literature, and the experts' opinions must be logically connected to the data from which the conclusions are drawn.

Because of the importance placed on children's forensic interviews, lawyers should examine investigators' training and interviewing skills.[151] MHPs' abilities to conduct competent interviews with children about sexual abuse allegations are critical because most researchers agree that what children—particularly preschoolers—"remember" or relate depends so much on the MHPs' interview skills and how MHPs conduct their interviews.[152] Key components of reliable forensic interviews include: how interviewers prepare for and conceptually approach the interviews, how interviewers present themselves to the children they interview, and how interviewers elicit information from those children.[153]

Given the importance of quality, competent forensic interviews, interviewers bear much responsibility.[154] However, not all interviews must be "ideal" to yield reliable information from children. Wood and Garven distinguished between clumsy interviews and improper interviews.[155] In clumsy interviews, interviewers may fail to use some recommended interview techniques. Ceci et al. also note that even interviews conducted with weakly suggestive techniques do not seriously compromise the accuracy of the children's reports.[156] Nevertheless, clumsy interviews still may yield less reliable information from children and the perception that those children's reports are less credible.[157]

In contrast, improper interviews include incentive-laden questions and other social reinforcements that seriously compromise, if not destroy, the reliability of interviewed children's elicited reports.[158] Reliability concerns increase when interviewers—often with confirmatory bias mind-sets—repeatedly ask children suggestion-laced questions coupled with stereotype inductions and atmospheres of accusation.[159] Add to this that children lodging sexual abuse allegations typically experience several interviews—from professionals as well as untrained adults—during the investigation period.[160]

The remainder of this chapter will examine approaches to interviews and interview techniques that may foster or compromise the reliability of children's reports.

Concerns of Problem Forensic Interviews

Interviewer Mind-Set and Confirmatory Bias

While many factors may influence children's susceptibility to suggestive questions in forensic child sexual abuse interviews, interviewer-confirmatory bias, when present, infuses and colors the "entire architecture" of those interviews.[161] Interviewers with confirmatory bias quickly decide—before or during interviews—the validity of allegations without adequately weighing evidence or plausible alternative explanations for the allegations.[162] Such interviewers seek confirming information—often through suggestive questioning or other reinforcing social behaviors—or ignore other evidence to confirm their set beliefs about the allegations.

Lawyers may expose sources of confirmatory bias when they explore the approaches forensic interviewers bring to sexual abuse cases. As noted earlier, MHPs differ conceptually in the ways they address sexual abuse concerns. Some "approach an allegation of sexual abuse with a clear understanding of who has a vested interest in lying and who in telling the truth."[163] Others assert that "either you believe the child's story or you do not."[164] And still other MHPs note that the purpose of forensic interviews is to explore and evaluate alternative hypotheses or explanations about the allegations without preconceptions before reaching conclusions.[165] These differing conceptual approaches may orient forensic interviews toward either hypothesis-confirming or hypothesis-testing methodologies;[166] the former points to confirmatory bias, while the latter signals a scientific–critical thinking approach to the allegations.

Besides attending to the conceptual approaches forensic interviewers bring to their investigative tasks, noting interviewers' pre-interview preparations may offer hints about whether the interviewers are sensitive to the possibility of confirmation bias. For instance, some MHPs believe that a blind interview with the child—where the professional has no information about the sexual abuse allegations or of the alleged perpetrator—best keeps them from developing confirmation bias. The rationale is that the interviewer then will be less likely to ask the child leading questions about the abuse allegations.[167] But other MHPs note that blind interviewing reduces interviewers' abilities to consider alternative explanations about the meaning of the children's statements[168]—this is especially critical when the children are young, when information upon which allegations are based may be ambiguous, or when allegations arise in a context of complicated and angry relationships between significant adults in the children's lives.[169] Most authors support the view that interviewers should prepare before interviewing children about sexual abuse allegations by familiarizing themselves with the allegations and by collecting information that might help them clarify details during interviews and consider alternate explanations for the allegations.[170]

Interviewer Questions

Types of Questions Children respond differently to different kinds of questions. In forensic interviews, the kinds of questions asked and the interview context impact the reliability of children's statements. But, again, keep in mind that children often are asked to report their experiences to others prior to structured forensic interviews; parents, law enforcement personnel, therapists, and teachers often "informally" interview children. The concerns raised in this section also apply to these "informal" interviews and reemphasize the need to track the "chain of custody" of children's memories in cases with sexual abuse allegations.

The psychological and child abuse literature refer to two types of interview questions: open-ended versus specific questions.[171] Open-ended questions (e.g., "What was school like for you last week?") usually require several-word responses and do not suggest answers.[172] Specific questions (e.g., "What is the name of your math teacher?") are more detail oriented.[173] Psychological research has demonstrated that children respond differently to these two types of questions: children provide fewer details in response to open-ended questions than they do to specific questions,[174] but their responses to open-ended questions are more accurate than their responses to specific questions.[175] In sum, asking many specific questions at the wrong time in interviews and in the wrong way may compromise the reliability of children's statements and, thereby, the interview's reliability.[176]

Why the difference in both details and accuracy rates of children's responses to open-ended versus specific questions? We noted earlier that when children respond to open-ended questions, they use recall memory processes to choose how they will answer. In contrast, specific questions tap into recognition memory and may focus children on less salient details—to the children—of the alleged events or suggest to the children unclear or no longer remembered details.[177] In addition, research has shown that young children, following social convention rules, often try to answer specific questions that we know they cannot answer accurately.[178] Also, children do not always realize when they fail to comprehend a question, and they rarely ask for clarification.[179]

Usually, adult-child conversations are highly structured, specific-question oriented, and directed by adults.[180] Children generally assume that adults already know the answers to questions they ask, with the goal to determine which answers the adults prefer.[181] Conventions of conversation demand that children cooperate and try to answer the questions.[182] These conventions cause problems when children are asked to respond to yes-no questions.[183]

Understanding the types of questions interviewers ask will enable lawyers to gauge the forensic interview's quality—as well as the quality of previous "informal" interviews of the child that may have affected the reliability of the child's current statements. In considering the research, Poole and Lamb reviewed a range of interview questions from least suggestive to most suggestive. They note that when conducting forensic interviews, MHPs should question children in the least suggestive manner possible.[184] Types of questions include the following:

- *Free narrative questions* ask children to describe events in their own words.[185]

  "Tell me everything you can about that, even things you don't think are important."

- *Open-ended questions* ask children to select details they will discuss.[186]

  "You said your mother took you to her boyfriend's house. Tell me about that time."

- *Specific but nonleading questions* ask for details about matters that children already have mentioned.[187] Interviewers should ask these questions only when the details are important because children may try to answer specific questions even when they do not have relevant information to do so.[188]

  "Do you remember what you were doing when he told you to come into the room?"

- *Closed questions*, such as multiple-choice or yes-no questions, allow only limited response options, although multiple-choice questions are preferable to yes-no questions.[189]

  "Did that happen in the hallway, the bedroom, or some other place?"

  "Did your dad tell you not to say anything about what happened?"

- *Explicitly leading questions* suggest the desired answer or contain information the child has not yet volunteered.[190]

  "You told your dad that your mom hurt you, didn't you?"

In sum, open-ended questions pull from children's recall memories about situations and events. Specific questions are targeted and pull from recognition memory, opening children up to social demand characteristics and conventions of interactions with adults and other errors that may result from interview contexts.[191] As a result, children's reports are more likely impaired when forensic interviewers rely on specific questions, including yes-no questions.[192]

Other Interview Question Concerns The *language* interviewers use to question children may also impact children's reports. In a well-known older study, adults viewed film of automobile accidents and were asked to estimate the speed of the involved cars. Subjects asked how fast the cars were traveling when the cars "smashed" into each other were more likely to report having seen broken glass than subjects who were asked how fast the cars were traveling when the cars "hit" each other.[193] Language matters. Adults' mischaracterizations of children's experiences explicitly or unwittingly conveyed to children—before or during forensic interviews—may color or alter children's perceptions of their experiences and their reports of those experiences.[194]

Another interviewer question concern involves *repeated questioning* of children. Repeating specific—especially yes-no—as opposed to open-ended questions to children several times within an interview or over several interviews can lead children to change their original answers or incorporate into their reports elements of others' questions that were not part of the original statements.[195] Preschoolers are particularly vulnerable to this problem.[196] Research notes that some repeated questioning may help young children preserve memories of events.[197] But repeating the same specific questions in interviews or over several interviews (remember, children may be "informally" interviewed several times before the forensic interview) presents significant reliability risks on two counts: the impact of the implicit social demands in children's interactions with adults, and the impact of explicit suggestions.[198] For example, adults generally do not repeat questions to a child unless the child failed to understand the question or failed to give the desired answer.[199] In studies, young children sometimes changed their answers in response to repeated specific questions.[200] Further, children showed more confidence in their responses to repeated specific questions than they showed in their original responses, and increasing numbers of children guessed when repeatedly questioned about information they did not have.[201]

Poole and White showed a difference between repeating open-ended questions versus specific questions to children. They concluded that repeating open-ended questions within an interview does not compromise children's reports, but repeating specific questions draws out inconsistent responses from children and speculation about what the right answer should be.[202] Finally, when misleading information or explicit suggestions—often through interviewer or confirmation bias—are presented to children through repeated questions, the reliability of the children's reports may become seriously compromised.[203]

Finally, Walker and Hunt noted three faulty question techniques that compromised interview integrity in Child Protective Services interviews they analyzed.[204] One faulty technique included cases in which the interviewer *modified the child's statement* by rewording it in a way that changed the statement's meaning, or the interviewer claimed that the child made a statement that the child had not made.[205] This technique increases the likelihood that the child could become inappropriately compliant.[206] A second faulty technique was noted in which the interviewer used *forced-choice questions* that limited the responses the child could give. For example, the interviewer might ask the child if the shirt the man wore was black or yellow, forcing the child to respond only to those choices.[207] This technique introduces the possibility that the child would choose one of the interviewer's options, whether or not either was correct.[208] A third faulty technique asked the child *multi-part questions*. For instance, the interviewer might ask if Bob wore a black coat, or did John wear a yellow coat.[209] Such multi-part questions increase the possibility that the child may become confused.[210] And, unfortunately, children do not always realize when they fail to understand a question, and they rarely ask for clarification.[211]

How interviewers ask questions matters. Make sure that interviewers follow Lyon's advice: Let the child supply the details.[212] But it is up to interviewers to ensure that their questions allow the child to supply reliable information.

Interviewer Status

Interviewer status may also affect how children report their experiences. Children attend to the social power and status of their interviewers. For example, adults have high status in young children's eyes:[213] children are more likely to believe adults than other children, more willing to comply with adults' wishes or agendas, and more likely to incorporate adults' beliefs into their own reports.[214] Also, not surprisingly, children accord police officers high status. It is not uncommon for children who voice statements interpreted as sexual abuse allegations to be interviewed by police officers or other authorities recognizable by dress or other status symbols—often well before formal forensic interviews are conducted. In one interesting study, some four-year-olds were interviewed by a policeman who told them that a babysitter they were to meet might have done something bad. Those children gave fewer accurate statements and more inaccurate statements about their encounters with the babysitter than did children who had not met the policeman and other children in an observer control group.[215] Although other young children interviewed by the policeman gave accurate statements,[216] the author, citing this study, noted that an accusatory or intimidating context can lead to increased errors in children's reports.[217]

Use of Anatomically Detailed Dolls

The use of Anatomically Detailed (AD) dolls as interview aids for children in sexual abuse investigations has been fraught with controversy. Proponents assert that the dolls may play important and valid roles in clinical assessment of child sexual abuse.[218] They claim that the dolls help young children with limited cognitive and language skills to recall their experiences accurately through nonverbal means and to overcome the embarrassment of disclosing details of their alleged abuse experiences.[219] Others suggest that AD dolls serve a number of functions: a comforter to the child during the interview, an interview icebreaker to talk about sexuality, an anatomical model for naming body parts, a demonstration aid to show what happened, a memory stimulus to trigger memory of sexual experiences, and a diagnostic screen.[220] Still other proponents use AD dolls as projective tests, interpreting children's interactions with the dolls as consistent with hypotheses that the children had been abused.[221]

In contrast, those who question the use of AD dolls as interview aids for young children in sexual abuse investigations point to the lack of standardized interview procedures as a shortcoming. Interviews vary in the number of interview sessions, the number of dolls presented to the child, the presentation of the dolls to the child as dressed or undressed, and the anatomical features of the dolls. In addition, those questioning the use of AD dolls conclude that there is no scientific evidence to justify clinical or forensic diagnosis of abuse based on doll play and that such doll play does not even provide incremental validity to the decision about whether abuse occurred.[222]

Given these competing positions, the American Psychological Association (APA) appointed a committee to address the scientific basis for the use of AD dolls in sexual abuse evaluations. The committee's 1991 statement[223] reflected "competing political entities within APA,"[224] essentially noting the concerns of each position and proposing cautions in the use of "doll-centered assessment of sexual abuse."[225] Subsequently, APA commissioned a working group of scholars to conduct a literature review of the scientific and clinical knowledge of AD doll use in sexual abuse investigations.[226] The review concluded that trained professional interviewers may still use AD dolls as communication tools with five caveats:[227]

1. AD dolls are not a psychological test with predictive (or postdictive) validity per se.[228]
2. Definitive statements about child sexual abuse cannot be made based on spontaneous or guided "doll *play*" (emphasis in original) alone. A clinical interview by a skilled clinician is not play.[229]
3. Particular caution is called for when interpreting the reports of children age four and under, at least when affirmations to leading questions about "being touched" are concerned and when repeated misleading questioning has been used.[230]
4. In light of current knowledge, the scholars recommended that APA reconsider whether valid "doll-centered assessment" techniques exist and whether they still "may be the best available practical solution" for the pressing and frequent problem of investigation of child sexual abuse.[231]
5. Special recognition of normative differences between children of different racial groups and socioeconomic strata should be a part of training professionals who use AD dolls in clinical inquiry.[232]

Despite the continued use of AD dolls by some professionals in their sexual abuse interviews with children, several concerns to which lawyers should attend have been raised in the literature. First, young children, particularly preschoolers, may lack the cognitive skills to reliably make use of AD dolls.[233] To use AD dolls to relate their experiences, children must (1) have "representational insight"—an understanding that dolls are objects and symbols that represent their own bodies;[234] (2) be able to map their own experiences accurately onto the dolls;[235] and (3) keep the symbolic purpose of the dolls in mind and not stray off into unrelated behavior with the dolls during the interview.[236] Children under four years old have particular difficulties with these cognitive skills.[237]

One study looked at the influence of AD dolls on three- to four-year-old children's reports of a routine medical exam during which half the children received a genital exam and half did not.[238] Immediately after the exam, children in both groups were asked to demonstrate various events on an AD doll and on their own bodies. In sum, no age differences were evident on measures that assessed reports of genital touching, regardless of how the children were questioned.[239] Children in both age groups frequently erred when telling or showing on the dolls and when showing on their own bodies whether and how the doctor had touched their buttocks and genitals during the exam.[240] In addition, children in both groups showed a comparable number of sexualized behaviors with a plastic spoon the doctor did not use when asked with specific, suggestive questioning to show on the doll how they had been touched by the doctor.[241] As a result of these findings, the study's authors concluded that AD dolls should not be used in forensic interviews with children younger than five years old.[242]

A second concern to which lawyers should attend that has been raised in the literature is that children offered AD dolls by interviewers will explore or show play behaviors that could be misunderstood by some as portraying sexual abuse concerns.[243] Summary of the research has shown that play with AD dolls explicitly demonstrating intercourse or oral-genital contact was rare with samples of children not referred to clinics. But young children who interact with AD dolls commonly explore the dolls' genitals, anuses, and breasts.[244] In one study of two- to five-year-old children, a large number of presumed non-sexually abused toddler and preschool children spontaneously undressed the AD dolls presented to them by interviewers.[245] The majority of those children explored the AD dolls' genitals, anuses, and breasts.[246]

A third concern to which lawyers should attend that has been raised in the litera-ture is that without shared understandings, interviewers' biases may too easily influence interpretations of children's interactions with AD dolls.[247] For example, if a child puts a finger into the AD doll's anal opening, does this represent a sexual abuse reenactment or merely the child's exploration of the new doll? As noted earlier, there are no validated, objective standards to address this question. Instead, the answer lies with the inter-viewer's interpretation—and perhaps professional background and experiences.[248] In an older survey study, professionals—child protective workers, physicians, MHPs, and law enforcement officers—differed in what they considered children's normal behaviors with AD dolls.[249]

In sum, MHPs have not reached consensus about the value of using AD dolls to interview young children in sexual abuse investigations.[250] At best, recommendations by professional organizations for the use of AD dolls by forensic interviewers are qualified. Bruck et al. conclude that in light of "the mounting negative evidence on doll-assisted interviews, coupled with the slender (almost nonexistent) evidence that the dolls actu-ally improve reporting for younger children," AD dolls "probably should not be used in interviews with children below the age of 5 years."[251] Consequently, MHPs who use AD dolls in their interviews should bear the burden of showing that doll interviews are the best of the available alternatives to elicit reliable statements from children about their experiences.[252]

The Forensic Interview Structure—Basic Principles

Purposes of Forensic Interviews

While the forensic interview is often viewed as a key component in sexual abuse cases, its results may not yield reliable information from the child about the allegations no matter how clear the child's reports about the allegations may seem. Many concerns, addressed in this chapter, may color or corrupt the reliability of children's statements. The most pernicious concern is confirmatory bias—the tendency to seek information that confirms conclusions already reached while ignoring disconfirming information.[253] In addition, the effects on children of prior "informal interviews" by parents or other family members, therapists, or even lawyers may compromise the reliability of chil-dren's statements in the formal forensic interviews. And, as noted earlier, children may incorporate other inaccurate information into their reports of their experiences. In sum, explicit "coaching" or "scripting" of a child is not the only way to corrupt a structured, well-conducted forensic interview.

Lawyers also should ensure that experts, particularly investigative interviewers and evaluators, are able to articulate the difference between therapeutic and forensic inter-views. As noted in this book's first section, therapeutic and forensic roles are defined by different relationships and different tasks. The therapist's responsibility is to the child or parent patient, and the therapist's emphasis is one of helping as opposed to obtain-ing facts for use in court;[254] the role of advocate is inappropriate for the fact-finding mission.[255] Understandably, therapists' relationships with their patients easily give rise to confirmatory bias if therapists give expert opinions about the sexual abuse allega-tions. As a result, numerous professional guidelines explicitly state that the forensic and therapy roles should be filled by different professionals.[256]

In contrast, competent forensic interviewers seek two goals: to obtain reliable statements from children about the children's experiences and the associated abuse allegations—from the children's perspectives—and to explore plausible alternative explanations for the allegations and the children's statements about those allegations.[257] The first goal seeks to minimize the effects of suggestibility in the interviewer-child relationship, the interviewer questions, and the interviewer demeanor. In addition, this goal allows children to determine the vocabulary and specific content of the interview as much as possible.[258] The second goal seeks to challenge confirmatory biases that could prevent the interviewer from understanding the nature of the allegations under investigation.[259]

The Research-Based Protocol

At this time, there is no "official" protocol that MHPs follow when they conduct forensic interviews in child sexual abuse cases. But there is a consensus regarding procedures for conducting high-quality forensic interviews of children.[260] A common strategy in the various guidelines and protocols is to eliminate suggestive question styles and behaviors or statements that reinforce children's reports and otherwise impair accuracy of children's reports.[261] These protocols or guidelines apply research findings discussed in this chapter to enhance the quality and reliability of children's reports and, consequently, share many features.[262] The literature indicates that interviewers who use research-based protocols or guidelines obtain higher quality information from their child interviewees than when they use unstructured, non-protocol interviews.[263] Nevertheless, research suggests that only a small fraction of interviewers typically ask open-ended questions when interviewing children—the kinds of questions likely to elicit the most reliable reports from children—because children are more likely to resist providing free-narrative accounts.[264]

Describing a protocol in detail is beyond the scope of this chapter. Debra Poole and Michael Lamb in their book *Investigative Interviews of Children* provide an excellent discussion of the science of interviewing children and descriptions of research-based protocols for interviewing children about sexual abuse allegations. Forensic interviews represented by those protocols incorporate much of the research described in this chapter.

The forensic interview begins when the interviewer *establishes rapport with the child* while gaining information about whether the child can participate.[265] To relate information accurately, children must be able to attend to the interviewer, they must understand what the interviewer is asking, and they must be motivated to provide information.[266]

Next, the interviewer explains that *the child has the right to say "I don't know"* if a question is asked that the child is unable to answer or understand.[267] This step alerts children that they do not have to "cooperate" with the "answer" they might assume the interviewer would want to hear—a conventional assumption children have in their conversations with adults.[268]

The interviewer then conducts a practice interview using *open-ended questions* to ask the child, for example, to recall a recent significant event or to describe a typical morning at home before leaving for school.[269] This step allows the child to describe nonthreatening events in free-narrative form, giving the child practice using recall memory to describe events and details in his or her own words.

The *interview topic is introduced* to the child in the least suggestive way possible.[270] Questions like "Do you know why you are here?" or "What is the reason you came to talk with me today?" adequately introduce the interview's purpose.[271] At this stage, the interviewer should avoid introducing a particular individual or action and avoid using words that imply harm such as "hurt," "bad," or "abuse."[272] These words invoke problems with *negative stereotyping* that could affect the way children cognitively organize their experiences and color the reports of their experiences. In addition, experts should be careful not to reinforce—positively or negatively—the child or the child's statements during the interview.[273]

From this point, the flow of the forensic interview should simulate a *funnel*, starting with open-ended questions that elicit free-narrative descriptions from the child and then proceeding, with caution, to more direct questions, seeking carefully to clarify elements the child introduced earlier.[274] It is always preferable to attempt more open-ended prompts before asking more specific questions;[275] for example, "I understand someone has been bothering you" is preferable to "Your mom said your father tried to touch your privates in the shower."[276] Then, the interviewer returns to open-ended questions to allow the child to relate more information—if there is more to relate.[277] The interview ends after discussion over neutral topics.[278]

Adequately analyzing forensic interviews of children requires more than just this brief outline.[279] And recall that "clumsy" interviews that fail to use some recommended interview techniques[280] or even interviews conducted with weakly suggestive techniques may not seriously compromise the accuracy of children's reports.[281] But lawyers will be able to recognize many improper interviews when they apply concepts discussed in this chapter and the brief interview outline just presented. Improper interviews generate unreliable information. Experts who base their conclusions and opinions on such unreliable information will be exposing confirmatory biases in their approaches to the sexual abuse allegations.

The Forensic Interview in Context

As noted earlier, the forensic interview often is viewed as the key piece of evidence in child sexual abuse allegation cases. But if MHP experts do not place the interview, no matter how apparently reliable, in the context of a broader picture, they will be particularly vulnerable to confirmatory bias, if not other biases as well. Recall that the primary method of combating confirmatory bias is to consider plausible alternative explanations of the allegations. Given that "the entire motivational, cognitive, and physical environment needs to be taken into consideration" in addressing the reliability of children's statements in sexual abuse cases,[282] the forensic interview is one piece of the puzzle, albeit often important, when trying to understand the nature of sexual abuse allegations. The other puzzle pieces include reviews of other professional, legal, and police records, interviews with relevant people involved in the child's life and with the case, and assessments of the child and parents. This comprehensive approach reflects the MHP's assumption that sexual abuse allegations are complex, requires evaluations that reflect that complexity, and enhances the reliability of the expert's testimony.[283] In contrast, experts content only with the child's statements, even from a competently conducted forensic interview, and, perhaps, the complaining parent's reports assume that children's reports are unaffected by the research discussed in this chapter.[284] Limited information hampers the expert's ability to explore plausible alternative explanations of the allegations, thereby hindering opportunities to consider the allegations from a scientific–critical thinking mind-set. Such limitations provide fertile ground for confirmatory bias to infect the expert's conclusions and, thereby, to compromise the reliability of the expert's testimony, opening the gate to *Frye-Daubert* concerns. These principles are the same when experts evaluate and/or testify about other family law issues.

NOTES

1.   *See* Amos Tversky & Daniel Kahneman, *Judgment and Uncertainty: Heuristics and Biases*, 185 SCIENCE 1124 (1974).

2.   *See* David Martindale, *Confirmatory Bias and Confirmatory Distortion*, 2(1/2) J. CHILD CUSTODY 31 (2005) (Martindale refers to this as "confirmatory distortion," or the deliberate attempt to skew reporting to bolster a position).

3.   CAROLE WADE & CAROL TAVRIS, PSYCHOLOGY 325 (7th ed. 2003).

4.   *See* Steve Herman, *Improving Decision Making in Forensic Child Sexual Abuse Evaluations*, 29 LAW & HUM. BEHAV. 87, 88 (2005).

5.   Watkins v. Telsmith, Inc., 121 F.3d 984, 991 (5th Cir. 1997).

6.   Kumho Tire Co., Ltd. v. Carmichael, 526 U.S. 137, 152 (1999).

7.   *See* General Electric Co. v. Joiner, 522 U.S. 136, 146 (1997).

8.   *See* Jeffrey J. Haugaard, *The Challenge of Defining Child Sexual Abuse*, 55 AM. PSYCHOL. 1036, 1036 (2000).

9.   Celia B. Fisher & Katherine A. Whiting, *How Valid Are Child Sexual Abuse Validations?*, *in* EXPERT WITNESSES IN CHILD ABUSE CASES 159, 162 (S.J. Ceci & H. Hembrooke eds., 1998).

10.   *Id.*

11.   WILLIAM N. FRIEDRICH, PSYCHOLOGICAL ASSESSMENT OF SEXUALLY ABUSED CHILDREN AND THEIR FAMILIES 55 (2002) (also, Friedrich notes that neither is there a single profile of an incestuous father or sex offender).

12.   *Id.* at 56.

13.   *See* Kathleen A. Kendall-Tackett et al., *Impact of Sexual Abuse on Children: A Review and Synthesis of Recent Empirical Studies*, 113 PSYCHOL. BULL. 164, 173 (1993).

14.   Celia B. Fisher, *American Psychological Association's (1992) Ethics Code and the Validation of Sexual Abuse in Day-Care Settings*, 1 PSYCHOL. PUB. POL'Y & L. 461, 472 (1995).

15.   *See* Kendall-Tackett et al., *supra* note 13; Margaret A. Hagan, *Faith in the Model and Resistance to Research*, 10 CLINICAL PSYCHOL: SCI. & PRAC. 344 (2003).

16.   *See* Kendall-Tackett et al., *supra* note 13, at 173.

17.   *Id.*

18.   *See* THOMAS M. ACHENBACH, MANUAL FOR THE CHILD BEHAVIOR CHECKLIST/4–18 AND 1991 PROFILE 128–47 (1991).

19.   *Id.* at 120.

20.   Kendall-Tackett et al., *supra* note 13, at 171.

21.   *Id.*

22.   William N. Friedrich et al., *Normative Sexual Behavior in Children: A Contemporary Sample*, 101 PEDIATRICS e9 (1998), http://www.pediatrics.org/cgi/content/full101/4/e9.

23.   *Id.* (Friedrich noted that sexual behavior in children can be sorted into several categories: adherence to personal boundaries, exhibitionism, gender role behavior, self-stimulation, sexual anxiety, sexual interest, sexual intrusiveness, sexual knowledge, and voyeuristic behavior).

24.   *Id.* at 2.

25.   William N. Friedrich, *Letters to the Editor: In Reply*, 103 PEDIATRICS 853 (1999).

26.   Friedrich et al., *supra* note 22, at e6.

27. *Id.*

28. *Id.*

29. *Id.*

30. *Id.*

31. *Id.*

32. *See* Richard A. Warshak, *Letters to the Editor,* 103 PEDIATRICS 853 (1999); *and see* Friedrich, *supra* note 25, at 853.

33. Friedrich, *supra* note 25, at 853.

34. Gerald P. Koocher et al., *Psychological Science and the Use of Anatomically-Detailed Dolls in Child Sexual-Abuse Assessments,* 118 PSYCHOL. BULL. 199, 206 (1995).

35. *See* Sally L. Davies, Danya Glaser & Ruth Kossoff, *Children's Sexual Play and Behavior in Pre-School Settings: Staff's Perceptions, Reports, and Responses,* 24 CHILD ABUSE & NEGLECT 1329 (2000).

36. *See* Kerry M. Drach, Joyce Wientzen & Lawrence R. Ricci, *The Diagnostic Utility of Sexual Behavior Problems in Diagnosing Sexual Abuse in a Forensic Child Abuse Evaluation Clinic,* 25 CHILD ABUSE & NEGLECT 489 (2001).

37. *See* Bill Friedrich, *Correlates of Sexual Behavior in Young Children,* 2 J. CHILD CUSTODY 41, 47 (2005).

38. Toni Cavanaugh Johnson, *Young Children's Problematic Behaviors, Unsubstantiated Allegations of Child Sexual Abuse, and Family Boundaries in Child Custody Disputes,* 2 J. CHILD CUSTODY 111, 114 (2005).

39. *Id.* at 114–16.

40. *Id.* at 125.

41. David A. Wolfe & Barbara L. Legate, *Expert Opinion on Child Sexual Abuse: Separating Myths from Reality,* 10 CLINICAL PSYCHOL.: SCI. & PRAC. 339, 341 (2003).

42. *See* Kathryn Kuehnle, *Critical Issues in Child Sexual Abuse Evaluations* 4 (Mar. 7, 2002) (Workshop materials presented at the American Academy of Forensic Psychology, quoted from KATHRYN KUEHNLE, ASSESSING ALLEGATIONS OF CHILD SEXUAL ABUSE (1996)); *see also* Kathryn Kuehnle, *Evaluating Claims of Child Sexual Abuse in Child Custody Cases* (Apr. 8, 2006) (Fourth Family Law Conference, Bend, OR), www.ojd.state.or.us/osca/cpsd/courtimprovement/familylaw/documents/Dr.Kuehnle.ppt.

43. *See* Commonwealth v. Dunkle, 602 A.2d 830 (Pa. 1992); *see also* SUZANNE M. SGROI, HANDBOOK OF CLINICAL INTERVENTION IN CHILD SEXUAL ABUSE (1982).

44. Roland C. Summit, *The Child Sexual Abuse Accommodation Syndrome,* 7 CHILD ABUSE & NEGLECT 177, 181 (1983).

45. *Id.* at 182–83.

46. *Id.* at 184.

47. *Id.* at 186.

48. *Id.* at 188.

49. *Id.*

50. *Id.* at 191.

51. Kamala London et al., *Disclosure of Child Sexual Abuse: What Does the Research Tell Us About the Ways That Children Tell?,* 11 PSYCHOL. PUB. POL'Y & L. 194, 195 (2005) (citing R.K. Oates & A.C. Donnelly, *Influential Papers in Child Abuse,* 21 CHILD ABUSE & NEGLECT 319 (1997) (noted that professionals rated Summit's 1983 article as particularly influential on the topic of child sexual abuse)).

52. *See* ANN M. HARALAMBIE, CHILD SEXUAL ABUSE IN CIVIL CASES 41 (1999).

53. *See Dunkle,* 602 A.2d; State v. Michaels, 642 A.2d 1372 (N.J. 1994); State v. Foret, 628 So.2d 1116, 1124 (La. 1993).

54. *See, e.g.,* Steward v. State, 652 N.E.2d 490 (Ind. 1995); *Dunkle,* 602 A.2d; HARALAMBIE, *supra* note 52, at 41; London et al., *supra* note 51, at 197.

55. Roland C. Summit, *Abuse of Child Sexual Abuse Accommodation Syndrome,* 1 J. CHILD SEXUAL ABUSE 153, 156 (1992).

56. *Id.*

57. *See* Mary Ann Mason, *Expert Testimony Regarding the Characteristics of Sexually Abused Children: A Controversy on Both Sides of the Bench, in* EXPERT WITNESSES IN CHILD ABUSE CASES 217, 227 (Stephen J. Ceci & Helene Hembrooke eds., 1998).

58. *See* Margaret Bull Kovera & Eugene Borgida, *Expert Scientific Testimony on Child Witnesses in the Age of Daubert, in* EXPERT WITNESSES IN CHILD ABUSE CASES 185, 198, *supra* note 57; *see, e.g.,* State v. J.Q., 617 A.2d 1196 (N.J. 1993); *see also* Mason, *supra* note 57, at 227.

59. Lucy McGough, *A Legal Commentary: The Impact of Daubert on 21st-Century Child Sexual Abuse Prosecutions, in* EXPERT WITNESSES IN CHILD ABUSE CASES 265, 274, *supra* note 57.

60. Mason, *supra* note 57, at 232.

61. *See Foret,* 628 So.2d at 1129.

62. London et al., *supra* note 51, at 196.

63. HARALAMBIE, *supra* note 52, at 40.

64. Brett C. Trowbridge, *The Admissibility of Expert Testimony in Washington on Post Traumatic Stress Disorder and Related Trauma Syndromes: Avoiding the Battle of the Experts by Restoring the Use of Objective Psychological Testimony in the Courtroom,* 27 SEATTLE U. L. REV. 453, 474 (2003).

65. John E.B. Myers, *Expert Testimony Describing Psychological Syndromes,* 24 PAC. L.J. 1449, 1453 (1993).

66. *See* John A. Zervopoulos, *Robinson/Daubert and Mental Health Testimony: The Sky Is Not Falling,* 64 TEX. B.J. 350, 359 (2001).

67. London et al., *supra* note 51.

68. *Id.* at 198.

69. *Id.* at 203. (London et al. also noted the primary limitation of retrospective studies: the accuracy of the informants' reports. For example, it is possible that some adults were abused but continued to deny the abuse, that some adults had not been abused but claimed to have been, or that some adults may have disclosed their abuse in childhood despite their reports to the contrary).

70. Irit Hershkowitz, Omer Lanes & Michael E. Lamb, *Exploring the Disclosure of Child Sexual Abuse with Alleged Victims and Their Parents,* 31 CHILD ABUSE & NEGLECT 111 (2007).

71. London et al., *supra* note 51, at 197.

72. *Id.* at 216.

73. *Id.*

74. *Id.* at 219.

75. Maggie Bruck & Stephen Ceci, *Forensic Developmental Psychology: Unveiling Four Common Misconceptions,* 13 CURRENT DIRECTIONS IN PSYCHOL. SCI. 229, 230 (2004).

76. London et al., *supra* note 51, at 217.

77. *Id.* at 217.

78. *Id.* at 217–18.

79. Stephen J. Ceci & Maggie Bruck, *Suggestibility of the Child Witness: A Historical Review and Synthesis,* 113 PSYCHOL. BULL. 403, 433 (1993).

80. *See* Kathleen Coulborn Faller, *Is the Child Victim of Sexual Abuse Telling the Truth?,* 8 CHILD ABUSE & NEGLECT 473 (1984); *see also* Mason, *supra* note 57, at 221.

81. Faller, *supra* note 80.

82. *Id.*

83. *Id.*
84. *Id.*
85. *See* London et al., *supra* note 51, at 196.
86. *See, e.g.,* Kuehnle, *supra* note 42.
87. STEPHEN J. CECI & MAGGIE BRUCK, JEOPARDY IN THE COURTROOM 63 (1995).
88. DEBRA A. POOLE & MICHAEL E. LAMB, INVESTIGATIVE INTERVIEWS OF CHILDREN 69 (1998).
89. *Id.*
90. Marcia K. Johnson, *Memory and Reality,* 61 AMER. PSYCHOL. 760, 767 (2006).
91. *Id.* at 40–44.
92. Michael E. Lamb, Kathleen J. Sternberg & Phillip W. Esplin, *Making Children Into Competent Witnesses,* 1 PSYCHOL. PUB. POL'Y & L. 438, 439 (1995).
93. *Id.* at 439–40.
94. *Id.* at 439.
95. *Id.*
96. *Id.* at 440.
97. *Id.*
98. *Id.*
99. *Id.*
100. *Id.*
101. *Id.*
102. *See* CECI & BRUCK, *supra* note 87, at 44–45.
103. *Id.* at 44.
104. *Id.*
105. *Id.* at 45.
106. *Id.*
107. *Id.*
108. *Id.*
109. *Id.* at 271.
110. Bruck & Ceci, *supra* note 75, at 231; *see also* Maggie Bruck, Stephen Ceci & L. Melnyk, *External and Internal Sources of Variation in the Creation of False Reports in Children,* LEARNING & INDIVIDUAL DIFFERENCES 289, 292 (1997).
111. *See* Elizabeth F. Loftus & J.C. Palmer, *Reconstruction of Automobile Destruction,* 13 J. VERBAL LEARNING 585 (1974).
112. Bruck & Ceci, *supra* note 75, at 231.
113. Elizabeth F. Loftus & Hunter G. Hoffman, *Misinformation and Memory: The Creation of New Memories,* 118 J. EXPERIMENTAL PSYCHOL.: GEN. 100, 103 (1989); *see* Elizabeth F. Loftus, *Make-Believe Memories,* 58 AMER. PSYCHOL. 867 (2003).
114. Gail S. Goodman, *Wailing Babies in Her Wake,* 60 AMER. PSYCHOL. 872, 874 (2005).
115. *See* POOLE & LAMB, *supra* note 88, at 105 (citing Lucy S. McGough, *Commentary: Achieving Real Reform—The Case for American Interviewing Protocols, in* 61 (4–5, Serial no. 248) MONOGRAPHS OF THE SOCIETY FOR RESEARCH IN CHILD DEVELOPMENT 108 (1996)).
116. Debra Ann Poole & D. Stephen Lindsay, *Children's Eyewitness Reports After Exposure to Misinformation from Parents,* 7 J. EXPERIMENTAL PSYCHOL.: APPLIED 27 (2001).
117. Michelle D. Leichtman & Stephen J. Ceci, *The Effects of Stereotypes and Suggestions on Preschoolers' Reports,* 31 DEV. PSYCHOL. 568, 569–70 (1995).
118. POOLE & LAMB, *supra* note 88, at 69.
119. *See* Leichtman & Ceci, *supra* note 117, at 568.
120. *Id.* at 569.

121.   Maggie Bruck & Stephen J. Ceci, *Amicus Brief for the Case of State of New Jersey v. Michaels Presented by Committee of Concerned Scientists*, 1 Psychol. Pub. Pol'y & L. 272, 287 (1995).

122.   Leichtman & Ceci, *supra* note 117, at 568.

123.   *Id.* at 575; *see also* Stephen J. Lepore & Barbara Sesco, *Distorting Children's Reports and Interpretations of Events Through Suggestion*, 79 J. Applied Psychol. 108 (1994) (finding that four- to six-year-olds will produce misleading reports about their interactions with either familiar or unfamiliar adults when they are prompted to do so by an opinionated adult interviewer).

124.   *See* Joan B. Kelly & Janet R. Johnston, *The Alienated Child: A Reformulation of Parental Alienation Syndrome*, 39 Fam. Ct. Rev. 249, 254 (2001) (noting that these children "are responding to complex and frightening dynamics within the divorce process itself, to an array of parental behaviors, and also to their own vulnerabilities towards the parent they are rejecting"); *see also* Richard A. Warshak, *Bringing Sense to Parental Alienation: A Look at the Disputes and the Evidence*, 37 Fam. L.Q. 273, 286 (2003) (noting that research on memory, suggestibility, stereotype induction, social influence, and coercive influence may help to explain how one parent could exert enough influence over a child to cause that child to lose affection and respect for the other parent and the rejected parent's relatives) (citing Ceci & Bruck, *supra* note 87 for the noted research)).

125.   Leichtman & Ceci, *supra* note 117, at 574.

126.   Stephen J. Ceci et al., *Repeatedly Thinking About a Non-Event: Source Misattributions Among Preschoolers*, 3 Consciousness & Cognition 388 (1994).

127.   Stephen J. Ceci et al., *The Possible Role of Source Misattributions in the Creation of False Beliefs Among Preschoolers*, 42 Int'l J. Clinical & Experimental Hypnosis 304 (1994), cited in Poole & Lamb, *supra* note 88, at 61.

128.   *Id.*

129.   *Id.*

130.   Poole & Lamb, *supra* note 88, at 42–45.

131.   *See* Nancy E. Walker, *Forensic Interviews of Children: The Components of Scientific Validity and Legal Admissibility*, 65 Law & Contemp. Probs. 149, 157 (2002).

132.   Poole & Lamb, *supra* note 88, at 43.

133.   *See* Poole & Lindsay, *supra* note 116, at 27.

134.   *Id.*

135.   Poole & Lindsay, *supra* note 116, at 39.

136.   *Id.* at 46.

137.   Sena Garven et al., *More Than Suggestion: The Effect of Interviewing Techniques from the McMartin Preschool Case*, 83 J. Applied Psychol. 347, 356 (1998).

138.   *Id.; also see* Dalia Gilboa & Charles W. Greenbaum, *Adults' Warmth, Type of Verbal Reinforcer, and Children's Learning*, 43 Psychol. Rep. 223 (1978).

139.   *See* Karen L. Salekin, *The Suggestive Interview and the Taint Hearing: How Much Is Too Much?*, 5(4) J. Forensic Psychol. Prac. 49, 54 (2005).

140.   *Id.* at 55.

141.   *Id.*

142.   *Id.*

143.   John E.B. Myers, *New Era of Skepticism Regarding Children's Credibility*, 1 Psychol. Pub. Pol'y & L. 387, 394 (1995).

144.   Thomas D. Lyon, *The New Wave in Children's Suggestibility Research: A Critique*, Cornell L. Rev. 1004, 1013–14 (1999).

145.   Thomas D. Lyon, *False Allegations and False Denials in Child Sexual Abuse*, 1 Psychol. Pub. Pol'y & L. 429, 429 (1995).

146.   *Id.* at 430.
147.   Stephen J. Ceci, Maggie Bruck & Robert Rosenthal, *Children's Allegations of Sexual Abuse: Forensic and Scientific Issues,* 1 PSYCHOL. PUB. POL'Y & L. 494, 503 (1995).
148.   *Id.* at 505.
149.   *Id.*
150.   *See* John Doris et al., *Training in Child Protective Services,* 1 PSYCHOL. PUB. POL'Y & L. 479, 480 (1995).
151.   *Id.*
152.   Michael Lamb et al., *supra* note 92, at 444; see also Walker, *supra* note 131, at 150 (research since the McMartin trial in the late 1980s shows that the skill of the interviewer directly influences whether a child relates a true memory, discusses a false belief, affirms details suggested by others, embellishes fantasies, or provides no information at all).
153.   *See* POOLE & LAMB, *supra* note 88.
154.   Lindsay E. Cronch et al., *Forensic Interviewing in Child Sexual Abuse Cases: Current Techniques and Future Directions,* 11 AGGRESSION & VIOLENT BEH. 195, 196 (2006).
155.   J.M. Wood & S. Garven, *How Sexual Abuse Interviews Go Astray: Implications for Prosecutors, Police, and Child Protection Services,* 5 CHILD MALTREATMENT 109 (2000).
156.   Stephen J. Ceci et al., *Children's Allegations of Sexual Abuse: Forensic and Scientific Issues; A Reply to Commentators,* 1 PSYCHOL. PUB. POL'Y & L. 494, 501 (1995).
157.   Wood & Garven, *supra* note 155.
158.   *Id.*
159.   *Id.*
160.   Ceci et al., *supra* note 156, at 501.
161.   Bruck & Ceci, *supra* note 75, at 230.
162.   *Id.*
163.   Faller, *supra* note 80, at 473.
164.   SGROI, *supra* note 43, at 69.
165.   Lamb et al., *supra* note 92, at 441.
166.   *See* POOLE & LAMB, *supra* note 88, at 109.
167.   *See* Julie Cantlon et al., *Outcome-Based Practice: Disclosure Rates of Child Sexual Abuse Comparing Allegation Blind and Allegation Informed Structured Interviews,* 20 CHILD ABUSE & NEGLECT 1113 (1996).
168.   POOLE & LAMB, *supra* note 88, at 112.
169.   *Id.*
170.   *Id.* at 113; *see also* Salekin, *supra* note 139, at 52.
171.   POOLE & LAMB, *supra* note 88, at 52.
172.   *Id.*
173.   *Id.*
174.   *See* POOLE & LAMB, *supra* note 88, at 52 (citing K.J. Sternberg et al., *The Relationship Between Investigative Utterance Types and the Informativeness of Child Witnesses,* 17 J. APPLIED DEV. PSYCHOL. 439 (1996)).
175.   *Id.*
176.   POOLE & LAMB, *supra* note 88, at 53.
177.   *Id.* at 53.
178.   *See* Debra A. Poole & L.T. White, *Two Years Later: Effects of Question Repetition and Retention Interval on the Eyewitness Testimony of Children and Adults,* 29 DEV. PSYCHOL. 844 (1993).
179.   POOLE & LAMB, *supra* note 88, at 155.
180.   *Id.* at 76–77.

181.   *Id.* at 77.

182.   *Id.* at 54.

183.   *Id.*

184.   *Id.* at 146.

185.   *Id.*

186.   *Id.*

187.   *Id.*

188.   *Id.*

189.   *Id.*

190.   *Id.* at 147.

191.   Lamb et al., *supra* note 92, at 440.

192.   POOLE & LAMB, *supra* note 88, at 55.

193.   Loftus & Palmer, *supra* note 111, at 585.

194.   POOLE & LAMB, supra note 88, at 59.

195.   Bruck & Ceci, *supra* note 121, at 279; *see also* Poole & White, *supra* note 178, at 844.

196.   *Id.*

197.   *See* POOLE & LAMB, *supra* note 88, at 55.

198.   *Id.* at 56.

199.   *See* M. Siegel et al., *Misleading Children: Causal Attributions for Inconsistency Under Repeated Questioning,* 45 J. EXPERIMENTAL CHILD PSYCHOL. 438 (1988).

200.   *Id.*

201.   Poole & White, *supra* note 178.

202.   *Id.*

203.   *See* W.S. Cassell et al., *Developmental Patterns of Eyewitness Responses to Repeated and Increasingly Suggestive Questions,* 61 J. EXPERIMENTAL CHILD PSYCHOL. 116 (1996); POOLE & LAMB, *supra* note 88, at 56.

204.   Walker, *supra* note 131, at 162. (Walker noted that she and Jennifer Hunt had conducted further analyses of questions from forty-two Child Protective Services interviews of children who alleged that they had been sexually abused; *see* Nancy E. Walker & Jennifer S. Hunt, *Interviewing Child Victim-Witnesses: How You Ask Is What You Get, in* EYEWITNESS MEMORY: THEORETICAL AND APPLIED PERSPECTIVES 55 (Charles P. Thompson et al. eds., 1998). For the original analysis, *see* Amye R. Warren et al., *"It Sounds Good in Theory, But . . .": Do Investigative Interviewers Follow Guidelines Based on Memory Research?,* 1 CHILD MALTREATMENT 231 (1996)).

205.   Walker, *supra* note 131, at 162.

206.   *Id.* at 163.

207.   *Id.* at 162.

208.   *Id.* at 163.

209.   *Id.* at 162.

210.   *Id.* at 163; *see also* Nancy Walker Perry et al., *When Lawyers Question Children: Is Justice Served?,* 19 LAW & HUM. BEHAV. 609 (1995) (questions that included multiple parts with mutually exclusive responses were the most difficult to answer; those that included negatives, double negatives, or difficult vocabulary also posed significant problems).

211.   POOLE & LAMB, *supra* note 88, at 155.

212.   Thomas D. Lyon, *Speaking with Children: Advice from Investigative Interviewers, in* HANDBOOK FOR THE TREATMENT OF ABUSED AND NEGLECTED CHILDREN 65 (P. Forrest Talley ed., 2005).

213.   CECI & BRUCK, *supra* note 87, at 258.

214.   Bruck & Ceci, *supra* note 121, at 285; CECI & BRUCK *supra* note 87, at 152.

215.   Ann E. Tobey & Gail S. Goodman, *Children's Eyewitness Memory: Effects of Participation and Forensic Context,* 16 CHILD ABUSE & NEGLECT 779, 793 (1992).

216.   *Id.* at 794.

217.   Gail S. Goodman, *Understanding and Improving Children's Testimony,* 22 CHILD. TODAY 13, 15 (1993).

218.   Koocher et al., *supra* note 34, at 199–200.

219.   Anne Hungerford, *The Use of Anatomically Detailed Dolls in Forensic Investigations: Developmental Considerations,* 5 J. FORENSIC PSYCHOL. PRAC. 75, 77 (2005).

220.   M.D. Everson & B.W. Boat, *Putting the Anatomical Doll Controversy in Perspective: An Examination of the Major Uses and Criticisms of the Dolls in Child Sexual Abuse Evaluations,* 18 CHILD ABUSE & NEGLECT 113 (1994).

221.   Bruck & Ceci, *supra* note 121, at 290.

222.   G. Wolfner et al., *The Use of Anatomical Dolls in Sexual Abuse Evaluations: The State of the Science,* 2 APPLIED & PREVENTIVE PSYCHOL. 1 (1993).

223.   American Psychological Association, *Proceedings of the American Psychological Association, Incorporated, for the Year 1990,* 46 AM. PSYCHOL. 689, 722 (1991).

224.   Koocher et al., *supra* note 34, at 199.

225.   American Psychological Association, *supra* note 223.

226.   *Id.*

227.   Koocher et al., *supra* note 34, at 218.

228.   *Id.*

229.   *Id.*

230.   *Id.*

231.   *Id.*

232.   *Id.*

233.   Jason J. Dickinson et al., *Back to the Future: A Comment on the Use of Anatomical Dolls in Forensic Interviews,* 5 J. FORENSIC PSYCHOL. PRAC. 63, 66 (2005).

234.   *Id.*

235.   *Id.*

236.   *Id.*

237.   *See id.; see also* Judy S. Deloache & Donald P. Marzolf, *The Use of Dolls to Interview Young Children: Issues of Symbolic Representation,* 60 J. EXPERIMENTAL CHILD PSYCHOL. 155 (1995).

238.   Maggie Bruck, Stephen J. Ceci & Emmett Francoeur, *Children's Use of Anatomically Detailed Dolls to Report Genital Touching in a Medical Examination: Developmental and Gender Comparisons,* 6 J. EXPERIMENTAL PSYCHOL.: APPLIED 74 (2000).

239.   *Id.* at 79.

240.   *Id.*

241.   *Id.*

242.   *Id.* at 82.

243.   Dickinson et al., *supra* note 233, at 67.

244.   *See* POOLE & LAMB, *supra* note 88, at 187.

245.   B.W. Boat & M.D. Everson, *Exploration of Anatomical Dolls by Nonreferred Preschool-Aged Children: Comparisons by Age, Gender, Race, and Socioeconomic Status,* 18 CHILD ABUSE & NEGLECT 139, 145 (1994).

246.   *Id.*

247.   Dickinson et al., *supra* note 233, at 68.

248.   *Id.* at 70.

249.   *See* B.W. Boat & M.D. Everson, *Use of Anatomical Dolls Among Professionals in Sexual Abuse Evaluations,* 12 CHILD ABUSE & NEGLECT 171 (1988).

250.   POOLE & LAMB, *supra* note 88, at 193.

251.   Bruck, Ceci & Francoeur, *supra* note 238, at 82.

252.   Dickinson et al., *supra* note 233 at 72.

253.   POOLE & LAMB, *supra* note 88, at 225; CECI & BRUCK, *supra* note 87, at 296.

254.   CECI & BRUCK, *supra* note 87, at 290.

255.   Salekin, *supra* note 139, at 51.

256.   *Id.* (American Academy of Child and Adolescent Psychiatry (1988); the American Psychological Association's *Guidelines for Child Custody Evaluations in Divorce Proceedings* (1994); American Professional Society on the Abuse of Children (1990)).

257.   *See* POOLE & LAMB, *supra* note 88, at 109.

258.   *Id.*

259.   *Id.*

260.   Walker, *supra* note 131, at 169, 171. (Michigan has enacted legislation mandating use of the *State of Michigan Forensic Interviewing Protocol* "to obtain a statement from a child, in a developmentally-sensitive, unbiased and truthseeking manner, that will support accurate and fair decision-making in the criminal justice and child welfare systems." This protocol is similar to the NICHD protocol.); *see also* POOLE & LAMB, *supra* note 88, at 120 (noting that "there is remarkable overlap in the interview guidelines from various research groups and professional panels").

261.   POOLE & LAMB, *supra* note 88, at 81.

262.   Such protocols include the Cognitive Interview, the Structured Interview, the Memorandum of Good Practice, the Step-Wise Interview, the National Institute of Child Health and Human Development (NICHD) Interview Protocol, and Guidelines for Psychosocial Evaluation of Suspected Sexual Abuse in Young Children (2d ed. 1997); *also see* POOLE & LAMB, *supra* note 88, at 120.

263.   *See* Hershkowitz et al., *supra* note 70, at 99; *see also* Y. Orbach et al., *Assessing the Value of Structured Protocols for Forensic Interviews of Alleged Child Abuse Victims,* 24 CHILD ABUSE & NEGLECT 733 (2000).

264.   *See, e.g.,* Walker, *supra* note 131, at 167 (citing Nancy E. Walker & Jennifer S. Hunt, *Interviewing Child Victim-Witnesses: How You Ask Is What You Get, in* EYEWITNESS MEMORY: THEORETICAL AND APPLIED PERSPECTIVES 64 (Charles P. Thompson et al. eds., 1998)).

265.   POOLE & LAMB, *supra* note 88, at 121.

266.   *Id.* at x.

267.   *Id.* at 145.

268.   *Id.* at 54; *see also* ANNE GRAFFAM WALKER, HANDBOOK ON QUESTIONING CHILDREN: A LINGUISTIC PERSPECTIVE 60 (2d ed. 1999).

269.   POOLE & LAMB, *supra* note 88, at 145.

270.   *Id.*

271.   *Id.* at 134.

272.   *Id.*

273.   *See* Wood & Garven, *supra* note 155.

274.   Kuehnle, *supra* note 42.

275.   POOLE & LAMB, *supra* note 88, at 134.

276.   Example adapted from POOLE & LAMB, *supra* note 88, at 134.

277.   POOLE & LAMB, *supra* note 88, at 134.

278.   *Id.* at 145.

279.   *See* POOLE & LAMB, *supra* note 88; *see also* WALKER, *supra* note 268.

280.   Wood & Garven, *supra* note 155.

281.   Ceci et al., *supra* note 156, at 501.

282.   Ceci et al., *supra* note 147, at 505.

283.   *See* KUEHNLE, ASSESSING ALLEGATIONS, *supra* note 42, at 115.

284.   *See id.*

PART 3

Obtaining Mental Health Records

CHAPTER 9

Negotiating the Mental Health Records Maze

Parents' emotional states and children's developmental adjustments are relevant concerns when courts address the best interests of the child. Pre-litigation mental health records often document those family concerns. Records may provide insight about how family problems began and were addressed during the marriage. They may also provide helpful checks on spouses' reports of issues in the marriage. For instance, records may provide more objective data on sources of a parent's depression and on attempts to treat the depression. Or records may document reasons for marital problems from the more objective eye of a therapist than from spouses who may try to minimize or exaggerate those problems amid a contentious divorce. In addition, records may reflect evidence of domestic violence during the marriage and the nature and extent of physical altercations that may have attended marital conflicts. Conversely, a spouse, during the divorce, may be raising domestic violence allegations from the past that were never raised in counseling during the time the violence was alleged to have occurred. Finally, records might document children's specific problems; their overall academic, emotional, and social development; and their relationships with their parents.

Lawyers may encounter roadblocks when they try to access mental health records of parents and children and use those records in court. First, lawyers must consider psychotherapist-patient confidentiality concerns when they seek release of mental health records. Lawyers may also be required to deal with the protective provisions of the Privacy Rule of HIPAA—the federal Health Insurance Portability and Accountability Act of 1996[1]—when they try to access those records. After confidentiality issues are addressed, lawyers must consider whether a psychotherapist-patient privilege might prevent the disclosure or use of those records in court. Lawyers and psychologists may clash over whether and to whom psychologists should release the raw data and protocols of psychological tests that were administered to the parties before or during the divorce process. Full treatment of these overlapping issues is beyond the scope of this chapter. But understanding key concerns and rationales about confidentiality, privacy, and privilege and about psychologists and test data will help lawyers tailor their efforts to obtain mental health records or resist those records' disclosure. In particular, lawyers should closely attend to the rationales supporting these issues and invoke those rationales as they negotiate the mental health records maze.

CONFIDENTIALITY

Confidentiality involves ethical and legal obligations for MHPs.[2] The general rule is that MHPs do not permit the unauthorized release of patient information except in specific situations as required or permitted by law.[3] The rationale is that effective psychotherapy depends upon a relationship of confidence and trust in which the patient is willing to relate personally sensitive concerns to an MHP.[4] The mere possibility that those concerns will be disclosed outside the psychotherapy relationship may impede development of the confidential relationship necessary for successful treatment.[5]

But confidentiality is not absolute. Exceptions to confidentiality are determined by MHPs' ethics codes and state and federal laws. Exceptions include written authorization from the patient and various public policy reasons.[6] For instance, a Texas MHP, on receipt of a written request from the patient to examine or copy the patient's mental health records, shall make the information available not later than fifteen days after receiving the request.[7] But the MHP may deny a patient access to a confidential record made of that patient if the MHP "determines that release of that portion would be harmful to the patient's physical, mental, or emotional health."[8] The MHP, however, must follow a procedure that informs the patient why the record request is being denied. In such a case, the patient may request that, in lieu of releasing the records to the patient, the records be sent to another MHP who will be treating the patient "for the same or a related condition" as the MHP denying access.[9] Public policy exceptions to patients' right to confidential communications with MHPs include: when MHPs suspect child abuse; when patients raise their own mental or emotional status as part of a legal proceeding; or when patients file malpractice suits against MHPs.[10]

Confidentiality of mental health records may present other complications if the spouses engaged in marriage therapy together. For example, the American Association of Marriage and Family Therapist's Ethics Code (hereinafter *AAMFT Ethics Code*) notes that because of "unique confidentiality concerns" in the marital or family counseling relationship that includes more than one person, "therapists respect and guard the confidences of each individual client."[11] The *AAMFT Ethics Code* states that the therapist may not reveal any individual's confidences to others in the client unit without the prior written permission of that individual.[12]

Likewise, the *Ethical Principles of Psychologists and Code of Conduct* (hereinafter *APA Ethics Code*) gives little guidance to psychologists about how to manage confidentiality issues in marriage therapy. First, a psychologist is obligated to discuss with couples at the outset the "relevant limits of confidentiality" and the "foreseeable uses of the information generated" in the therapy.[13] Later, if the psychologist is required to perform potentially conflicting roles—such as a family therapist and then a witness summoned by one party in divorce proceedings—the psychologist "takes reasonable steps to clarify and modify, or withdraw from, roles appropriately."[14]

The APA's *Record Keeping Guidelines* are unclear about how psychologists should manage record requests when it is not apparent who should have access to records generated in prior marriage therapy in divorce situations when one spouse or parent objects to the records' release.[15] If one were to apply an example in the *Guidelines* regarding divorced parents' access to their children's records, the psychologist might, in such situations, seek the court's direction about how to handle the records' release.[16]

State law may offer more specific guidance about how MHPs should handle the release of such "mixed" records. For instance, Texas regulations direct an MHP to delete confidential information about another person who has not consented to the release.[17] But MHPs may not delete information relating to the patient that another person has provided, or the identity of the person responsible for that information.[18]

Rules regarding confidentiality with minors present other concerns and vary among the states. For example, in Texas, while statutes indicate that an MHP shall make available a child's confidential psychotherapy records to a parent,[19] "parents cannot always be deemed to be acting on the child's behalf."[20] Therefore, an MHP "is not required to provide access to a child's confidential records if a parent who requests them is not acting 'on behalf of' the child."[21] Examples include a parent who has sexually abused a child and later demands access to the child's records, or parents embroiled in a divorce who may be driven by their own litigation concerns when seeking the child's mental health records and may not be acting on the child's behalf.[22] But parents denied their children's mental health records may then choose another professional who would treat the child for the same or a related condition to examine and copy the records, or they may petition the district court for relief.[23]

New York State statutes also limit parental access to their children's mental health records under limited circumstances. In one case, the MHP *shall not* disclose information in those records if the MHP determines that disclosure would be detrimental to the child's treatment, to the MHP's relationship with the child, or to the child's relationship with his or her parents.[24] In addition, the MHP *may* withhold information from the child's parents if the child is over twelve years old and objects to the disclosure.[25]

Lawyers trying to obtain mental health records should familiarize themselves with the state provisions governing the confidentiality of those records, the ethical mandates of the MHP's particular discipline, and the rationales that support confidentiality in psychotherapist-patient relationships. Such knowledge will enable lawyers to manage or negotiate many disagreements with MHPs about confidentiality issues. For example, the *APA Ethics Code* notes that "if psychologists' ethical responsibilities conflict with law, regulations, or other governing legal authority, psychologists make known their adherence to the Ethics Code and take steps to resolve the conflict."[26] Then, if the conflict cannot be resolved, "psychologists may adhere to the requirements of law, regulations, or other governing legal authority."[27] Negotiations with MHPs may include proposals of tailored protective orders, carefully crafted to safeguard certain private or nonrelevant information.

PRIVACY AND HIPAA REQUIREMENTS

Privacy concerns, embodied in requirements of HIPAA's Privacy Rule,[28] represent a second issue—overlapping with confidentiality and privilege issues—which lawyers may deal with when they seek to obtain mental health records in a lawsuit. HIPAA was passed by Congress in 1996 to establish and formalize minimal standards for the electronic exchange, privacy, and security of health, including mental health, information. The following material is designed to acquaint lawyers with basic HIPAA principles, not to provide a comprehensive HIPAA guide. More detailed HIPAA information and answers to questions may be found at the HIPAA website that lists responses to *Frequently Asked HIPAA Questions*.[29]

To begin, lawyers should note three key points about HIPAA. First, HIPAA did not create physician-patient or medical records privileges.[30] Rather, HIPAA is "purely procedural" in character.[31] Therefore, while objections in court to the use of HIPAA to gain access to mental health or medical records would often be based on a privilege— for example, the psychotherapist-patient privilege—the source of the privilege would be found elsewhere than in the HIPAA regulations themselves.[32] Second, the HIPAA requirements for disclosure are imposed on the health care provider, not on the lawyer attempting to obtain the records.[33] That is, it is the health provider's responsibility to ensure that HIPAA requirements are met before disclosing patient records.

The third key point lawyers should note is HIPAA's preemption provision: when HIPAA's privacy provisions conflict with provisions of a state's privacy laws, the provisions that give greater protection to patients' privacy or right to access their own health information take precedence.[34] HIPAA's privacy rule preempts on a provision-by-provision basis, not law-by-law. Lawyers should know the privacy and confidentiality provisions in their own states to ensure which rules will be applicable. Many states note on their Internet websites which provisions in their records statutes follow HIPAA rules or state laws.

HIPAA's Privacy Rule sets conditions for the control, access, and use of patients' information.[35] The Privacy Rule applies to *covered entities*, defined as health care providers who transmit or hire others to transmit patients' identifiable health information in electronic form; health plans; and health clearinghouses.[36] HIPAA defines such individual identifiable health information that is held or transmitted by a covered entity or its business associate, in any form or media, whether electronic, paper, or oral as *Protected Health Information*.[37] For instance, many MHPs with psychotherapy practices could be covered entities; some MHPs who limit their clinical practices and do not file insurance electronically, if at all, may not fall under HIPAA's auspices. However, MHPs who electronically transmit protected health information of any patients in their practices, including billing statements, to insurance companies would be covered entities, even if the protected health information of a party in a lawsuit was not electronically transmitted. Hospitals, health maintenance organizations, and health insurance carriers certainly are covered entities.[38]

Covered entities *must* disclose patients' protected health information in only two situations: first, to individuals or their personal representatives when they request access to, or an accounting of disclosures of, their protected health information, and, second, to the Department of Health and Human Services in investigation, review, or enforcement actions.[39]

Otherwise, covered entities are *permitted, but not required*, to use and disclose protected health information without an individual's authorization in certain situations.[40] Among those situations, three are more likely relevant in family law cases.[41]

- *To report victims of abuse, neglect, or domestic violence.* Under certain conditions, covered entities may disclose protected health information about an individual whom the covered entity reasonably believes to be a victim of abuse, neglect, or domestic violence to government authorities legally authorized to receive such reports.[42]

- *To avert serious threat to health and safety.* Under certain conditions, covered entities may, consistent with applicable law and standards of ethical conduct and in good faith,[43] disclose protected health information that they believe is necessary to prevent or lessen a serious and imminent threat to a person or the public[44] when such disclosure is made to someone they believe can prevent or lessen the threat, including the target of the threat.[45]
- *For judicial and administrative proceedings.* Under certain conditions, covered entities may disclose protected health information in a judicial or administrative proceeding in response to a court order[46] or a subpoena.[47] If a covered entity receives a court order to disclose protected health information, the disclosure must be limited to the protected health information expressly authorized by the order.[48]

If the covered entity receives a subpoena unaccompanied by a court order to disclose a patient's protected health information, the covered entity may disclose the information after certain conditions are met. The covered entity should receive "satisfactory assurance" from the party seeking the information that reasonable efforts have been made by that party to ensure that the patient has been given notice of the request.[49] Alternatively, the covered entity should receive "satisfactory assurance" from the party seeking the information that reasonable efforts have been made by that party to secure a "qualified protective order"[50] that (1) prohibits the parties from using or disclosing the protected health information for any purpose other than the litigation for which the information was requested and (2) requires the return to the covered entity or destruction of the protected health information at the litigation's end.[51] Finally, a covered entity may disclose protected health information in response to a subpoena without receiving "satisfactory assurance" from the patient if the covered entity makes reasonable efforts to provide notice to the individual or to seek a "qualified protective order."[52]

In sum, a lawyer may gain access to protected health information of parties to a lawsuit in three ways: by direct authorization of the patient, by court order, or by subpoena. Covered entities must comply with written requests by the patient, but may comply with court orders or subpoenas. If the lawyer does not provide the covered entity with an authorization containing the statements required by HIPAA, a subpoena containing the representations required by HIPAA, or a court order, the covered entity is precluded from disclosing protected health information.[53] Finally, covered entities may deny access to individuals' protected health information but must follow certain procedures following such denial.[54]

As might be expected, a child's protected health information under HIPAA's Privacy Rule raises special concerns. The Privacy Rule requires covered entities to treat "personal representatives" the same as individuals with respect to uses and disclosures of the individuals' protected health information.[55] In most cases, parents are the personal representatives for their minor child. In some uncommon situations when a parent is not considered a minor child's personal representative, the Privacy Rule defers to state and other law to determine the rights of parents to access and control the protected health information of their minor child.[56] If state and other law is silent concerning parental access to a minor's protected health information, a covered entity may provide or deny a parent access to the minor's health information, provided the decision is made by a licensed health care professional in the exercise of professional judgment.[57]

Some tips for lawyers: If a covered entity disputes whether the lawyer's authorization form is HIPAA-compliant, that issue may be resolved by the lawyer's using the covered entity's own authorization form.[58] Recall that it is the covered entity that must comply with HIPAA procedures in order to release patient information. The lawyer may also ask the court to order the party to make a HIPAA request for access to his or her own records; the lawyer then should bring the HIPAA authorization forms for the party's signature to the court hearing.[59]

PSYCHOTHERAPIST–PATIENT PRIVILEGE

While confidentiality principles and HIPAA address conditions under which MHPs may disclose patient information outside the psychotherapy relationship, the psychotherapist-patient privilege speaks to conditions under which patients may keep their records from being used in court or keep MHPs from testifying in court about information generated and developed in psychotherapy. The rationale? Privileges arise from public policy decisions that the nature of certain relationships—for example, attorney-client, physician-patient, penitent-clergyman, and husband-wife—require some confidentiality even though those relationships could yield relevant evidence.[60] But privileges are strictly construed and must outweigh the fundamental principle that all relevant evidence should be heard.[61]

In *Jaffee v. Redmond*,[62] the U.S. Supreme Court held that, in federal courts, a psychotherapist privilege covers confidential communications made to licensed psychotherapists—including licensed psychiatrists, psychologists, and social workers—in the course of psychotherapy. The holding was not grounded in a Constitution-based privacy notion. Rather, it interprets the Federal Rules of Evidence applied in cases tried in federal courts.[63] The Court noted that the psychotherapist-patient privilege is based on an essential need for confidence and trust,[64] and that if the privilege were rejected, confidential conversations between psychotherapists and their patients would be chilled.[65] Thus, the privilege serves the public interest by facilitating treatment for individuals wishing to deal with emotional concerns, and private interests by protecting confidential psychotherapist-patient communications from involuntary disclosure.[66]

While the federal courts' broad recognition of a psychotherapist-patient privilege is recent, all fifty states and the District of Columbia had enacted some form of psychotherapist-patient privilege[67]—*Jaffee* presented no new evidence or arguments about the importance of privilege that state courts and legislatures had not already considered.[68] The general rule is that the patient owns the privilege. The MHP may claim the privilege, but only on the patient's behalf. The protections provided by the privilege vary among the states.[69] But, as with confidentiality, the psychotherapist-patient privilege is not absolute. Each state notes certain exceptions:

- when patients waive in writing the right to the privilege of confidentiality of any information[70]
- when patients place their mental status into litigation as part of their claim or defense[71]
- when patients submit themselves to court-ordered examinations relating to their mental or emotional conditions[72]
- when patients initiate legal or administrative proceedings against an MHP[73]

As with confidentiality, privilege issues related to records or testimony that arise from marriage counseling may present complications. States differ in how they handle these issues. For example, in some states, not all persons who conduct marriage counseling—psychologists, psychiatrists, social workers, marriage and family therapists, clergy—may fall under the privilege umbrella;[74] other states allow spouses who engage in marriage counseling from a broad range of professionals to claim the psychotherapist-patient privilege.[75] States also differ in whether both spouses[76] or only one[77] must waive the privilege to preclude records disclosure or testimony by the marriage therapist. Lawyers should be familiar with how their own states address these issues.

While the mental health records of parents in a child custody dispute may seem relevant for the court's consideration, the contents of those records may not automatically justify piercing the psychotherapist-patient privilege. Some jurisdictions in which mental health records had been exceptions to the psychotherapist-patient privilege in child custody disputes now require a balancing test to determine whether those records are privileged or excepted from the privilege. These courts seek to balance the need to protect children's well-being and the compelling public policy of encouraging treatment for parents' emotional problems.[78] For example, in Texas, the trial court will gauge whether the precise need for the information is outweighed by legitimate privacy interests protected by the privilege.[79] In New Jersey, if the court perceives that information gained by independent court-appointed experts is inadequate, the court may consider piercing the psychotherapist-patient privilege. But for the court to conduct an *in camera* review of the mental health records to rule on the matter, the party seeking to pierce the privilege must make a *prima facie* showing that: (1) there must be a legitimate need for the evidence; (2) the evidence must be relevant and material to the issue before the court; and (3) by a fair preponderance of the evidence, the information cannot be secured from any less intrusive source.[80] Nevertheless, only in the most compelling circumstances should the courts permit the privilege to be pierced.[81]

Some jurisdictions allow parties in a child custody case to assert the psychotherapist-patient privilege if relevant mental health information can be gained instead by an independent court-appointed psychological or psychiatric evaluation. New Jersey courts, cited earlier, require that the first source of information about the parents' mental health should be court-appointed independent experts or experts hired by the parties for litigation purposes rather than MHPs who have established relationships with the parties.[82] In Florida, because a parent's psychological state may help the trial court determine the child's best interest, the trial court may order an independent psychological evaluation in lieu of requiring the parent to waive the psychotherapist-patient privilege and produce records from previous counseling.[83] The privilege would also protect counseling records from being disclosed to the evaluator conducting the independent psychological evaluation.[84] In sum, an independent psychological evaluation is the court's method for balancing the need to determine the parents' mental health as it relates to the child's best interest, and the need to maintain the confidentiality between a treating psychotherapist and patient.[85]

Nevertheless, Florida courts do not routinely order independent evaluations. Rather, only in situations in which "calamitous events," such as an attempted suicide or behaviors that place the child at direct significant risk, occur during a pending child custody dispute have courts found that the parent's mental health is sufficiently at issue to warrant piercing the psychotherapist-patient privilege.[86] A parent's present ability and condition is most relevant to the trial court when the court decides child custody issues.[87]

Therefore, courts should order those evaluations only upon a showing of good cause—that is, evidence that the parent has been unable to meet the child's special needs.[88] Conclusory allegations alone do not compel a court-appointed evaluation.[89]

In addition, Florida appellate courts have ruled that in a divorce proceeding in which child custody is disputed, a party does not make his or her mental health "an element of his claim or defense" simply by requesting custody of a child.[90] Also, mere allegations that a parent is mentally unstable are not sufficient to place that parent's mental health at issue and pierce the psychotherapist-patient privilege.[91]

Finally, information gathered and relied upon in a court-appointed child custody evaluation usually is not confidential for purposes of the case and generally is excepted from the psychotherapist-patient privilege. Nevertheless, courts have imposed some interesting restrictions on evaluation records and reports. For instance, in California, the court may appoint an expert to conduct an evaluation, submit a report, and testify at trial.[92] But once submitted, the report "shall be placed in the confidential portion of the court file of the proceeding"[93] and may only be disclosed to the parents and their attorneys, counsel appointed for the child, selected people related to the court, and "any other person upon order of the court for good cause."[94] In Texas, communications to an MHP in the course of a court-appointed evaluation will not be privileged "only with respect to issues involving the patient's mental or emotional health."[95] But courts will be careful to impose appropriate safeguards against unauthorized disclosure.[96]

An interesting New York opinion used the best-interest-of-the-child standard to protect the disclosure of records from a court-appointed child custody evaluation.[97] The court noted that a court-appointed neutral forensic psychologist in a contested custody proceeding is unlike a retained expert in other cases. While a retained expert's report is introduced at trial to advocate a position of a party, the court-appointed expert's report is intended to provide the court "with an unbiased professional opinion on the often difficult psycho-social issues that are before the court in a custody dispute."[98] The court further noted that for custody litigation to be successful, the court's concern for the best interests of the child "must apply not only with respect to the result, but in the means used to reach that result, as well."[99] The court expressed concern that while disclosure of the court-appointed expert's evaluation records would be useful for cross-examining the expert, such disclosure could negatively impact future relationships of the parties themselves.[100] The court proposed a balancing test to decide in each case the benefits versus the detriments of the records' disclosure and noted that a showing of bias or other reason to doubt the report's credibility, other than mere displeasure with the report's conclusions, would cause the balance to weigh in favor of disclosure.[101]

How might lawyers use these issues in arguments over the disclosure of records from court-appointed evaluations? In general, disclosing those records in the context of the case is preferred because those records contain relevant information, and they presumably address issues on which the court will make decisions. Although a minority of jurisdictions find that records of a court-appointed evaluator should not be disclosed, the use of the best-interest-of-the-child standard by courts in those jurisdictions to manage the disclosure of records generated in a court-appointed evaluation presents an interesting base from which to argue against disclosure in a jurisdiction in which disclosure is normally permitted. For example, if there is a realistic potential that one of the parents might misuse those records by reporting or publishing the contents of those records to nonparties outside the lawsuit, such actions could compromise the child(ren)'s best interests, invoking both case-specific and public policy concerns which may weigh against disclosure.[102] In such cases, lawyers might argue that the best-interest-of-the-child standard is more than a statement of the primary criterion for deciding custody matters; "it is an expression of the court's special responsibility to safeguard the interests of the child at the center of a custody dispute because the child cannot be presumed to be protected by the adversarial process."[103]

In addition, lawyers who keep in mind rationales for the psychotherapist-patient privilege will be able to sharpen their arguments to the court on this issue. As noted earlier, privileged information is often relevant information kept out of evidence for public policy reasons. But public policy rationales that support privileges may cut both ways. On the one hand, those rationales support confidentiality and privileges for certain private relationships that courts and legislatures deem important for the public good.[104] On the other hand, privileges must be strictly construed because they may exclude relevant evidence and, thereby, hamper the court's means for ascertaining the truth.[105] The party asserting a privilege has the burden of producing evidence to support the elements of the privilege claim.[106] The party opposing the privilege claim may, if applicable, assert an exception to the privilege. Or, the party may ask the court for an *in camera* inspection of the records at issue. Upon *in camera* inspection, the court may use a balancing test to ensure that the precise need for the information is not outweighed by legitimate privacy issues protected by the privilege and determine what parts of the records should be admitted.[107] Again, lawyers familiar with their jurisdictions' rules of evidence on privilege issues will be best able to decide whether to propose a privilege or how to argue for the most narrowly tailored grant of the privilege that will allow the court to consider relevant evidence.

PSYCHOLOGISTS, TEST DATA, AND TEST MATERIALS

A vigorously debated question among lawyers and psychologists is whether psychologists, even when presented with a valid patient authorization or when directed by subpoena, should release raw psychological test data or results to non-psychologists.[108] The question's problem involves balancing discovery rules, designed to provide full disclosure of everything on which a party will rely at trial, against psychologists' scientific, ethical, and contractual obligations.[109] In addition, test publishers, asserting proprietary interests in the testing instruments they developed and sell, as well as copyright and trade secret laws, claim a stake in the issue.[110] When faced with the demand to produce those materials, psychologists often ask lawyers to direct them to send those materials to a person "qualified to use such information," usually another psychologist.[111] For lawyers, this issue may result in discovery obstacles; for psychologists, this issue raises ethical dilemmas and legal exposure.[112]

This records disclosure problem arose from concerns raised in the since revised 1992 *APA Ethics Code* that psychological test data, results, and materials could be misused.[113] Many of these concerns focused on lawyers' demands for psychological records to prepare for depositions or cross-examinations of opposing psychologist experts.[114] Several rationales for opposing or limiting disclosure of test data, results, and materials sup-ported the Ethics Code provision:

- people untrained in the use of psychological testing would misuse or misinterpret test results[115]
- public dissemination of test information such as manuals and protocols could slowly erode the validity and reliability of the test instruments as test items became more widely available[116]
- test publishers have a copyright interest in the test information that required protection[117]
- psychologists may have a contractual or other legal obligation due to copyright laws not to disclose such information[118]

The APA's current Ethics Code,[119] adopted in June 2003, ostensibly clarified the issue of what materials from patients' records psychologists may release upon proper demand. The current *APA Ethics Code* distinguishes between test data and test materials. Test data "refers to raw and scaled scores, client/patient responses to test questions or stim-uli, and psychologists' notes and recordings concerning client/patient statements and behavior during examination."[120] *APA Ethics Code* Standard 9.04 states that "pursuant to a client/patient release, psychologists provide test data to the client/patient or other persons identified in the release." But psychologists may withhold test data "to protect a client/patient or others from substantial harm or misuse or misrepresentation of the data or the test."[121] Finally, "in the absence of a client/patient release, psychologists pro-vide test data only as required by law or court order."[122] Client consent is the touchstone for when, and to whom, test data are to be released, following the trend in state laws and federal regulations—for example, HIPAA—that affords patients greater control over their health information.[123]

Test materials, distinguished from test data, "refers to manuals, instruments, pro-tocols, and test questions or stimuli and does not include test data. . . ."[124] *APA Ethics Code* Standard 9.11 notes that test materials do not include test data as defined earlier; as opposed to test data, test materials do not include anything unique to a particular patient.[125] Psychologists are to make reasonable efforts to maintain the integrity and security of test materials.[126]

Despite the attempts of the 2003 *APA Ethics Code* to distinguish test data from test materials, many psychologists still are uncertain about how to handle requests to release those records.[127] For instance, the 2003 *APA Ethics Code* indicates that psychologists may refrain from releasing test data to protect a patient from misuse or misinterpreta-tion of the data or the test. Psychologists might argue that because it would be unlikely that people without training would attempt to interpret psychological tests appropri-ately, the contemplated misuse and misinterpretation of test data would not occur.[128] But psychologists who consider releasing test data under this rationale are cautioned to review relevant state law or HIPAA regulations that may prohibit releasing test data except to "another qualified professional" or pursuant to a court order.[129]

Some psychologists also believe that the 2003 *APA Ethics Code* distinction between test data and test materials is artificial.[130] For example, examinee responses (test data) in many neuropsychological tests are the same as the stimuli (test materials) provided by the examiner—a list of words which examinees must repeat from memory.[131] Or con-sider test protocols that contain both examinee responses and the test items on the same pages.[132] In both of these examples, what are test data, and what are test materials? The Ethics Code tried to resolve this problem by classifying these as test data, that is, information collected by the psychologist that is unique to a particular patient.[133]

Nevertheless, the 2003 *APA Ethics Code* instructs psychologists "to maintain the integrity and security of test materials and other assessment techniques consistent with laws and contractual obligations, and in a manner that permits adherence to this *APA Ethics Code*."[134] But how do psychologists protect test integrity and security in the last example when both the test questions and answers are on the same page and psychologists are to produce test data? Other guidelines, both pre-and post-HIPAA, also emphasize the safeguarding of test materials,[135] and some psychologists warn that without protections, "the worldwide dissemination of these materials via the Internet is virtually assured."[136] In addition, test publishers have issued papers emphasizing that test materials are considered confidential information and that trade secrets must be protected.[137] The papers emphasize that the publishers have "required the completion of a Test User Agreement which prohibits purchasers (qualified professionals) from copying and releasing the tests to others who are not qualified to interpret the results or do not have the same ethical obligations to maintain test security."[138]

Despite this apparent emphasis of ethical codes and guidelines that psychologists maintain the security of test materials to avoid misuse, misinterpretation, and, ultimately, harmful effects,[139] some psychologists have asserted that the field's unwillingness to provide raw data to the courts has damaged their professional reputations, has undermined their credibility as professional scientists, and, ultimately, has not served consumers' best interests.[140] These psychologists have suggested that the APA, in concert with the American Bar Association, develop procedures for temporary disclosure of psychological test information, after which the material would be sealed or returned to the psychologist.[141]

STRATEGIES FOR NEGOTIATING THE MENTAL HEALTH RECORDS MAZE

The interactions of confidentiality issues, HIPAA requirements, the psychotherapist-patient privilege, and other protections against the disclosure of some mental health records content may confuse lawyers and MHPs when they try to negotiate access to mental health records. Courts may also be confused about these issues, particularly when compelling case facts beg for mental health information that could inform difficult best-interest-of-the-child decisions.

Lawyers will need to be clear and, at times, creative in their arguments for or against the disclosure of mental health records, particularly as some states uphold the psychotherapist-patient privilege less strictly than others. In addition to practice tips offered throughout this chapter, consider the following when organizing your arguments:

- Know your state laws and case law about the confidentiality of mental health records, which state law provisions preempt HIPAA regulations, and the court's evidence rules concerning the psychotherapist-patient privilege.
- Understand the rationales for the confidentiality of mental health records and the psychotherapist-patient privilege.

- Learn how other jurisdictions differ in the ways they manage and decide these issues, and consider using the rationales from those decisions in your arguments. Several were noted in this chapter.
- Depending on your position and your court's rules of procedure, consider asking the court to review the mental health records *in camera* to support a decision about whether the records, in part or all, should be disclosed. If you oppose *in camera* review of the records, *Jaffee* may be cited as opposing *in camera* review of mental health records because such judicial scrutiny and evaluation "would eviscerate the effectiveness of the privilege."[142]
- If you seek or oppose the records disclosure but believe that the court will not fully support the privilege, consider proposing qualified protective orders to circumscribe only information that is truly relevant to the case. Or urge the court to apply a balancing test, as applied in some states and discussed earlier, to determine the relevancy of different aspects of the records. If you oppose disclosure, note *Jaffee*'s rejection of the notion that a court may use a balancing test to decide whether to support the privilege using the same rationale as *Jaffee*'s rejection of judicial scrutiny of mental health records noted earlier.[143]
- Incorporate and emphasize reasons that the best interest of the child should be considered in your arguments for seeking or resisting disclosure of mental health records.

Lawyers who are able to negotiate the mental health records maze will be better equipped to apply to their cases the emotional, legal, and psychological perspectives described in this book. Records may provide history and insight into a family's emotional issues, document the methods MHPs used to generate data that supports their conclusions and expert opinions, and expose the rationales by which MHPs connected their data to their conclusions and expert opinions.

In this book's first paragraph, we asserted that "How do you know what you say you know?" is the family lawyer's central challenge to MHPs. As we have noted, addressing this challenge may be difficult, depending on the lawyer's knowledge of MHPs' qualifications, methods, and mind-sets, and on the lawyer's access to records that could document case concerns. In addition, MHPs may hide, intentionally or unintentionally, the reasoning by which they tie their data to their conclusions and opinions. But lawyers can expose and manage these issues. Lawyers who use the model presented in this book to address the central challenge to MHPs will sharpen their own experts' presentations, effectively critique their opponents' experts, and provide the court a roadmap for their *Frye-Daubert* analyses.

NOTES

1. Pub. L. No. 104–191, 42 U.S.C. § 1320d-1, *et seq.*
2. *See* American Psychological Association, *Ethical Principles of Psychologists and Code of Conduct*, 57 AM. PSYCHOL. 1597 (2002) [hereinafter *APA Ethics Code*], Standard 4.01. ("Psychologists have a primary obligation and take reasonable precautions to protect confidential information . . . ."); *see also* TEX. HEALTH & SAFETY CODE ANN. § 611.002 (a) ("Communications between a patient and a professional, and records of the identity, diagnosis, evaluation, or treatment of a patient that are created or maintained by a professional, are confidential.").
3. BRUCE E. BENNETT ET AL., ASSESSING AND MANAGING RISK IN PSYCHOLOGICAL PRACTICE: AN INDIVIDUALIZED APPROACH 106 (2006).

4. Salvatore Cullari, *The Client's Perspective of Psychotherapy, in* Counseling and Psychotherapy 104 (Salvatore Cullari ed., 2001); *see also* Jaffee v. Redmond, 518 U.S. 1 (1996).

5. Cullari, *supra* note 4; *see also Jaffee,* 518 U.S. 1, 10 n.9 (1996) (referring to studies and authorities cited in the Brief for American Psychiatric Association et al. as Amici Curiae 14–17, and the Brief for American Psychological Association as Amicus Curiae 12–17).

6. Bennett et al., *supra* note 3, at 106.

7. Tex. Health & Safety Code Ann. § 611.008 (a).

8. *Id.* at § 611.0045 (b).

9. *Id.* at § 611.045 (e).

10. Bennett et al., *supra* note 3, at 106–107.

11. Principle II: Confidentiality (2001), http://www.aamft.org/resources/lrm_plan/ethics/ethicscode2001.asp.

12. *Id.* at Principle II, 2.2.

13. *See APA Ethics Code, supra* note 2, at Standard 4.02 (a) and (b).

14. *Id.* at Standard 10.02 (b).

15. American Psychological Association, *Record Keeping Guidelines,* 7–8 (2007), http://www.apa.org/practice/recordkeeping.pdf.

16. *Id.* at 8.

17. Tex. Health & Safety Code Ann. § 611.0045 (g).

18. *Id.*

19. *See id.* at § 611.0045 (f) and § 611.004 (4).

20. Abrams v. Jones, 35 S.W.3d 620, 625 (Tex. 2000).

21. *Id.* at 625–26.

22. *Id.* at 625.

23. *Id.*

24. N.Y. Mental Hyg. Law § 33.16 (b)(3) (McKinney 2004).

25. *Id.* at § 33.16 (c)(2).

26. *APA Ethics Code, supra* note 2, at Standard 1.02.

27. *Id.*

28. *See Summary of the HIPAA Privacy Rule* at http://hhs.gov/ocr/privacysummary.pdf.

29. *See* http://www.hipaadvisory.com/action/faqs/faq_main.htm and then click on "Privacy," type "Judicial and Administrative Proceedings" into FAQ request, and click on search.

30. Northwestern Memorial Hospital v. Ashcroft, 362 F.3d 923, 926 (7th Cir. 2004).

31. *Id.*

32. *Id.*

33. Kathryn Lanigan Wieser & Lindley Bain, *Discovery of Medical and Psychological Information, or How to Avoid HIPAASTERIA,* 6th Annual Family Law on the Front Lines Conference 2 (June 22–23, 2006).

34. 45 C.F.R. § 160.203 (b).

35. *See Summary of the HIPAA Privacy Rule* at http://hhs.gov/ocr/privacysummary.pdf.

36. 45 C.F.R. § 160.103 (3).

37. 45 C.F.R. § 160.103.

38. 45 C.F.R. § 160.103 (3).

39. 45 C.F.R. § 164.502 (a)(2).

40. *See* 45 C.F.R. § 164.512.

41. *See* Wieser & Bain, *supra* note 33, at 3.

42. 45 C.F.R. § 164.512 (c)(1).

43. 45 C.F.R. § 164.512 (j)(1).

44. 45 C.F.R. § 164.512 (j)(1)(i)(A).

45. 45 C.F.R. § 164.512 (j)(1)(i)(B).
46. 45 C.F.R. § 164.512 (e)(1)(i).
47. 45 C.F.R. § 164.512 (e)(1)(ii).
48. 45 C.F.R. § 164.512 (e)(1)(i).
49. 45 C.F.R. § 164.512 (e)(1)(ii)(A).
50. 45 C.F.R. § 164.512 (e)(1)(ii)(B).
51. 45 C.F.R. § 164.512 (e)(1)(v)(A) and (B).
52. 45 C.F.R. § 164.512 (e)(1)(vi).
53. Wieser & Bain, *supra* note 33, at 2.
54. 45 C.F.R. § 164.524.
55. 45 C.F.R. § 164.502 (g)(3)(i).
56. 45 C.F.R. § 164.502 (g)(3)(i)(B).
57. 45 C.F.R. § 164.502 (g)(3)(ii)(C).
58. Judith A. Langer, *The HIPAA Privacy Rules: Disclosures of Protected Health Information in Legal Proceedings,* 78(4) WISC. LAW. (April 2005).
59. Wieser & Bain, *supra* note 33, at 9.
60. EDWARD J. IMWINKELREID, EVIDENTIARY FOUNDATIONS 150 (2d ed. 1989).
61. *See* Trammel v. U.S., 445 U.S. 40, 50 (1980).
62. 518 U.S. 1 (1996).
63. Daniel W. Shuman & William Foote, *Jaffee v. Redmond's Impact: Life After the Supreme Court's Recognition of a Psychotherapist-Patient Privilege,* 30 PROF. PSYCHOL.: RES. & PRAC. 479, 479 (1999).
64. *Jaffee,* 518 U.S. at 10, citing *Trammel,* 445 U.S. at 51.
65. *Jaffee,* 518 U.S. at 11–12.
66. *Id.* at 11.
67. *Id.* at 12.
68. Shuman & Foote, *supra* note 63, at 479.
69. BENNETT ET AL., *supra* note 3, at 109.
70. *See, e.g.,* TEX. R. EVID. 510 (d)(2).
71. *See, e.g.,* TEX. R. EVID. 510 (d)(5).
72. *See, e.g.,* TEX. R. EVID. 510 (d)(4).
73. *See, e.g.,* TEX. R. EVID. 510 (d)(1).
74. *See* Carlton D. Stansbury, *Discovery and Admissibility of Mental Health Records in Custody Disputes,* Paper from ABA Section of Family Law Teleconference 5 (Mar. 1, 2005).
75. *See* Wichansky v. Wichansky, 313 A.2d 222 (N.J. Ch. 1973) ("nothing in this act ['Practicing Marriage Counseling Act'] shall be construed to prevent qualified members of other professional groups such as social workers, psychologists, physicians, attorneys at law, members of the clergy, or guidance counselors from doing work of a marriage and family counseling nature consistent with the accepted standards of their respective profession"); *see also, e.g.,* Kinsella v. Kinsella, 696 A.2d 556, 571 (N.J. 1997) (relied on N.J. Rules of Evidence 510: Marriage Counselor Privilege stating that "[a] communication between a marriage and family therapist and the person or persons in therapy shall be confidential and its secrecy preserved . . .").
76. *See, e.g.,* Wheelahan v. Wheelahan, 557 So. 2d 1046 (La. App., 4th Cir. 1990), *writ denied,* 559 So. 2d 1379 (La. 1990) (both spouses must waive the privilege before the contents of counseling are disclosed).
77. *See* Redding v. Virginia Mason Medical Center, 878 P.2d 483 (Wash. App. 1994) ("In litigation arising between the joint patients, the psychologist-patient privilege does not protect statements made by one of them to a therapist during a joint counseling session.").
78. *See Kinsella,* 696 A.2d at 584.

79. Tex. R. Evid. 510 (*Comment to 1998 change* referencing R.K. v. Ramirez, 887 S.W.2d 836 (Tex. 1994)).

80. *Kinsella,* 696 A.2d at 572.

81. *Id.* at 584.

82. *Id.* at 583.

83. *See* Loughlin v. Loughlin, 935 So. 2d 82 (Fla. Dist. Ct. App. 2006).

84. McIntyre v. McIntyre, 404 So. 2d 208, 209 (Fla. Dist. Ct. App. 1981).

85. *See* Leonard v. Leonard, 673 So. 2d 97 (Fla. Dist. Ct. App. 1996); *Loughlin,* 935 So. 2d 82.

86. *See* Miraglia v. Miraglia, 462 So. 2d 507 (Fla. Dist. Ct. App. 1984); *see also* O'Neill v. O'Neill, 823 So. 2d 837 (Fla. Dist. Ct. App. 2002); *see also Kinsella,* 696 A.2d at 583 (as part of a balancing analysis in New Jersey courts, the court's decision to order disclosure of parents' mental health records must be based on independent evidence of potential for harm to the child—for example, the fact of a recent hospitalization, the opinion of the expert, or the court's own observations).

87. Schouw v. Schouw, 593 So. 2d 1200, 1201 (Fla. Dist. Ct. App. 1992).

88. *Id.* at 1201.

89. Williams v. Williams, 550 So. 2d 166 (Fla. Dist. Ct. App. 1989).

90. *McIntyre,* 404 So. 2d at 209; *see also Kinsella,* 696 A.2d at 580–81 ("Courts that have ordered disclosure of treatment records, in addition to relying on independent psychological evaluations, typically have been confronted with evidence of recent or continuing serious mental illness bearing on potential unfitness.").

91. *McIntyre,* 404 So. 2d at 209.

92. Cal. Evid. Code § 730.

93. Cal. Fam. Code § 3025.5.

94. Cal. Fam. Code § 3025.5 (a)–(d).

95. Tex. R. Evid. 510 (d)(4).

96. *Id.*

97. Ochs v. Ochs, 749 N.Y.S.2d 650 (Sup. Ct. Westchester Co. 2002).

98. *Id.* at 652; *see also* Delcourt v. Silverman, 919 S.W.2d 777, 783 (Tex. App. Houston [14th Dist.] 1996, *writ denied*) (held that court-appointed psychologists who conduct child custody evaluations are entitled to absolute immunity in their function to provide information essential to the decision-making process and that when a court appoints a mental health professional to examine the child and parents in a custody proceeding, the professional is acting as a fact finder for the court).

99. *Ochs,* 749 N.Y.S.2d at 653.

100. *Id.*

101. *Id.* at 656; *see also* Drago v. Tishman Constr. Corp., 777 N.Y.S.2d 889, 892 (Sup. Ct. New York Co. 2004) (only in child custody disputes have reasons been found to limit the disclosure of raw test results and related notes).

102. *See, e.g., Abrams,* 35 S.W.3d at 625 (indicating that an MHP is not required to disclose a child's confidential records if a parent requesting them is not acting "on behalf of the child"; a parent embroiled in a divorce who may be driven by his or her own litigation concerns when seeking the child's mental health records may not be acting on the child's behalf).

103. *Kinsella,* 696 A.2d at 577–78.

104. *Jaffee,* 518 U.S. at 11.

105. *Trammel,* 445 U.S. at 50.

106. Imwinkelried, *supra* note 60, at 151.

107. *See Ramirez,* 887 S.W.2d at 836.

108. Rita Chadda & Steven J. Stein, *Test Publisher's Perspective: Release of Test Data to Non-Psychologists,* 5(2) J. Forensic Psychol. Prac. 59, 60 (2005).

109.   SHANE S. BUSH, MARY A. CONNELL & ROBERT L. DENNEY, ETHICAL PRACTICE IN FOREN-SIC PSYCHOLOGY 103 (2006) (citing D.L. Rapp & P.S. Ferber, *To Release, or Not to Release Raw Test Data, That Is the Question, in* HANDBOOK OF FORENSIC NEUROPSYCHOLOGY 337, 342 (2003)).
110.   *Id.*
111.   *See* American Psychological Association, Ethical Principles of Psychologists and Code of Conduct, 47 AM. PSYCHOL. 1597 (1992) [hereinafter 1992 *APA Ethics Code*].
112.   *See* Marcia M. Andberg, Caught in the Middle: Ethical/Legal Mandates and Test Security 5 (July 28, 2004) (unpublished manuscript presented at the 2004 American Psychological Association Convention, Honolulu, Haw.).
113.   1992 *APA Ethics* Code, *supra* note 111 (Section 2.02 (b) states, "[P]sychologists refrain from misuse of assessment techniques, interventions, results, and interpretations and take reasonable steps to prevent others from misusing the information these techniques provide. This includes refraining from releasing raw test results or raw data to persons, other than to patients or clients as appropriate, who are not qualified to use such information.").
114.   *See* Committee on Legal Issues, American Psychological Association, *Strategies for Private Practitioners Coping with Subpoenas or Compelled Testimony for Client Records or Test Data,* 27 PROF. PSYCHOL.: RES. & PRAC. 245 (1996).
115.   *Id.* at 247.
116.   American Psychological Association, *Editorial Test Security: Protecting the Integrity of Tests,* 54 AM. PSYCHOL. 1078 (1999).
117.   Committee on Legal Issues, *supra* note 114, at 248.
118.   *Id.*
119.   *APA Ethics Code, supra* note 2.
120.   *Id.* at Standard 9.04 (a).
121.   *Id.*
122.   *Id.* at Standard 9.04 (b).
123.   Stephen Behnke, *Release of Test Data and APA's New Ethics Code,* 34 MONITOR ON PSY-CHOL. 70 (2003).
124.   *APA Ethics Code, supra* note 2, at Standard 9.11.
125.   Behnke, *supra* note 123, at 70.
126.   *APA Ethics Code, supra* note 2, at Standard 9.11.
127.   Shane S. Bush & Thomas A. Martin, *The Ethical and Clinical Practice of Disclosing Raw Test Data: Addressing the Ongoing Debate,* 13 APPLIED NEUROPSYCHOL. 115, 115 (2006).
128.   BUSH ET AL., *supra* note 109, at 105.
129.   Celia B. Fisher, *Test Data Standard Most Notable Change in New APA Ethics Code,* 12 NAT'L PSYCHOL. 12 (2003); *see also,* e.g., 22 TEX. ADMIN. CODE § 465.22 (c)(4).
130.   Bush & Martin, *supra* note 127, at 119.
131.   *Id.*
132.   Chadda & Stein, *supra* note 108, at 64.
133.   Behnke, *supra* note 123, at 70.
134.   *APA Ethics Code, supra* note 2, at Standard 9.11.
135.   AMERICAN EDUCATIONAL RESEARCH ASSOCIATION ET AL., STANDARDS FOR EDUCATIONAL AND PSYCHOLOGICAL TESTING 129 (1999); Committee on Ethical Guidelines for Forensic Psychologists, *Specialty Guidelines for Forensic Psychologists,* 15 LAW & HUM. BEHAV. 655 (1991); National Academy of Neuropsychology; *Test Security: Official Statement of the National Academy of Neuropsychology,* 15 ARCHIVES OF CLINICAL NEUROPSYCHOL. 383 (2000) (this statement was updated in 2003; *see* at nanonline.org (click on PAIC tab and then on Position Papers)).
136.   Richard Rogers, *APA 2002 Ethics, Amphibiology, and the Release of Psychological Test Records: A Counterperspective to Erard,* 82 J. PERSONALITY ASSESSMENT 31 (2004).

137. *See* Harcourt HIPAA Position Statement, http://harcourtassessment.com/hai/images/ pdf/legal/HIPAA_Position.pdf; *see also* MHS Test Disclosure Policy, http://www.mhs.com/Test Discloser.asp?id=MHS (adopted by leading Canadian test publishers and the Canadian Psychological Association).

138. MHS Test Disclosure Policy, *supra* note 137.

139. Bush & Martin, *supra* note 127, at 122.

140. Paul R. Lees-Haley, John C. Courtney & Juliet P. Dinkins, *Revisiting the Need for Reform in the Disclosure of Tests and Raw Test Data to the Courts: The 2002 APA Ethics Code Has Not Solved Our Dilemma,* 5(2) J. FORENSIC PSYCHOL. PRAC. 71, 72 (2005).

141. *Id.* at 79.

142. *Jaffee,* 518 U.S. at 18; *see also* Newton v. Kemna, 354 F.3d 776 (8th Cir. 2004).

143. *Jaffee,* 518 U.S. at 18.

Appendix
Internet Sources for Relevant Mental Health Ethical Codes and Guidelines

American Academy of Child and Adolescent Psychiatry, *Practice Parameters for Child Custody Evaluation* (1997), *available at* http://www.aacap.org/galleries/PracticeParameters/Custody.pdf.

American Academy of Psychiatry and the Law, *Ethics Guidelines for the Practice of Forensic Psychiatry* (2005), *available at* https://www.aapl.org/pdf/ETHICSGDLNS.pdf.

American Psychological Association, *Guidelines for Child Custody Evaluations in Divorce Proceedings*, 47 AM. PSYCHOL. 677 (1994), *available at* http://www.apa.org/practice/childcustody.html.

American Psychological Association, *Ethical Principles of Psychologists and Code of Conduct*, 57 AM. PSYCHOL. 1597 (2002), *available at* http://www.apa.org/ethics/code2002.html.

Association of Family and Conciliation Courts, *Model Standards of Practice for Child Custody Evaluation*, 45 FAM. CT. REV. 70 (2007), *available at* http://www.afccnet.org (search for Resource Center, then follow "Standards of Practice," then follow "Model Standards of Practice for Child Custody Evaluation").

Committee on Ethical Guidelines for Forensic Psychologists, *Specialty Guidelines for Forensic Psychologists*, 15 LAW & HUM. BEHAV. 655 (1991), *available at* http://www.ap-ls.org/links/professionalsgfp.html.

See also, http://www.kspope.com (search "ethics codes," then follow for links to therapy, counseling, forensic and related ethics (and practice) codes developed by professional organizations).

Index